INTERNATIONAL PERSPECTIVES

ON SPORT

AND EXERCISE PSYCHOLOGY

Sidónio Serpa
Faculty of Human Movement
Technical University of Lisbon

José Alves
Superior School of Education
Polytechnic Institute of Guarda

Vítor Pataco
Sports Institute
Ministry of Education

Editors

Vítor Ferreira
Faculty of Human Movement
Technical University of Lisbon

Assistant Editor

Based on the keynote addresses of the 8th World Congress of Sport Psychology, 1993, organized by the International Society of Sport Psychology, Portuguese Society of Sport Psychology and Technical University of Lisbon (Faculty of Human Movement)

FITNESS INFORMATION TECHNOLOGY, INC.
MORGANTOWN, WV 26504

Library of Congress Catalog Card Number: 94-71468

ISBN 0-9627926-5-9

Cover Design: James M. Williams
Copyeditor: Sandra R. Woods
Printed by: BookCrafters

Printed in the United States of America
10 9 8 7 6 5 4 3 2 1

Fitness Information Technology, Inc.
P. O. Box 4425, University Avenue
Morgantown, WV 26504 USA
(800)-477-4348
(304)-599-3482

Contents

Contents

About the Editors

Sidónio Serpa took his university degree in physical education in 1975 in the Superior Institute of Physical Education of Lisbon and in psychology in 1983 in the Superior Institute of Applied Psychology, Lisbon. Presently finishing his doctoral thesis, he has a master's degree in Sport Sciences from the Faculty of Human Movement of the Technical University of Lisbon where he also has been Assistant Professor of Sport Psychology since 1985. He has been invited to attend conferences in Portugal and abroad and has published in different national and international journals. Being a former gymnast and gymnastics coach, he was Assistant Professor of Gymnastics at his University (1975/1980), developed national and international activities in this field and presented top-level teams of group gymnastics in several countries. Sidónio Serpa was the Chairman of the 8th World Congress of Sport Psychology, and is President of the Portuguese Society of Sport Psychology, member of the managing Council of International Society of Sport Psychology (ISSP), representative of Portugal at European Federation of Sport Psychology (FEPSAC), psychologist of elite athletes and member of the Editorial board of the *International Journal of Sport Psychology* (IJSP) and other journals.

José Alves took his university degree in physical education in the Superior Institute of Physical Education of Lisbon and in psychology in the Superior Institute of Applied Psychology, Lisbon. Dr. Alves has a master's degree in Physical Education, and he is a Ph.D. in Psychology in the field of cognitive psychology where he published about 30 articles; he also is an expert in neurolinguistic programming from the French Institute of NLP of Paris. He has been working for the last 13 years in the area of sport psychology as a professor of undergraduate and graduate courses in the Faculty of Human Movement of the Technical University of Lisbon, in the Superior Institute of Applied Psychology and in the Superior School of Education of the

Polytechnic Institute of Guarda where he presently is the Director of the Department of Physical Education. José Alves also works as psychologist of elite athletes, often participates in workshops for coaches, is a consultant in communication and leadership and was the Co-Chairman of the Organizing and Local Scientific Committees of the 8th World Congress of Sport Psychology.

Vítor Pataco finished his university degree studies in physical education in 1988 in the Faculty of Human Movement of the Technical University of Lisbon with a thesis on leadership in sports and he is now finishing his master's degree in organizational sciences applied to sport in the same Faculty. Since he is deeply interested in the psychological aspects of sports, he has been participating in research projects in this area and has presented several works in national and international congresses and conferences as well as has published on this topic. Pataco is a former handball player and a track and field competitor and is now a track and field coach of elite athletes also working in the Institute of Sports of the Portuguese Ministry of Education. Being the General Secretary of the Portuguese Society of Sport Psychology, he was the General Secretary of the 8th World Congress of Sport Psychology Organizing Committee.

Vítor Ferreira took his university degree in physical education in 1984 in the Superior Institute of Physical Education of the Technical University of Lisbon. He also took his master's degree in educational sciences in 1990 in the Faculty of Human Movement of the Technical University of Lisbon with a thesis on the subject "Simple Reaction Time, Choice Reaction Time and Decision Time. Comparative Study on Olympic Male Gymnasts of Different Practice Levels." He has been working in the psychology area on the subjects "Leadership" and "Attention/Concentration" too. Since 1984 he has been Assistant Professor in his Faculty and presently he is Assistant Professor of Sport Pedagogy and he is preparing a doctoral thesis in observation competency. Vítor Ferreira is member of the Portuguese Society of Sport Psychology, and he was a member of the Organizing Committee of the 8th World Congress of Sport Psychology.

About the Contributors

Dr. Bruce Abernethy is Professor and Head of the Department of Human Movement Studies at The University of Queensland in Brisbane, Australia. His principal research interest is in the nature of perceptual and motor expertise in the performance of natural actions. Professor Abernethy's research work has been supported by the Australian Sports Commission's Applied Sports Research Program, the Australian Research Council and Worksafe Australia and has resulted in publications in a wide range of international journals. He is an International Fellow of the American Academy of Kinesiology and Physical Education and a Foundation Board Member of the Australian Association for Exercise and Sport Science. Professor Abernethy is the current editor of the *Australian Journal of Science and Medicine in Sport*, a current editorial board member of *Human Movement Science* and *Current Psychology of Cognition/Cahiers de Psychologie Cognitive* and a former editorial board member of the *International Journal of Sport Psychology*.

Dr. Stuart Biddle is Senior Lecturer in the School of Education, University of Exeter, England where he is Course Director of the MSc degree in Exercise and Sport Psychology. He is President of FEPSAC, the European Federation of Sports Psychology. In addition, Dr. Biddle is International Associate Editor for *The Sport Psychologist*. His research interests include motivational aspects of sport and exercise, with a particular interest in the two areas of health-related exercise and attribution theory. In 1991 his book (co-authored with Dr. Nanette Mutrie), *Psychology of Physical Activity and Exercise: A Health-Related Perspective*, was published by Springer-Verlag, and in 1994 he edited the text *Exercise and Sport Psychology: A European Perspective*, published by Human Kinetics. Dr. Biddle is the co-ordinator of an Inter-University Cooperation Programme, funded by the ERASMUS Bureau of the European

Union, designed to establish a European Masters degree in Exercise and Sport Psychology.

Dr. Albert V. Carron is a Professor in the Faculty of Kinesiology at the University of Western Ontario. Over the past 25 years, Carron has presented numerous research papers and invited addresses and has been the author or co-author of a number of refereed articles, chapters in books, monographs and books. The latter includes *Social Psychology of Sport, Motivation: Implications for Coaching and Teaching*, and *Group Dynamics in Sport*. He has been President of the Canadian Association of Sport Sciences, a member of the Sports Medicine Council of Canada, on the executive board of the Association for the Advancement of Applied Sport Psychology, on the Editorial Board of the *Journal of Sport and Exercise Psychology*, and a Section Editor for *Canadian Journal of Sport Sciences*. He is currently a Section Editor for the *Journal of Applied Sport Psychology*.

Dr. Joan L. Duda, Full Professor in Sport/Exercise Psychology and Director of the Sport and Health Psychology Laboratory, is in the Departments of Health, Kinesiology and Leisure and Psychological Sciences at Purdue University. She has published over 70 papers in scientific journals/books/proceedings and has made over a 100 presentations at professional meetings in the United States and abroad. She is Editor of the *Journal of Applied Sport Psychology* and is on the Editorial Board of the *Journal of Sport and Exercise Psychology*. Dr. Duda is a Fellow and Certified Consultant in the Association for the Advancement of Applied Sport Psychology, Active Member of NASESCLA and Division 47 of the APA, and on the Manangement Council of the International Society of Sport Psychology. She is currently the Sport Psychology Consultant for the US Gymnastics Federation Women's Program.

Dr. Kari Fasting is Professor at the Norwegian University of Sport and Physical Education in Oslo. Her field is social science, particularly social psychology and sociology. Her publications concern gender and sport, women and sport, sport and leisure quality of life, health and unemployment. Kari Fasting was the first president of the Norwegian Society for Sport Science in Norway (1980-1985), and has been elected

President of the International Committee for Sociology of Sport (ICSS) (1992-1996).

Dr. Dieter Hackfort is Professor of sport psychology at the University of the Federal Defence in Munich and has been Head of the Institute for Sport Science and Sports since 1991.Main areas of research are the development of action theory and empirical methods in the frame of this perspective; emotions in sports, so-called negative emotions (especially anxiety) as well as positive emotions (fun, pride etc.); self-presentation; and issues referring to health in sports as well as health by sports. He is past president of the ASP (the national sport psychology association in Germany), current Treasurer of the International Society of Sport Psychology (ISSP), scientific counselor of the national organization for top athletics, and counselor for various national teams/Olympic teams. Dr. Hackfort is also editor/co-editor of national and international book series in sport science and he is on the editorial board of various international journals. As a reward his research was honored by the highest grants in sport science in Germany.

Dr. James E. Loehr is presently co-director of the private enterprise, LGE Sport Science, located in Tampa, Florida. He has long been recognized as an authority on mental toughness training for sport. Dr. Loehr is former Director of Sports Science for the United States Tennis Association. He is an author, lecturer, and *Tennis* magazine editor. He has worked with over 75 tennis stars, including Martina Navratilova, Gabriela Sabatini, and Jim Courier, as well as many other world-class athletes in other sports. Dr. Loehr has the unique ability to synthesize research and to generate practical programs for high-performance athletes. He is the only person in the United States to be awarded the highest designation of master professional by both the US Professional Tennis Association and the US Professional Tennis Registry.

Dr. Bruce C. Ogilvie is currently Professor Emeritus of Psychology at San Jose State University, California. Dr. Ogilvie has developed important work for many years in the area of sport psychology being a pioneer in the application of psychology for the enhancement of human performance. His work as scientist and consultant psychologist has been published in more than 120 articles in the area of sport, human performance, youth sports and psychological issues in sport and exercise. He has been working during the past 35 years as a consultant to professional, national, intercollegiate athletes and teams, and his present service area is crisis intervention, to individuals and teams. Dr. Ogilvie is a member of the U.S.O.C. Sport Psychology Registry, and he is Fellow of APA, Division 47, Sport and Exercise Psychology, Fellow of the American Association for the Advancement of Applied Sport Psychology; Fellow of the International Society of Sport Psychology; and Fellow of the American College of Sports Medicine.

Dr. Hubert Ripoll has directed the Laboratory of Sport Neurosciences of the National Institute of Sport and Physical Education, Paris. He is now Professor at the University of Poitiers Laboratory of Behavior and Cognitive Neurosciences in Sport and Physical Activities. He carries out research in sport in the field of cognitive neurosciences and psychology. He has edited two books in French: in 1982 Neurobiologie des Comportements Moteurs [Neurobiology of Motor Behavior]; in 1989 Neurosciences du Sport [Neurosciences of Sport], and in 1991 a special issue of I.J.S.P. (*22,* 3/4), Information Processing and Decision Making in Sport. He is a Vice President of the French Society of Sport Psychology (S.F.P.S.).

Dr. Robert W. Schutz is a Professor and Director of the School of Human Kinetics at the University of British Columbia. He received his Ph.D. from the University of Wisconsin, Madison, in 1971, and has published widely in the areas of multivariate analysis, generalizability theory, attitude measurement, and mathematical analysis of the strategies in sport. He is a past president of the Canadian Association of Sport Sciences, past president of the North American Society for the Psychology of Sport and Physical Activity, and a Corresponding Fellow of the American Academy of Physical Education.

Dr. Robert N. Singer is Professor and Chair of the Department of Exercise and Sport Sciences at the University of Florida, Gainesville. He served two 4-year terms (1985 - 1993) as President of the International Society of Sport Psychology and he is now its Past President. In 1993, he became President-Elect of the Division of Exercise and Sport Psychology in the American Psychological Association. Dr. Singer has been involved in international activities for many years, having lectured and consulted in many countries throughout the world on a wide range of themes. In addition, he was appointed as Head of the Sport Psychology Division of the first Sport Medicine Council of the United States Olympic Committee in 1978. He has authored or edited 15 books, and is co-editor of the *Handbook of Research on Sport Psychology*, which was published in 1993 by Macmillan Company. He is currently on the editorial boards of three research journals of sport psychology.

Dr. Francisco Sobral was for several years Professor at the Technical University of Lisbon and he is President of the Portuguese Society of Physical Education. He received his Ph.D. from his university in 1981, and has, since then, published widely in the fields of kinanthropometry and human biology applied to the specific problems of training and performance of children and youth. He is a member of the International Society for the Advancement of Kinanthropometry, and also affiliated to several biological and anthropological international societies. Presently Dr. Sobral is the Chairman of the Sport and Physical Education Sciences Course of the University of Coimbra.

Dr. Miroslav Vanek is Professor Emeritus of the Faculty of Physical Education and Sport, University of Charles in Prague (Czech Republic) where he has been a member of the staff since 1950. Dr. Vanek studied and took his Ph.D. (*Fear, Anxiety and Courage in Physical Education*) in 1952 in this University, department of Psychology and Physical Education. Then in 1962 he defended there the CSc. (Candidate of Psychological Sciences, which was the Soviet and Communist equivalent for the occidental Ph.D.) with the thesis *The Psychological Preparation of Athletes*, became associate professor in 1964 and defended his doctorate of psychological sciences (*The Personality in Sports*) in 1981. Born in Prague in 1923, Dr. Vanek was total Einsatz in a German factory during the World War II. He has been a member of the Managing Council of ISSP since its foundation and President for the period 1973-1985 and has published 17 books as well as about 260 articles in different journals. Perhaps his best known book, translated in several languages, is the classic *Psychology and Superior Athlete* with Bryant Cratty, published in 1970 by Macmillan. Dr. Vanek, who also worked as a psychologist (volunteer) with several former Czechoslovak

Olympic teams from 1964-1980 and national ice hockey teams, has different awards, medals and the Philip Noel-Baker prize by ICSSPE.

Preface

Those who are interested in the area of sport psychology will find in the chapters of this book important elements for a better understanding of this field of knowledge, both from the research and practice points of view. Historical and overall perspectives, the state-of-the-art of outstanding topics and practical intervention issues are developed by the prestigious international contributors in the 13 chapters that the editors tried to organize in a logic and coherent volume.

To begin with, the reader has two texts that help him/her to understand the general and conceptual development of sport psychology throughout the years and political situations. As a matter of fact, in chapter 1, Robert Singer gives a developmental perspective of sport psychology that concerns research and professional intervention and also discusses its expanding areas and the impact of former congresses in world sport psychology. Then, he interprets the concept of "integration" with regard to the future and further research fields leading to the notion of knowledge expansion in connection with other scientific areas and having in mind that sport psychology has its place in contributing to the achievement and welfare of people practicing physical activities.

In chapter 2, Miroslav Vanek, one of the most attentive witnesses and important figures of contemporary sport psychology, gives us the privilege of contributing an article where he develops his interpretation of the evolution of this sport field in relation to the history of the International Society of Sport Psychology. Vanek takes each four-year period and the corresponding decisive "bridges" which are the World Congresses and the General Assemblies of ISSP and makes the connection with the decisive personal and political influences that took place in a time when the "Cold War" was omnipresent in every activity.

The reader then will find a series of chapters dealing with research in sport psychology and reviewing the international scientific production concerning cognitive psychology, social psychology and two other domains of psychology connected to such everyday physical activities as those in the fields of wellness and school sport. Robert Schutz, in chapter 3, introduces this group of articles by discussing the methodological problems related to research development in sport psychology and having in mind the complexity and appropriate procedures that must lead to positive scientific results. In fact, according to him, if the researcher is not aware of the most problematic issues concerning methodology and measurement, the scientific process and its conclusions may be negatively affected. Schutz finishes his chapter by noting and discussing what he considers to be 10 of the most important methodological problems in contemporary sport psychology research.

Bruce Abernethy, in chapter 4, calls the reader's attention to the need for understanding the skills acquisition processes in order to enable a good and effective intervention in motor learning and sport training and shows us that the sport expertise area has been occupying a central place in research within cognitive psychology. An overview of research concerning perceptual, cognitive and ecological elements of sport expertise is finally done by the author, who also discusses its relation with enhancing strategies of motor performance.

Hubert Ripoll's chapter 5 deals with other topics in cognitive psychology. Cognition and Decision Making concerns the effective and fast information treatment in order to solve the various and complex sport situations which are associated with the motor constraints of sport tasks. The author discusses the informational demands inherent to different types of sport situations considering that performance may be improved when these characteristics are known.

Chapters 6 to 9 give the readers different perspectives in the field of sport social psychology. Albert Carron initiates the series with an interesting analysis of group dynamics in sport where he develops the operational and relational group mechanisms after clarifying the notion of group in the sport context. A conceptual model concerning the dynamics of sport groups and related outcomes is presented. Carron also provides an overview of the research undertaken by himself in collaboration with students and colleagues for many years and suggests some potential areas of study in this field.

Stuart Biddle, in chapter 7, reviews contemporary issues in motivation in sport and exercise psychology from analyzing the articles published in the most important international journals of sport psychology. This enables the author to call the reader's attention to the most popular topics associated with the motivation concept, topics which are very much related to self-perception and social-cognition perspectives. A critical analysis of methodological aspects regarding this area of research is done as well as the key issues in the study of motivation in sport and exercise psychology are pointed out.

Joan Duda is responsible for chapter 8, in which she discusses contemporary social-cognitive theories in relation to goal perspectives and achievement motivation. Laboratory experiments will be described and the recent research will be reviewed leading to relevant relations connecting goal perspectives and various meaningful issues in the sport context.

Gender is the main topic of chapter 9. Here, Kari Fasting clarifies this concept in relation to its socio-cultural dimension and compares it to the biological sex perspective. She develops an overview on the researchers' approaches during the latest years and their relating theoretical conceptions. These topics are also discussed in the sport framework considering future developments in what concerns consequences and implications.

Physical activity, health and wellness are concepts that sport and exercise psychology have increasingly been studying in their relations for the past few years. Dieter Hackfort analyzes in chapter 10 what has been produced, starting with the clarification of the concepts of "Psychological Health" and "Mental Health." Plausibilities and contradictions are critically analyzed from the methodological aspects concerning the research described by him in his review.

Francisco Sobral's chapter 11 deals with the relationship between physical education and sport in school and psychological consequences in children and youngsters. In his approach, Sobral highlights the concepts and beliefs inherent to the nature, purposes and outcomes of physical education and school sport according to the large amount of research produced in the latest years. He proposes a multidisciplinary and multimethod approach connected to the complexity of the phenomenon and describes psychological consequences concluding with some questions that he considers not to have been studied enough.

The main topic of the last two chapters is psychological professional practice in the sport context. Bruce Ogilvie, in chapter 12, uses some examples that he easily can find from his large experience as sport psychologist to discuss the need for adequate training in concrete and specific sport situations in order to promote effective intervention skills in graduate students. The author considers the sport context as highly complex organizations and argues that there is a need for training in the field of organizational psychology because of the large number of social psychological crises that take place in sport.

The last chapter of this book concerns a cognitive-behavioral model of practical intervention in sport context developed by James Loehr for helping tennis players to enhance their competitive performances. The origin of this model was a complete and rigorous study of top-level players in contrast to unsuccessful ones during that fundamental moment which is the "between-point". The author presents a four-stage sequence of thinking and acting as well as the training sequence leading to mental and physical routines that have been used by a large number of players all over the world in a very encouraging way.

Now it is time for the reader to use this volume and be in touch with the international perspectives of sport and exercise psychology. The contributors from the European, American and Australian continents will help you on that. Have a nice reading!

Sidónio Serpa
José Alves
Vítor Pataco

Foreword

Modern society is constantly demanding higher performances of men and women in all the fields of their activities. "Always better", "always more", "always more efficient" are present goals in the daily life of common people as well as of organizational management, scientific production or sport competition.

Also in the sport context the rigour and specificity of technical and scientific resources are being developed in order to promote the enhancement of athletes and the quality of the work. Sport psychology aims at these goals too.

The development of this science can be understood as being a result of the evolution of both general psychology and sport that met in a certain point of their "ways". As a matter of fact, sport psychology is a result of the institutionalization of psychology as an independent science, which influenced different areas of human activity, and of the enormous increase of the social importance of sport that determined the concerns with its scientific fundaments.

Although Cruz (1991) asserts that the origin of sport psychology is connected to Wundt's laboratory in Leipzig and all the following research on reaction time and motor behavior, he also admits that at that time psychology and sport were not yet related. According to Feige (1977), the interest with the psychological aspects of sport activity began already by the end of the nineteenth century with Fitz and Tripllet in the United States and Schultze in Germany.

It has been a long time since these individual works initiated the scientific production in psychology of exercise and sport. Motor learning was the first main topic but at the very beginning we can find some concerns with the psychological factors of sport practice as in the studies of Grifith regarding American football and basketball which were produced in the twenties (Cruz, 1991; Serpa, 1993).

Pierre de Coubertin understood the importance of this new field and in 1913, associated with the General Assembly of the International Olympic Committee in Lausanne, he organized the "International Congress of Sport Psychology and Physiology" that was perhaps the first international scientific event where sport psychology was discussed and where he made his own contribution (Brito, 1981; Feige, 1977).

It was after the World War II that special increase of research and practical intervention in this field took place both in the North American continent and Eastern European countries although in Western Europe it had its development only in the late fifties (Cruz, 1991).

The official recognition of sport psychology as a new field of applied psychology finally took place after the Firsth World Congress of Sport Psychology, which was held in Rome in 1965. It was really the beginning of a new era! Not only research and practical intervention but also scientific international cooperation developed. National and international societies appeared, and journals on this topic began to be published.

The development of this new sport science also originated new fields of research corresponding to social and scientific concerns. Schilling (1992) notes how new tendencies appear in each World Congress since the heterogeneous program in Rome where 216 papers from 27 countries were presented. Social psychology of sport in Washington, performance enhancement in Madrid, personality in Prague, children in sport in Ottawa, motor learning in Copenhagen and welfare and exercise in Singapore seem to be, according to Shilling, the most popular topics with along the World congresses. Meanwhile, a "common stream" concerning motor learning, social-psychological issues, coaching and performance enhancement have been keeping the place in the conference rooms.

In 1993 Lisbon received 628 participants in the 8th World Congress of Sport Psychology coming from 43 countries of the five continents. A total of 409 scientific contributions were presented and the previous research tendencies were confirmed. The most popular topic was "coaching and psychology" but the quantity and quality of papers concerning cognition issues revealed the importance of this field in the sport psychologists' concerns. Also the number of papers regarding health and wellness shows us that scientific production in sport and exercise psychology corresponds to the development of daily life sport in the world. On the other hand, the contributions on the topic "measurement and methodological issues" are an important sign of the scientists' worries about the quality of research as well as the social and cultural aspects discussed by a number of participants relate sport and its psychological outcomes with the wider social context.

Prestigious scientists from different countries introduced each section giving their points of view. No doubt they are influenced by their experience and interests, but surely their contributions also are a product of particular cultural influences received in their countries. It was the international perspectives presented in the Congress!

The keynote addresses -- some of them reviewed -- are published in this volume as well as Dr. Vanek's conference about the evolution of ISSP and Sport Psychology and Dr. Ogilvie's contribution concerning practical professional issues.

All 13 articles will give the reader an important and interesting outlook on "International Perspectives on Sport and Exercise Psychology."

Sidónio Serpa

References

Brito, A. (1981). A Psicologia Desportiva em Portugal. In J. Lourenço (Ed), *I Jornadas de Informação Científico-Desportiva* (pp.34-37). Estudos e Investigação, 6, Lisboa: IND.

Cruz, J. (1991). Historia de la Psicologia del Deporte. J. Cruz & J. Riera, (Eds.) *Psicologia del deporte, aplicaciones y perspectivas* (pp.13-42). Barcelona: Martinez Roca.

Feige, K. (1977). O desenvolvimento da Psicologia Desportiva. Brito (Ed) (1981), *Textos de Apoio de Psicologia Desportiva.* (pp.25-32). Lisbon: I.S.E.F. - Technical University of Lisbon.

Schilling, G. (1992). State-of-the-art review of Sport Psychology, *Sport Science Review, 1* (2), 1-12.

Serpa, S. (1993). O Psicólogo e a Intervenção no Desporto, *Revista Horizonte, 9* (53), 187-192.

Acknowledgments

The editors would like to express their appreciation to all those who have given their support to the work concerning the preparation of the 8th World Congress of Sport Psychology where this book was born. We wish to thank the ISSP Managing Council (1989/1993) for their confidence in the Portuguese proposal and for their assistance since the beginning. We particularly thank to Dr. Robert Singer and Dr. Denis Glencross, who together with Geoff Paull were always in the next working table despite being on two other continents.

We also express our appreciation to the Faculty of Human Movement of the Technical University of Lisbon and to the marvellous Portuguese team that co-operated with us including the administrative, teaching and student staff.

Our thanks to the authors who immediately gave their positive response to our wish of publishing this volume and to Dr. Andrew C. Ostrow, President, Fitness Information Technology, Inc., Publishers, who accepted our proposal to make this project possible.

And, last but not the least, our gratitude to all the work in promoting sport psychology in Portugal that Dr. António Paula-Brito has been doing for so many years.

Chapter 1

SPORT PSYCHOLOGY: AN INTEGRATED APPROACH

Robert N. Singer

It is truly interesting, if not difficult, to determine the evolution of sport psychology from its presumed beginnings to the present time. What trends are apparent? Can they help to reveal what we might expect to occur in the near future as to research and practical/professional activities? Will there be similar patterns of development throughout the world, or will cultural, economic, educational, and geographical factors influence alternative directions?

In regard to these and other related questions, sport psychology as well as every profession and/or discipline needs to periodically review what it has accomplished, and what it can and would like to accomplish, considering changing times, conditions, expectations, and possibilities. The challenge for leading sport psychologists from all parts of the world, whom others look up to for vision and inspiration, is to provide such insights. The 8th World Congress of Sport Psychology, sponsored by the International Society of Sport Psychology and generously hosted by Lisbon, is the latest and most significant moment in the history of international sport psychology. Perspectives can and should be presented on this occasion. They will be scrutinized seriously with the potential to shape our thinking about viable future directions in sport psychology; and, indeed, what we attempt to do in the name of sport psychology.

The intention in this paper will be to provide projections about the future, with special reference to approaches to research. The structure and theme of this Congress, entitled "Sport Psychology: An Integrated Approach," will serve as the launching pad for these ideas.

Where From Here?

Interesting and meaningful developments in research and professional services are becoming more apparent. The energies and activity of researchers have expanded the body of knowledge. The insightfulness and interests of performance enhancement and counseling specialists have led to the generation of a variety of education/intervention and counseling programs. From the more scholarly, contributing to the foundational knowledge of topics and themes, to the more practical, evolving support programs for athletes, recreational participants, and exercisers, major advancements have been shown.

Where from here? What should be the next meaningful step? Where is all this flourishing activity taking us, to progress the field even further?

This is the most exciting challenge: to predict future research directions. Other attempts have been made on occasion (e.g., Singer, 1986; Strean & Roberts, 1992). Such projections become more complex and therefore perplexing if one considers topical themes, type of focus (e.g., more applied vs. more basic), methodological approaches (e.g., quantitative vs. qualitative), and geographical/cultural factors (similarities and distinctions as to interests and approaches), to name a number of more obvious variables. I will reduce the myriad of considerations by calling for a greater integration in the future. Topics, methodologies, and potential collaborators can each reflect integrative approaches.

Integrating Possibilities

What do we mean by "integrated"? Webster's *New World Dictionary* says that the purpose of integration is "to make whole or complete by adding or bringing together parts." The goal in this Congress is to recognize the importance of striving to unite and to unify the expanding field of sport psychology. Presumably more powerful insights and contributions can be realized by this type of approach. Furthermore, if meaningful outcomes are perceived as possible, future activities in sport psychology will continually reflect attempts at integration.

What can be integrated? The integration of different types of research is a necessity, according to Brawley (1992). Schilling (1992), in an excellent overview of developments in sport psychology as reflected by themes in the previous seven ISSP- sponsored World Congresses, perceptibly speculated briefly about future directions in sport psychology. He called for different types of collaborations, a number of which we had in mind in advocating more integrated approaches for this Congress.

There are additional considerations as well. Each prior ISSP Congress emphasized specific themes that tended to broaden the scope of sport psychology. Whereas at first the primary emphasis in sport psychology was on the personality testing of athletes — to understand, to profile, and to predict successful achievers — the Seventh Congress in Singapore revealed the increasing recognition of health and exercise psychology for "average" people. In-between Congresses tended to expand the boundaries of sport psychology, and at the same time, showed the depth of study and applications unfolding for different topics in all parts of the world.

The next step, the one which we are confronted with, is to conceive of ways of exploring approaches that can become even more exciting and meaningful: to sport psychologists, the discipline/profession in general, and to various consumer groups (i.e., high-level athletes, participants at the recreational level, and those concerned with health and fitness). What does this mean? Briefly described, some examples are to:

(1) Undertake *multidisciplinary approaches to research*, in which, for example, cognitive, behavioral, physiological, kinematic, and other dependent measures may be studied together while addressing certain questions. Specialists from different fields could collaborate. The result would be a more comprehensive understanding of mechanisms and processes involved under specified conditions, and how they can provide a better window in the study of phenomena of interest.

(2) Involve *qualitative and quantitative methodologies* in the same investigations. Heretofore, they have been considered to be contrasting orientations, with arguments in favor of or against each approach. Yet, both methodologies can provide stronger collaborative data in expanding the knowledge base.

(3) Search for a possible resolution in the *conceptual orientations proposed for the understanding of motor behavior*. Information processing, communication, engineering, and ecological (perception-action theory) approaches stress different perspectives for the study of motor behavior. Could a bigger picture emerge in order to explain the possible ways that humans function in their attempts to achieve goals, master environments, and attain skill?

(4)   Study *cumulative performance-enhancement strategies* rather than singular strategies. In the real world of sport, for instance, an athlete doesn't prepare for a pending event with an isolated technique. Pre-performance routines are formulated, and at first they are quite complex. They include serial and interactive processes and procedures. After many experiences with them, the preparatory act is run off as if automatic. Considering each sport, or type of sport, are there preferred combinations of readying strategies that should be useful for most participants?

(5)   Integrate *conceptual orientations with practical concerns*, so that the match between both becomes obvious and stronger. The formulation of practical performance-enhancement techniques to foster better performance, for example, can be couched in theoretical frameworks on many occasions. The conceptual and scientific basis in support of proposed practical applications for psychological skills training programs enriches the body of knowledge and at the same time lends greater credibility to these programs.

These are illustrations of possible integration approaches in sport psychology. Let's explore each one in more depth.

Multidisciplinary Approaches to Research

The next sections on "Quantitative and Qualitative Approaches" and "Conceptualizations About Motor Behavior" suggest trends toward integrating concepts, research, and scholars representing different academic specializations. These trends will apparently continue. Traditional academic/department units limit the kinds of research that can be undertaken and completed satisfactorily. Cross-fertilization provides more insightful and comprehensive perspectives in dealing with substantial issues. Is it any wonder that new departments, centers, and institutes are being formed in universities throughout the world?

Indeed, the trend in major agencies to fund research grants shows favoritism toward interdisciplinary collaborative efforts. Static disciplines like chemistry and physics can probably proceed in traditional ways. However, behavior is dynamic in complex situations, requiring a variety of scholarly perspectives to "...afford a special window into the principles of behavior at several levels of descriptors" (Kelso, 1990, p. 249). This is what Gaddis (1992) called for to contribute to political theory and international relations (as indicated earlier in this paper).

In a pessimistic view of psychology, Scott (1991) stated that "psychology lacks a clear identity" (p. 975). The same statement could obviously be made about sport psychology. When viewing how psychology might be structured in the year 2050, Scott believes that "...it is inevitable and desirable that formal structures realign to match the needs of evolving academic disciplines whose process they are obliged to serve" (p. 976). An example would be the ties between psychology and biology in the form of behavioral neuroscience and cognitive neuroscience. Such integrations move beyond classic convenient boundaries. New alliances help to create more dynamic scientific specializations which may effectively deal with the needs of society.

Reflections have been made by prominent psychologists about psychology's past and future, and described by Boneau (1992). The respondents felt that considerable change had been made over the last 24 years with regard to subject matter/knowledge base as well as in application/professional practices. New alliances and expanded integrations of subject fields related to psychology and the study of behaviors were primary targets of conjecture.

In an analysis of the research on genetic traits, Lykken, McGue, Tellegen, and Bouchard (1992) studied competence in a number of circumstances. According to these researchers, genes alone do not describe "emergenic" traits, those that do not predictably run in families. Traditional twin studies are reviewed. Described are shortcomings in this approach in explaining emergenic traits (novel or emergent properties that result from the interaction of genetics and other factors, such as situational conditions. Examples of emergenic traits are teaching ability, creativity, parenting ability, and leadership, among other behaviors. Many approaches to research and ways to assess behaviors discussed by Lykken et al. (1992) provide a broader and more useful scope of analysis of the traits of interest in this conceptual paper.

In predicting psychological testing and assessment in the 21st century, Matarazzo (1992) states that clinical neuropsychologists "...will be using biological tests of intelligence and cognition that record individual differences in brain functions at the neuromolecular, neurophysiologic and neurochemical levels" (p. 1007). New paper and pencil inventories as well as biological measures for assessing differences in interests, attitudes, personality styles, and predispositions are projected by Matarazzo in the future.

From a more limited consideration, there is a trend toward the determination of a variety of dependent measures in the same study to raise the degree to which they go together. In a sense, this is an attempt to cross-validate the relationship of variables of interest or the effect of a manipulated independent variable in an experiment. It is not unusual to see physiological, behavioral, and kinematic dependent measures in a particular investigation. Archery performance was of interest to Landers, Boutcher, and Wang (1986), who tested amateur archers on a variety of measures to determine the relationship of a number of variables with shooting performance. Relative leg strength, reaction time, depth perception, endomorphy, imagery usage, confidence, and focus on past mistakes were found to be associated with performance.

A multimodal model approach to performance enhancement has been described by Davies and West (1991). It is a comprehensive and integrated approach to helping counsel collegiate athletes. Davies and West recommend that counseling sport psychologists use a modality profile for athletes, which would consist of measures of behavior, affect, sensations, imagery, cognitions, interpersonal relations, and biological functioning. Goggin and Meeuwsen (1992) reported a variety of measures in a comparison of age-related differences as associated with the control of spatial aiming movements.

The present trend toward integrating biological and psychological measures in the same research will apparently continue and become stronger. This requires a more comprehensive scholarly background on the part of researchers. It also calls for teams of researchers representing different specializations to integrate their efforts in determining appropriate research paradigms and dependent measures for the issues studied.

Quantitative and Qualitative Approaches to Methodology

As one might expect, traditional quantitative approaches as associated with the "hard" sciences (e.g., physics, chemistry, and physiology) embracing experimental and correlational methods have dominated the sport psychology literature. Such approaches are driven by the collection of numbers and the ability to analyze them statistically. In experimental research, quantitative data serve as the basis for determining cause and effect circumstances.

As an alternative, qualitative approaches are gaining much greater support and acceptance, which is the case in education, sociology, and anthropology. The reliance is on words; the data are verbal. Words in the form of observations, interviews, and the like constitute the data. In qualitative methods, the emphasis is on field research and typically on natural environments. The researcher has to assess the situation of interest, be insightful, and make interpretations using scientifically accepted techniques. Quantitative methods usually rely on manipulated conditions, on "hard" data—numbers. Computers crunch numbers for the purpose of statistical analyses. Judgments of data interpretations rely on the outcome of these analyses; statistical significance or the absence of it. A good deal of the research in which quantitative methods are used takes place in laboratory settings.

However, due to the desire to understand psychological and cognitive processes associated with highly skilled athletic performance, and to obtain more ecologically evolved data (which critics complain laboratory settings do not produce satisfactorily), qualitative methods have become increasingly popular with sport psychology researchers. This is evident when one scans recent publications of sport psychology journals.

Indeed, further and more extreme challenges to experimental methods and quantitative statistics have been made by Cziko (1992). He disclaims their role for educational research by arguing that the unpredictability of human behavior is counter to deterministic perspectives. Furthermore, he feels that individual differences are great and that it is unrealistic to expect convenient, conforming data. People vary in many ways from each other and over time. Cziko's disenchantment with traditional experimental methods in contributing meaningfully to educational research is expressed in his thoughts that "... the most we can ever realistically hope to achieve in educational research is not prediction and control but rather only temporary understanding" (Cziko, 1989, p.17).

From another specialization orientation (in this case, political science and international relations), Gaddis (1992) also expresses concern over traditional research attempts to resolve issues. The basis for his concerns was triggered by the inability of political theory to predict the end of the Soviet Union and the political upheavals in other countries in Eastern Europe in the same time period. Gaddis asks whether the science of the physical and natural sciences can be or should be applied effectively by the social sciences. Considering that sport psychology would probably be classified as a social science, his observations are of interest to us.

Gaddis (1992) reaffirms that classical scientific methods generate laws and predictions. They are associated with precise observations, vigorous quantification, and the reproducibility of results. But, Gaddis asks, can they accommodate indeterminacy, irregularity, and unpredictability? The complexity of human behavior, especially in competitive sport environments, may make it virtually impossible to understand with classic research approaches. So many variables interact. Classical researchers know, according to Gaddis, "... that if they do not impose ... exclusions, controls, and quantifications, complications will quickly overwhelm their analyses, and predictability will suffer" (p. A44).

So, the question is how to account for reality. Gaddis (1992) calls for a liberation from simplistic experimentation and meaningless generalizations. However, unlike Cziko, Gaddis does not plead for a complete rejection of experimental, deterministic, and quantitative approaches to research. Instead, he suggests the use of a composite of approaches to understand, predict, and influence behaviors. Why shouldn't good scientists make use of all of the tools at their disposal? Gaddis recommends that political scientists include more than just theory, observation, and calculation. The other options for them might include "... narrative, analogy, paradox, irony, intuition, imagination, and —not least in importance—style" (Gaddis, 1992, p. A44). Perhaps we sport psychologists need to be more creative, flexible, and imaginative as well.

Of course the primary purpose of experimental research and quantitative methods is indeed prediction: Given an experimental treatment, does it lead to significant effects? Sport psychology researchers in particular and researchers representing other specializations in general are not at all ready to discard the deterministic model of behavior as well as attempts to create research paradigms that might provide useful knowledge about cause and effect relationships. But more support for alternative concepts and methodological approaches is tending to lend much more credibility to qualitative techniques.

As has been pointed out, sport psychology researchers are increasingly using qualitative methods to obtain descriptive data to gain understandings about athletes and achieving in sport. Other types of problems and questions are also being studied in this manner. Insights gained are helpful in contributing to the body of knowledge as well as in providing implications for guidance and instruction. Qualitative research methodology and analyses were used by Gould, Eklund, and Jackson (1992a,b) to study mental preparation strategies, precompetitive cognition, and affect of the 1988 U.S. Olympic wrestling team. Extensive interviews provided an in-depth examination of these factors. Complex and lengthy procedures were designed to prepare and analyze the data.

As Leedy (1993) puts it, "Qualitative and quantitative data may compatibly live in the same base; the terms refer more to a global atmosphere in which the researcher attempts to solve the basic problems for research, not to any exclusive method of operation" (p. 142). Sport psychologists are discovering the limitations as well as the values of each type of research methodology.

Perhaps more future investigations will be designed to include both qualitative and quantitative data. Major outcomes would be (1) the acquisition of more comprehensive data associated with the research question(s), and (2) the use of both kinds of data to validate each other. Integrating both forms of data in the same investigation may be beneficial considering these perspectives. Merging approaches may also break down some of the walls that have divided researchers who have exclusively advocated one or the other approach.

Conceptualizations About Motor Behavior

The study of motor behavior is also dividing into camps. Traditional cognitive models (e.g., the information processing approach with specified sequences of operations from input to output) is being challenged by more global and dynamic attempts to approach the study of motor behavior in the context of action theory (perception and action interactions).

In the 1940s, major concepts were formulated as alternative perspectives to behaviorism for the understanding of how humans acquire knowledge and skill, maintain them over time, and even attain great levels of proficiency. Theoretical approaches and associated research were usually grouped as being aligned to information, cybernetic, and hierarchical control models (Singer, 1980). These models were especially appealing to motor behaviorists. Later, in the 1950s, the evolution of information processing perspectives within the cognitive psychology school of thought was to have a tremendous impact on scholars and practitioners (Bruner, Goodnow, & Austin, 1956; Miller, 1956; Newell & Simon, 1972). It still does today.

Attempts have been made to understand more about the performance state of the person (Glaser, 1990). Functions of cognitive operations on information processing, such as attention, memory, decision-making, and problem-solving, have been analyzed (Anderson, 1990; Bower & Hilgard, 1981). Some obvious pragmatic questions are: How can information processing operations be improved upon? What can a teacher or coach do to assist the student or athlete in the functioning of these operations, thereby leading to more efficient and effective learning, and improved performance? Perhaps an even more important concern is what people can do for themselves to attain proficiency, considering self-direction and self-regulatory strategies.

The information processing approach, with the identification of mental operations that systematically become activated, from selective attention to appropriate cues/information to response production, has been conveniently associated with flow diagrams and schematics. Are these models too simplistic? Do they fail to account for an accurate description of the dynamics that occur in real-world complex situations? Action theorists believe that this is the case.

Whereas sensation, perception, cognition, and action are traditionally studied as separate operations, an alternative view is that they interact and are not separable. Simplifying the concept, perception leads to action and action influences perception (Neumann & Prinz, 1990). Gibson's (1979) classic work on a comprehensive view of perceptual systems has been extended by Turvey and Carello (1986) and others. In essence, it is proposed that what is perceived depends on the action to be performed. As indicated by Tipper, Lortie, and Baylis (1992), "...speculations concerning the link between perception and action have interesting implications for the role of the active observer in selective attention tasks" (p. 893). Many other relationships are also being established.

While information processing models depended to a great extent on computer analogies of human behavior, the orientation of perception/action models seems to be closer to the biological sciences. Furthermore, Prinz (1990) states that "Unlike response-centered approaches to psychology, which consider the organism's activity more or less determined by the actual stimulus information, the action approach emphasizes intentional control as being simultaneous with (or even prior to) informational control of activity, assuming that intentional processes fix the rules for the selection and use of stimulus information" (p. 167). Prinz also suggests that the action approach stresses the environmental consequences that are associated with bodily actions. Meaningful interactions with the situation are more significant to understand than the movements themselves. He claims that perceptual codes and action codes are not separate.

Williams, Davids, Burwitz, and Williams (1992), in an excellent overview article, summarize the leading disagreements between information processing approaches and action approaches. Perspectives are of great interest to movement scientists. Williams et al. examine sport-related tasks and discuss the artificiality and limitations of laboratory-oriented research paradigms associated with cognitive psychology. Perception-action approaches try to be more ecologically valid, but not without their share of strengths and limitations as well.

Can information processing perspectives and action theory perspectives be reconciled? Williams et al. (1992) conclude their summary by exploring possibilities. They state that "...it is clearly evident that there are conceptual differences between the two approaches making the possibility of reconciliation difficult, but not impossible, to obtain at this point" (p. 189). Typically, in the history of psychology, alternative conceptual frameworks have been useful in different ways in studying and explaining phenomena of intent. Different approaches have involved increasing multidisciplinary collaborations. Bourne (1992) states that cognitive psychologists work integratively and effectively on research problems with linguists, computer scientists, and others interested in the cognitive sciences. Neumann (1990) concludes by pleading for a multidisciplinary approach for the understanding of an action-oriented view of visual attentions. According to him, psychological theories of visual attention should not ignore the relevant research from the neurosciences and related fields.

Not only can perception influence action and action influence perception, but it has also been speculated that behavior controls perception (Powers, 1973). In Powers' Perceptual Control Theory, activity is viewed as being neither controlled nor regulated. Rather, it is the sensory input that is controlled or regulated through the activity of the organism. Presumably perception and behavior influence each other reciprocally and simultaneously. According to Cziko (1992) it would be "... the reference signal of the system (the internal goal) that ultimately determines how the systems... will behave" (p. 15).

Other models of behavior have their strong advocates, too. Cognitive psychology has spawned connectionism: a computer-based neural approach to modeling the human systems (Bourne, 1992). Interconnected networks of elements are designed. Processing capabilities are presumed to be parallel and distributed in a mapping context. The notion of hierarchical control over behavior is rejected, as parallel and simultaneous processing elements are couched in a biological framework. Artificial neural networks are used to describe adaptive control and learning in situations.

Adaptive and flexible behaviors in response to environmental constraints are elaborated upon by Zanone and Kelso (1992). Proposed are nonlinear dynamical systems, rooted in physics and mathematics, to describe coordinated actions. A theory of synergetics to embrace pattern formation and self-organization is discussed by Kelso (1990). Laws to explain observations of phase transitions in human behavior are proposed in equilibrium systems. The behavioral and neural sciences are wedded in the analysis of the stability of behavioral patterns with the ability to change behavioral patterns.

In other words, as we can see, knowledge is enhanced through integrated approaches. The understanding of human movement behavior and skill is enriched through the challenges put forth from different perspectives and possible resolutions from integrated research activity.

Cumulative Performance-Enhancement Strategies

In the clean, classic tradition, one independent variable is manipulated to determine cause and effect relationships. Such approaches provide interesting and meaningful data on occasion. This is especially true in relatively simple tasks, as are routinely studied under controlled laboratory conditions.

But as has been argued up to now, thoughts are changing about the ecological validity of dealing with complex behaviors in such a simplistic fashion. For example, this is a leading reason why action theory is gaining popularity among motor behaviorists as an alternative to information processing approaches in which singular mental operations are analyzed as if they function independently of other operations involved in performing a task. However, even with information processing models it is possible to study the effects of combinatorial strategies in learning and performing complex sport skills.

Singer (1988b) analyzed the sequential cumulative strategies athletes probably use to effectively execute self-paced skills. Examples of such skills are serving in tennis, shooting a foul shot, and hitting a golf ball. There is time to prepare, the situation is stable and predictable, and the execution needs to be performed as if automatic (habitual). The cumulative strategy developed by Singer (the 5-Step Strategy) includes readying, imaging, focusing attention, executing with a quiet mind, and evaluating if time permits. It presumably should aid individuals at any level of proficiency in acquiring skill or performing at a high degree of excellence.

In one study, Singer and Suwanthada (1986) analyzed the effectiveness of the 5-Step Strategy in aiding beginners to learn a primary sport-type self-paced task as well as to generalize to two other tasks. Data confirmed this usefulness in all three tasks. In other studies involving key-pressing (Singer, Flora, & Abourzek, 1989) and sport-type tasks (Singer, DeFrancesco, & Randall, 1989), the 5-Step Strategy turned out to be more beneficial in contributing to achievement as compared to control conditions. Recently, Singer, Lidor, and Cauraugh (1993) compared the effectiveness of different types of learning strategies with a computer-managed ball-throwing task. The 5-Step Strategy and non-awareness strategy groups out-performed the awareness strategy and control groups.

An interesting research design was devised by Prapavessis, Grove, McNair, and Cable (1992). They used a single-subject design to study a small-bore rifle shooter and the effectiveness of an intervention program to reduce competitive anxiety. Many techniques were integrated (training in relaxation, thought stoppage, refocusing, coping statements, and biofeedback). Furthermore, many dimensions of anxiety were determined; and self-report, physiological, and behavioral measures were obtained.

More and more illustrations of proposals for considering cumulative strategies, versus singular ones, are appearing in the sport psychology literature in regard to maximizing athletic performance. In addition, more comprehensive programs over a reasonable period of time have been devised. Examples includes Hellstedt's (1987) program designed for use at a ski academy for young competitive skiers. Different mental/psychological skills were addressed during the precompetitive and competitive seasons. Various performance-enhancement interventions were introduced to an amateur boxer by Heyman (1987). This creative single-case study generated a number of issues about the development, application, and evaluation of interventions, with the intent of suggesting ways to develop better and more comprehensive approaches. Fenker and Lambiotte (1987) describe the development and implementation of a performance enhancement program used during the competitive season with a major college football team. They state that their evaluation indicated that many of the major goals of the program for the players, involving generating positive attitudes, developing a present-centered focus, and learning skills for relaxation and attention control, were accomplished.

Thus, whether for an isolated event, such as serving in tennis, or over a competitive season, various performance-enhancement techniques oriented to cumulatively contribute to achievement can indeed be formulated. Research designs that include such multiple procedures may be more related to sport-type conditions. The data provide support for the deployment and use of various mental/psychological skills in combination, not merely isolated skills which are rarely activated separate from each other in real-world sport settings.

Conceptual Orientations and Practical Concerns

A good deal of the research in sport psychology in the 1960s and 1970s was generated to satisfy the "rules" of the academic game, incorporating standard designs under tightly controlled conditions as associated with the natural sciences. With the contemporary movement of sport psychology under way, there was a self-perceived need in sport psychologists for respectability in universities. The legitimacy of our specialization would be demonstrated with laboratory studies, rigorous controls, and sophisticated statistics.

As the years have proceeded to the present time, more and more sport psychology students have declared war on such research approaches. The feeling is that conceptually driven studies conducted in artificial laboratory settings do not have any real-world applications. Many new comers to sport psychology are interested in pragmatic approaches to curricula and research. Data obtained under meaningful conditions and that can be directly applied in areas of personal interest are perceived to be preferable. Howell (1992) has noticed a similar trend with psychology students in general. He is concerned about more and more psychology students wanting applied courses and careers. According to him, there is a growing scientific deficit.

Howell (1992) raises the question "... is psychology headed for bankruptcy as a major producer of basic sciences and scientists?" (p. 21). He believes that psychology should be anchored in a body of knowledge. Those who practice it should be well versed in the values and methods of science. Professional practice should be grounded in science. The same arguments could (and should) be made for sport psychology. Should not sport psychology practitioners be well educated in scientific methods and in the available scholarly literature, in order to know what they can advocate on the basis of scientifically verified knowledge? What is not known? What guidance is intuitively delivered?

Besides such issues in the professional preparation of the sport psychologist, let us return to the the research generated and how investigations might be approached. Most of the research questions posed can be couched in a conceptual framework, with resultant data contributing to the body of knowledge *as well as* to practical knowledge useful in applied circumstances. Body of knowledge oriented research need not conflict with applied oriented research. Sport psychology is not a pure discipline, with a pure body of knowledge. As a sport science and a branch of psychology, much of our research by its very nature will have practical overtones implicitly offered or explicitly recognized. A conceptual perspective for undertaking a study provides the intellectual justification for pursuing rational questions.

As to educational research, Kaestle (1993) analyzed its perceived awful reputation and in what ways it might be considered to be meaningful. Researchers frequently identified major projects in which a union of theory and practice was demonstrated.

A good example of the wedding of the theoretical with the practical can be found in the work of psychologist Robert J. Sternberg. He has been concerned with practical intelligence. He is presently involved in a 6-year project to help teachers in being more flexible with students possessing different thinking styles and to encourage students in modifying their thinking styles to accommodate a variety of challenges (Jacobson, 1992). However, Sternberg's practical insights and contributions evolved from what he calls a triarchic theory of human intelligence. Presented in his book, *Beyond IQ* (Sternberg, 1985), the theory goes far beyond the typical equating of intelligence with scores on an IQ test. "The theory views intelligence as a range of behaviors that include people's internal approaches to problem-solving, how they deal with novel situations, and how they adapt to their environments or try to shape them" (Jacobson, 1992, p. A9).

To be successful, students need more than knowledge about a subject area. They have to develop common sense and practical judgment. Furthermore, achievement in many situations is determined through the effective identifying and solving of problems, using one's time efficiently, and collaborating well with others. Sternberg refers to such understandings as tacit knowledge. Some students seem to have it, while others do not. In any case, it is rarely taught in the schools. Sternberg's conceptual approach to intelligence has led to many applications in the schools.

As many sport psychology researchers demonstrate in their work, it is indeed possible, even desirable, to blend a conceptual framework for a methodological protocol that can lead to significant practical contributions. Substantive thinking leads to unique concepts, alternative procedural approaches to resolve issues, and more useful data. Sport psychology needs to consider its scientific legitimacy and body of knowledge, the primary sources for defensible practical application strategies.

Unity in Diversity

In summing up, it is apparent that one of the major reasons for the growth of sport psychology has been the diverse directions it has taken. There is appeal for many individuals with somewhat diverse interests. Yet, there must be threads of bonding in order for sport psychologists to feel that they have things in common.

We share concerns for human achievement and welfare—in and through the medium of movement. Sport, exercise, recreation, and play constitute this medium. Helping others to attain their goals ranging from reasonable performance satisfaction to performance excellence, and including self-realization and well-being, constitutes a primary service delivery mission. Research that contributes to realizing these services, as well as the many other perspectives of sport psychology described earler in this paper, strengthens the diverse structure of the field but at the same time unifies its significance as a social force. There can be unity in diversity.

Research fragmentation is dangerous. In-depth analyses of themes require integrative approaches to solving problems. Sport psychologists with different educational preparations and experiences should consider working together on research topics in which their unique expertise can lead to significant advancements in knowledge. The trend is to also collaborate with specialists from other disciplines, for the same reason.

Approaches to research, as has been pointed out, can include integrated and more comprehensive perspectives with regard to questions raised, methods devised, statistics used, and interpretations rendered. Of course, much depends on the research questions of interest as to the most satisfactory means selected in attempting to resolve them. Scientists need to be liberated on occasion from conventional thinking and science in order to create new visions and possibilities. By example, one exciting new perspective being advocated by some psychologists and educators to explain any dimension of life is chaos theory. Chaos theory evolved from the thinking of mathematicians, physicists, and others. It suggests that the world is not an orderly, predictable place. Things happen, and people behave, in nondeterministic and non linear ways.

Such thinking is quite revolutionary to many of us who believe that standard experiments can conveniently lead to generalizations about causal effects on predictable behaviors. Advocates of chaos theory believe that people may be as predictable and as unpredictable as the weather. They vary considerably in being attracted to particular end states, and in meeting stumbling blocks along the way, leading to chaos. But, from each chaotic experience, presumably new order emerges. DeAngelis (1993) sees psychologists potentially applying chaos theory to everything, from understanding the organization of the human brain and nervous system to clinical approaches to family and individual therapy. Chaos theory is quite different from Newtonian physics, which was predicated on an orderly world and predictable events from sufficient information. What the future of chaos theory is in science in general and psychology in particular is difficult to say at the present time.

The future of sport psychology will depend on minds that want to be challenged and which, in turn, will challenge others. Diverse opinions and concepts challenge sciences to advance to a higher state. Many times, divergencies become compromised and unified at a point in time. Then, new challenges arise. (Is this a form of chaos theory?) Unifying what sport psychology is all about in spite of diversity can be accomplished in certain ways and for certain purposes. This unification is needed for the continued advancement of sport psychology from at one time being considered as a frivolous and irrelevant passing fancy to a seriously accepted and recognized sport science and branch of psychology.

References

Anderson, J.R. (1990). *Cognitive psychology and its implications* (2nd ed.). New York: Freeman.

Boneau, C.A. (1992). Observations on psychology's past and future. *American Psychologist, 47*, 1586-1596.

Bourne, L.E. (1992, Sept./Oct.). Cognitive psychology: A brief overview. *Science Agenda*, Washington, DC: American Psychological Association, pp. 5 and 20.

Bower, G.H., & Hilgard, E.R. (1981). *Theories of learning* (5th ed.). Englewood Cliffs, NJ: Prentice-Hall.

Brawley, L.R. (1992). Dealing with reality in order to develop AAASP's future. *Journal of Applied Sport Psychology, 4*, 102-119.

Bruner, J.S., Goodnow, J., & Austin, G.A. (1956). *A study of thinking*. New York: Wiley.

Cziko, G.A. (1989). Unpredictability and indeterminism in human behavior: Arguments and implications for educational research. *Educational Researcher, 18*, 17-25.

Cziko, G.A. (1992). Purposeful behavior as the control of perception. *Educational Researcher, 21*, 10-18.

Davies, S., & West, J.D. (1991). A theoretical paradigm for performance enhancement: The multimodal approach. *The Sport Psychologist, 5*, 167-174.

DeAngelis, T. (1993, January). Chaos, chaos everywhere is what the theorists think. *The APA Monitor*, pp.1, 41.

Fenker, R.M., & Lambiotte, J.G. (1987). A performance enhancement for a college football team: One incredible season. *The Sport Psychologist, 1*, 224-236.

Gaddis, J.L. (1992, July). The Cold War's end dramatizes the failure of political theory. *The Chronicle of Higher Education*, p. A44.

Gibson, J.J. (1979). *The ecological approach to visual perception*. Boston: Houghton Mifflin.

Glaser, R. (1990). The reemergence of learning theory within instruction research. *American Psychologist, 45*, 29-39.

Goggin, N.L., & Meeuwsen, H.J. (1992). Age-related differences in the control of spatial aiming movements. *Research Quarterly for Exercise and Sport, 63*, 366-372.

Gould, D., Eklund, R.C., & Jackson, S.A. (1992a). 1988 U.S. Olympic wrestling excellence: I. Mental preparation, precompetitive cognition, and affect. *The Sport Psychologist, 6*, 358-382.

Gould, D., Eklund, R.C., & Jackson, S.A. (1992b). 1988 U.S. Olympic wrestling excellence: II. Thoughts and effect occurring during competition. *The Sport Psychologist, 6*, 383-402.

Hellstedt, J.D. (1987). Sport psychology at a ski academy: Teaching mental skills to young athletes. *The Sport Psychologist, 1*, 56-58.

Heyman, S.R. (1987). Research and interventions in sport psychology: Issues encountered in working with an amateur boxer. *The Sport Psychologist, 1*, 208-233.

Howell, W. (1992, December). Field's science deficit will have dire effects. *The APA Monitor*, p. 21.

Jacobson, R.L. (1992, October). Research on different ways of being smart leads to 6-year project on teaching and learning "practical intelligence" in schools. *The Chronicle of Higher Education*, pp. A9, A15.

Kaestle, C.F. (1993, Jan.-Feb.). The awful reputation of education research. *Educational Research*, pp. 23-31.

Kelso, J.A.S. (1990). Phase transitions: Foudations of behavior. In H. Haken & M. Stadler (Eds.), *Synergetics of cognition* (pp. 249-268). Berlin: Springer-Verlag.

Landers, D.M., Boutcher, S.H., & Wang, M.Q. (1986). A study of archery performance. *Research Quarterly for Exercise and Sport, 57*, 236-244.

Leedy, P.D. (1993). *Practical research: Planning and design*. New York: Macmillan.

Lykken, D.T., McGue, M., Tellegen, A., & Bouchard, T.J. (1992). Emergenesis: Genetic tracts that may not run in families. *American Psychologist, 47*, 1565-1577.

Matarazzo, J.D. (1992). Psychological testing and assessment in the 21st century. *American Psychologist, 47*, 1007-1018.

Miller, G.A. (1956). The magical number seven, plus or minus two: Some limits on our capacity for processing information. *Psychological Review, 63*, 81-97.

Neumann, O. (1990). Visual attention and action. In O. Newmann & W. Prinz (Eds.), *Relationships between perception and action* (pp. 227-268). New York: Springer-Verlag.

Neumann, O., & Prinz, W. (Eds.) (1990). *Relationships between perception and action*. New York: Springer-Verlag.

Newell, A., & Simon, H.A. (1972). *Human problem solving*. Englewood Cliffs, NJ: Prentice-Hall.

Powers, W.T. (1973). *Behavior: The control of perception*. Chicago: Aldine.

Prapavessis, J., Grove, R., McNair, P.J., & Cable, N.T. (1992). Self-regulation training, state anxiety, and sport performance: A psychophysiological case study. *The Sport Psychologist, 6*, 213-229.

Prinz, W. (1990). A common coding approach to perception and action. In O. Newmann & W. Prinz (Eds.), *Relationships between perception and action*. (pp. 167-195). New York: Springer-Verlag.

Schilling, G. (1992). State-of-the-art review of sport psychology. *Sport Science Review, 1*, 1-12.

Scott, T.R. (1991). A personal view of the future of psychology departments. *American Psychologist, 46*, 975-976.

Singer, R.N. (1980). *Motor learning and human performance* (3rd ed.). New York: Macmillan.

Singer, R.N. (1986). Current perspectives on motor learning and sport psychology. In L. E. Unesthal (Ed.), *Sport psychology in theory and practice*, (pp. 5 - 19). Orebro, Sweden: Veje.

Singer, R.N. (1988b). Strategies and metastrategies in learning and performing self-paced athletic skills. *The Sport Psychologist, 2,* 49-68.

Singer, R.N., DeFrancesco, C., & Randall, L.E. (1989). Effects of a global learning strategy practical in different contexts on primary and transfer self-paced motor tasks. *Journal of Sport and Exercise Psychology, 11,* 290-303.

Singer, R.N., Flora, L.A., & Abourezk, T.L. (1989). The effect of a five-step cognitive learning strategy on the acquisition of a complex motor task. *Journal of Applied Sport Psychology, 1,* 98-108.

Singer, R.N., Lidor, R., & Cauraugh, J.H. (1993). To be aware or not aware? What to think about while learning and performing a motor skill. *The Sport Psychologist. 7,* 19 - 30.

Singer, R.N., & Suwanthada, S. (1986). The generalizability effectiveness of a learning strategy on achievement in related closed motor skills. *Research Quarterly for Exercise and Sport, 57* (3), 305-213.

Sternberg, R.J. (1985). *Beyond IQ.* Boston: Harvard University Press.

Strean, W.B., & Roberts, G.C. (1992). Future directions in applied sport psychology research. *The Sport Psychologist, 6,* 55-65.

Tipper, S.P., Lortie, C., & Baylis, G.C. (1992). Selective reaching: Evidence for action-centered attention. *Journal of Experimental Psychology: Human Performance and Perception, 18,* 891-905.

Turvey, M.T., & Carello, C. (1986). The ecological approach to perceiving-acting: A pictorial essay. *Acta Psychologica, 63,* 133-155

Williams, A.M., Davids, K., Burwitz, L., & Williams, J.G. (1992). Perception and action in sport. *Journal of Human Movement Studies, 22,* 147-204.

Zanone, P.G., & Kelso, J.A.S. (1992). Learning and transfer as dynamical paradigms for behavioral change. In G.E. Stelmach & J. Requin (Eds.), *Tutorials in motor behavior II* (pp. 563-582). Holland: Elsevier Science Publishers

Chapter 2

REFLECTIONS ON THE INCEPTION, DEVELOP-MENT, AND PERSPECTIVES OF ISSP's IMAGE AND SELF-IMAGE

Miroslav Vanek

My ambition is to contribute toward an understanding of the background of the existence of our society. My reflections are based upon a study of a multitude of different documents, proceedings, meetings, and events, as well as human and literary sources. An important additional method, nevertheless, is the critical and self-critical retrospection relating my long-lasting and dedicated stay in the domain of sport psychology and ISSP. This approach tries not to be subjective even if it is a personal statement. But a qualified reflection is valuable in questioning our past activities as well as suggesting future activities. It helps to provide an adequate orientation of the actual determinants and stimulates a creative searching. Its goal is also to minimize the gap between the contemporary underestimated public image and overestimated self-image of sport psychology. I still remember the naive glorification of sport psychology in the recent past and its present pragmatic rejection, especially in sports in the post-communist countries.

Thus, many reasons exist for a realistic and penetrating reflection of the past. Please follow with me the main points I would like to make.

Inception of the Practice of Sport Psychology and the Foundation of ISSP

The use of psychology in sport settings was stimulated in the beginning of the '50s by the Sovietization of top-level sport. The benefits of the socialist system should, therefore, be strongly demonstrated. Among other training branches and a few sciences, a very difficult task was given to psychology. Soviet colleagues at that time undertook great experimental and analytical projects. But determined by the ideology of collectivism and voluntarism, they emphasized the volition for drill and winning as well as political morality as the main theme. Of course the inner motivation of the Soviets and other socialist athletes was a heavy struggle for life. The best of them also received better living conditions.

Similar political considerations related to sport psychology in the free world were partially introduced, but not initiated. Different related fields of study existed in different countries and institutions, for example, motor learning, sport education, etc. Such was also the case with approaches and methods. Nevertheless, it was top-level sport that opened the door of the sport sciences for psychology. This was paradoxically one of the small advantages of the cold war, and also the first step in the foundation of the ISSP. But political arguments by themselves could never convince the skeptical national and international sport scientific bodies to accept the most undisciplined of all disciplines. This took a certain period of time in which the sport psychological quantitative and qualitative indicators pushed the sport scientific societies in the first half of the '60s to its recognition during the Olympic Congress in Tokyo in 1964. For example, a session of sport psychology was held (keynoters were Kane, Vanek, and Matsuda), and in the following year the ISSP was baptized.

But before this big day, the quantity and quality of the bibliography in sport psychology should be indicated at that time. Olsen (1966) reported the development of the literature in sport psychology between the years 1898-1963. The total number of publications was 814, which was raised to 2,687 after the first ISSP Congress held in Rome in 1965. This more than triple augmentation was mostly the product of the ISSP Congress and it was a stimulus in the advancement of sport psychology. This quantitative indicator was impressive as was the diversity of the topics being addressed. But what about the quality? There were many different publications in the Olsen bibliography . More than 65% dealt with typical sport psychology areas (e.g., sport psychology, exercise psychology, motor learning, motor development, motor control, movement therapy); 20% belonged to the other humanistic sciences (philosophy, pedagogy, sociology); and the remaining 15% were represented in classical psychology (Wundt, Thorndike) or in classical physiology (Bechterey, Pavlov). The quality of the publications could be regarded positively even if the methodological approaches were very different.

Thus, the world of sport and sport sciences was ready to accept sport psychology. The official recognition was realized in April, 1965, with the Gala Congress Supershow in Rome. It was due to the efforts of Ferrucio Antonelli and a few of his colleagues from FIMS Groupment Latin (mostly psychiatrists) who firmly believed in sport psychology. Antonelli's professional reputation and social position were matched by his organizing and diplomatic abilities. He convinced many important institutions and personalities related to international sport, as well as the Italian government, including the Vatican. Antonelli obtained the favor of the Italian Olympic Committee, but not of the International Olympic Committee (IOC). The problem still exists. The medical section of the IOC as yet does not recognize sport psychology, even though ISSP has tried several times to gain recognition. The result of my last attempt in the second half of the '70s was the unfortunate request by the IOC to remove the Olympic rings from the ISSP logo.

By my criterion, the first Congress in Rome was very successful. It covered not only the topics and issues of all sport psychological branches, but also nearly all of the sport sciences of that time. Evident was the psychiatric emphasis in sport psychology.

During the Congress in Rome, ISSP was founded. There were no elections, no voting, no discussions. Everything was made ready with respect to the divided political world. The Statutes were only proclamative, the membership free. The structure of the first Managing

Council (MC) of ISSP was also interesting. Nine members and one at large were determined for the next Congress, which was to be held in Washington, D.C., in 1968. There were three psychiatrists, one sports medicine doctor, two psychologists, one physical educator, and two documentalists. The MC members were nominated according to language groups. It was a little bit naive (e.g., Vanek represented Slavian countries which did not exist). Only Kunath was nominated to represent East European countries. Such an ostrich policy shortly caused a heavy and long-lasting crisis in ISSP, especially because ISSP was in reality a European society, even though having two U.S. representatives. Nevertheless the foundation of ISSP quickly stimulated the origin of the national sport psychological societies in western Europe and in other continents. Highly interesting in this connection is that the Italian Society (AIPS) was founded late in March, 1974, by Antonelli. Could the interpretation of this event rest in Antonelli's strong personality? The image and self-image of ISSP at this point in time were at the highest level in its entire history.

The Development of ISSP in the Years 1965-1993

An analysis of this long period must begin with the nearly clinical death of the Society after the Washington Congress. Also, its slow take-off after the Congress in Madrid in 1973 must also be acknowledged.

Antonelli organized the sport psychology sessions and the ISSP agenda occasionally at the meetings of the FIMS Groupment Latin in Barcelona and Lisbon. The psychosomatic orientation of this group had a deep sensitivity for brief communications about sport psychology. But this existed only as an appendix. The ISSP MC never met together as the original team. The agenda "Business Meetings" were short and without discussions, while often improvisational in nature. The leadership of Antonelli, as the president of ISSP MC, was strong and decisions were deeply influenced by him.

Eric de Winter who died several years ago has a place in the annals of ISSP and FEPSAC, although he initiated a problematic relationship between him and ISSP. He worked as a physiotherapist in Paris. Using a psychosomatic approach, combined with autogenic training, he tried to discover an original and complex therapy. He published some articles before the Congress in Rome and organized some workshops. The social impact of being a member of an international society may be considered as a strong motivation for him. Not holding any academic degree, he could not be a member of the FIMS. So the ISSP was much easier for him. He participated in the MC meeting a day prior to the Congress in Washington. Then he left and reacted founding FEPSAC.

What were the reasons behind the problematic relationship between de Winter and ISSP? They included economic and organizing troubles of organizations, the U.S. concept of congresses, the nature of the U.S. universities and traditional competition, and especially the pre-congress dabble in politics.

The second ISSP Congress in Washington, D.C., in 1968 raised expectations for the quality of the meetings due to the high level of status of the U.S.A. But the reality was a general shortage of everything: no simultaneous translations, a small staff, no sponsors, no celebrities. I was sorry for Arthur Slater-Hammel, the lonely man. He was expected to provide direction for this Congress. At least the professional standard of the North American papers was very high. There were really good scientists studying human movement behavior as the product of the U.S. competitive university system. They showed friendly acceptance of others, critical thinking, and high self-confidence. I was able to understand these U.S. characteristics only during my stay in Los Angeles a few weaks later. But my reflection on this Congress is of a friendly community, pragmatic people with practical problem solutions, critical discussions, and human tolerance.

But I also remember the anticipation of a sinister political dualism in ISSP. The protesting absence of the Soviets and other colleagues from the satellite countries occupying Czechoslovakia stimulated a very angry reaction by Antonelli. He was undiplomatic, yes, but he would not tolerate this unbelievable event. I sent a protest letter to Antonelli in those terrible days, but he never should have used it as the President of an international body. Although he achieved to control the conflicts in Rome, the gap between the two political worlds was, due to the strong negation just before the Washington Congress, the deepest in the entire existence of ISSP. Paradoxically, the international power of politics never played a more important role in sport psychology. It was practically bridged over by the personal contacts and mutual respect which is literally documented in both of Salmela's *Sourcebooks* (1981, 1992).

The subsequent foundation of a socialistic FEPSAC as an antipode of the capitalistic ISSP created then a long-lasting situation until the 4th ISSP Congress in Prague. My memory of FEPSAC at that time is a nightmare. At this time, Emma Geron was a remarkable personality. Speaking French, she was, perhaps, the only person able to communicate with de Winter and they became the key-persons of FEPSAC with Geron as President and him as a strong-man. Meanwhile, he died and Geron fled to Israel during ISSP Congress held in Madrid in 1973. But she left it correctly. Winter in the position of Secretary General was replaced by Schilling, and this work oriented man became the next President of FEPSAC.

The image of ISSP was very low after the Washington Congress and its self-image was also diminished. My reflection of the period between the end of the '60s and '70s is influenced by the re-Sovietization of my country and an isolation of all affairs of the ISSP. There was surely some activity in the restoration of the fragile relations between the Eastern bloc countries and the free world, between ISSP and FEPSAC. Perhaps it was not so difficult, because the socialistic sport psychologists were highly "trip" motivated. An excellent medium was the German ASP organizing the FEPSAC Congress in Cologne (1972) and the psychological session during the Scientific Congress on behalf of the Olympic Games in Munich in 1972.

The ISSP Congress in Madrid in 1973 occurred in an atmosphere of quietness. But its calm was apparent only. The echo of the strong confrontation in 1968 resounded fully during the General Assembly in 1973. The election, particularly the cabinet (MC) nomination of the ISSP officials, evoked a contra Antonelli "revolution." The absolute chaos could not be controlled, especially when the only formal statute was useless. Finally, based on common sense the presidential elections were improvised. My being elected President was commented on by a Spanish colleague as a communist putsch. This was absurd, as the Congress was held in Madrid and there was but a small participant group from the Eastern bloc. It was just the Antonelli's loss.

In my reflection of the Madrid elections, I was dominated by the fear of the responsibility and of the absence of the know-how. It was so unexpected.

The situation of ISSP at that time was nebulous. There was a low image by others but a relatively heroic self-image especially of the MC members. The international tendencies and balances determined an unbelievable increasing of the MC number. In Rome in 1965, there were 9 members plus one at large on the MC. In Washington, there were 9 members plus 4 at large (2 of them were not present -- Kunath and Geron). In Madrid, 14 officials were on the MC, including 2 General Secretaries. The first MC meeting held in Madrid brought two important decisions. Herman Rieder accepted my proposal to work as the Secretary General. Also, Antonelli achieved to be given the position of Honorary President even though this was a very unusual protocol.

In order to overcome the many ISSP difficulties, there was only one way: hard work and modesty.

This was clear during the MC meeting in Prague in April of 1974. But it took a long time to get the support of the Czechoslovak Union of Sport and Physical Education, especially when the supreme decision institution was the Central Bureau of the Communist party. There was always a certain suspicion of Vanek's person, and the Communist control system worked permanently, even abroad.

In order to have effective activity and to operate in the spirit of its democratization, there was a need for continuous and open discussion among MC members. Rules and new statutes were needed, as well as a well-organized MC administration. I must reflect in this connection on the best person of my MC staff: Hermann Rieder. He was energetic but modest, strong in personality but kind, hard working but fair. I was a President with some ideas, but he did the job. And in addition, he introduced, as the President of ASP, several socialistic sport psychologists to international recognition through German translations. He also organized a few significant international events in Germany which helped to promote ISSP. Rieder and the German ASP were in the critical period between the Congresses in Madrid and Prague, a most important element for a new ISSP stability. This also increased through systematic meetings between the President and the General Secretary (Prague-Heidelberg) twice a year and the annual MC meetings. Many things were clarified, some problems solved, but also some new ones emerged. Positive relations between ISSP and FEPSAC surfaced during Schilling's presidency. Guido is a very good friend of mine but as FEPSAC President he was an opponent. (Once on a train from Magglingen he told me that "There are too many bosses in sport psychology." My reply was that FEPSAC is for Europe. ISSP will be for the other continents.)

The 4th ISSP Congress in Prague was not a bad one even if totally under the permanent survey of the state police. No posters were allowed, nor was the flag of Israel. A special ISSP flag was therefore designated. The keynoters were suggested mostly from the socialistic countries. I decided therefore to give 10 minutes for every speaker, except for the first speaker who was an obligatory nominated Marx-Leninist general psychologist. We created as a defense against it namely a small, but very cohesive and dedicated groups of experts-volunteers. They handled the psychological part of this congress with a professional pride, neglecting all political or ideological limits.

My thoughts on the Prague Congress were that there was a relatively lower level of sport psychology in Europe than in North America. I had a desire to transfer the ISSP management over the ocean. Among the MC members elected in Prague were officials from countries from different continents: Asia, Australia, North America, South America, and Africa. This was more important than the Congress itself. The younger, active, and well-educated members brought with them a significant impulse for a higher quality ISSP.

I had a good nose for motivated workers and I let them fulfill their tasks without any limitations. John Salmela very creatively finished and published his first *Sourcebook* and realized, with his Canadian collaborators, an excellent congress in Ottawa in 1981. The Congress was based upon the philosophy of well-being, scientific research, and practical applications. I remember the discussion during the General Assembly about the possibility of involving NASPSPA in ISSP. This was the only logical solution for the further internationalization of the Society. Even if Harris and Singer, the outstanding U.S. members of our MC tried to help me, I had to face the very pragmatic scientific American "sharks." I shall never forget the terms "visibility" and "credibility" in relation to ISSP. NASPSPA members were not going to agree to anything until they could realize that the relationship between both organizations could be mutually beneficial. The image of ISSP was slightly tarnished, but self-image increased as a result of the successful Congress. The joint commitment of NASPSPA and ISSP was completed just before the ISSP Congress in Copenhagen in 1985. It was a prosperous venture.

My reflections on this 6th Congress of the ISSP go in several directions. The business capacity of DIF, which was the main organizing institution in Denmark, demonstrated the perfect commercialization of a scientific event. This also was evident with the organizer of the Congress, Lars-Eric Unestahl, an excellent mental training specialist and also a tough dealer. I also reflect on Dorothy Harris, fighting for a woman presidency (to be President of ISSP) and finally on the election of Bob Singer. My psychosomatic difficulties which started five years earlier could be interpreted as the result of my presidential agony. But my friends recognized that I was just overstressed, and not only by the ISSP affairs. I was really happy when Bob Singer won the election as President. His worldwide reputation, art of communication, and sense of humor are very important parts of the President's actor image. But he is also a good organizer and tough-minded, even if always respecting the democratic approach and politeness. Having taught and advised many students from around the world, he could bring other countries into the ISSP Also his marketing skill would be very helpful.

This was demonstrated at the ISSP 7th Congress in Singapore in 1989. It was splendidly organized with excellent papers, many discussions, and in a friendly but also a very demanding atmosphere. A major continental society was formed: Asian South Pacific Association of Sport Psychology (ASPASP). My thoughts about ISSP at this time were very simple. My old dream was fulfilled. ISSP really had become an intercontinental society. But I was concerned about an emerging scientific and commercial perspective. Are we to be a Society wasting too much sport psychological science on ourselves? What is to be our involvement in the practice of sport and other physical activities? What is the philosophy of this totally renovated ISSP?

Perspectives of ISSP

The quantitative optimum has probably been reached by ISSP. This is demonstrated in Salmela's second *Sourcebook*. It is an excellent publication, even if there are also some small fictional accounts. The significance of Salmela's effort is without doubt. But the annals of ISSP also need a dedicated author. A person should be asked to elaborate on and to chronicle the 30 years of activities and history of ISSP in 1995 for the 30th anniversary. Personalities, annual reports, MC documents, etc., should be described. This would not be the history of sport psychology, but rather a critical and objective evaluation of ISSP.

But let me reflect now on research perspectives in sport psychology. Research directions and themes in sport psychology have been developed with a certain diversity of topics, methods, and issues. But after carefully studying Schilling's (1992) Sport Psychology Review I received the impression that themes will not expand much more. This state could be overcome by a new interpretation of basic research and its empirical applications (Nitsch, 1989). Basic research should be oriented to the study of human movement (*homo movens*) as integrated in kinanthropological dimensions. Psychology still studies the relations between psychic functions and human movement. But perhaps this is only a surface analysis of the deepest neurophysiological regulations (spinal to subcortical operations) that influence motor behavior. Muscle morphology and other factors might also be studied and integrated with these other perspectives.

Such basic research could be a new source of interpretation of the yet to be collected datum and it could also offer a new orientation to empirical explorations. Two lines could be followed. Considered could be psychological dimensions with their own terminology (motivation cognition, emotion, etc.) and also the dimensions of the different movement activities which are urgently needed in the everyday work of coaches, physical educators, managers, and the like.

This practical point of view is very important for sport psychology. The contemporary system of the psychologization of different educational programs is not very effective. Sport psychology should not only be an external part of them. It should be included in the everyday knowledge base of sport and physical activity specialists.

There exist enough good handbooks of general sport psychology, motor learning, exercise psychology, and other sport sciences, but the practitioners are not being helped enough. For example, what about the psychology of ski jumping or the psychological considerations in teaching physical education activities or the psychological preparation of the ice hockey team during the mezzocycle period? We can determine certain psychological characteristics of different sport activities. Antonelli and Salvini (1978) has done this in his huge handbook with the speculative descriptions of about 14 sports, including reference to the sporting child, woman, coach, referee, and spectator. But Gabler et al. (1979) found only few useful scientific references about the different sports.

All of these considerations would be a milestone in the recognition of the sport psychology as a useful specialization for the whole world of sport and its different fields (e.g., topsport, schoolsport, handicapped sport). This effort will not be easy and will take a long time. It should be started, with negotiations with the IOC, at the highest possible level. On the official list of the Olympic support service personnel are, of course, a physician and a physiotherapist. But not a psychologist. This is an old story, but the president of ISSP should regard it as a very important task to have sport psychologists accepted as legitimate contributors to an athlete's performance and well-being. Perhaps the main obstacle is the attitude of the IOC Medical Committee that may misunderstand the psychological approaches and consider it as potential doping. But psychologists in the world of sport have unique and very real positive roles and functions which include humanistic values. Singer (1984) indicates about nine practical professional involvements for sport psychologists, including being a scientist helping to overcome psychological obstacles, or being a spokesperson, not only for winners but also for losers in athletic competition.

The IOC should open then the doors to all international sport federations. It could be useful to organize the meetings of psychologists and coaches. The Canadian CAC in this style on behalf of the Olympic Games in Montreal in 1976 organized three symposia: An International Symposium on the Art and Science of Coaching (1972), a Science and the Athlete symposium (1974), and a Post-Olympic Games symposium (1976).

The ISSP Congresses have increasingly become scientific shows for the best scientists and prestigious participants. They cannot be either replaced or changed. But there is sufficient room for some smaller special workshops, symposia, and other forms of relatively inexpensive but effective meetings organized by the national bodies. And all of them, having a certain level of credibility, could be patronized by the ISSP logo.

The very unstable post-communist world with many local wars and a global economic recession leads me to two ideas. The old one is related to the still lasting memory of linguistic barriers associated with the Washington, D.C., Congress. I know that English was, during my Presidency, fixed as the official language of ISSP. But the absence of French stimulated the aggressive foundation of FEPSAC. In subsequent years, the domination of English-speaking conferences led to the loss of a scientific and very effective working francophone association ARPS, contacting not only the French-speaking European countries but also the French-speaking Arabic regions. We are surely not a selfish and megalomanic society, but a certain liaison between the ISSP, ARPS, and other similar bodies needs to be established.

Documentation and bibliographies also must be regarded as a very important qualitative indicator of the level of each science. Unfortunately, the excellent international services in the sport psychology documentation by Essing were terminated for ISSP use in 1974. The famous Documentation Center of the Sporthochschule in Köln was not able to continue this international activity for economic reasons. Its specific value for mutual understanding and overcoming linguistic barriers is very important. A possibility of a cross-cultural and cross-linguistic documentation in sport psychology should be therefore discussed by the MC of the ISSP with concern for these perspectives.

The second idea deals with economic troubles. The ISSP General Assembly should take into consideration a new type of membership: the Associated Membership for individuals and groups who are not able to pay the membership fee. They may not vote but they should have the possibility to discuss and to be elected into MC. I know nothing about the contemporary economic state of the ISSP, but the global shortage of everything in the post-communist countries and in the Third World could delay or totally destroy new developments in sport psychology. Humanistic missions have been included in each variation of the ISSP Statutes.

Helpful would be an MC whose officials should not only be distinguished scientists but also members with important public relations credentials for possible involvements of private as well as state institutions.

My reflections are finished. ISSP is an important, but also modest, scholarly, practical, and foremost a humanistic society. Thank you for your attention and patience. I wish ISSP a successful future which should be based upon an objective and prestigious image and an adequate self-image. Farewell and adieu!

References

Antonelli, F. (Ed.). (1966) . *Psicologia dello sport. Proceedings of the First International Congress of Sport Psychology.* Rome.

Antonelli, F. (1973). 3rd World Congress of ISSP. In L. Pozzi (Ed.), *International Journal of Sport Psychology.*

Antonelli, F., & Salvini, A. (1978). *Psicologia dello sport.* Rome.

Bundesistitut für Sportsvissenschaft (Ed.), (1972, February). *Sportpsychologie. III Europäischer Köngress für Sportpsychologie.* Schorndorf: Hofmann Verlag.

Feige, K. (1977). *The development of sport psychology.* Kiel: Bundesinstitut Für Sportwissenschaft.

Gabler, H., Eberspächer, H., Hahn, E., Kern, J. & Schilling, G. (1979). *Praxis der Psychologie im Leistungssport.* Berlin: Verlag Bartels und Wernitz.

Harris, D. (1977). A short history of the North American Society for the Psychology of Sport and Physical Activity. In K. Feige (Ed.), *The development of sport psychology* (pp. 95-101). Kiel: Bundesinstitut Für Sportwissenschaft.

Kenyon, G.S., & Grogg, T.M. (Eds.). (1970). Contemporary psychology of sport. *Proceedings of the Second International Congress of Sport Psychology* (p. 7). Chicago: The Athletic Institute.

Nitsch, J.R. (1989). Future trends in sport psychology and sport sciences. In C.K. Giam (Ed.), *Proceedings of the 7th World Congress in Sport Psychology* (pp. 200-203). Singapore: Singapore Sports Council.

Olsen, M.A. (1966). Sports psychology in the literature. In F. Antonelli (Ed.), *Proceedings of the First International Congress of Sport Psychology.* Rome.

Salmela, J.H. (Ed.). (1981). *The world sport psychology sourcebook.* New York: Mouvement Publications.

Salmela, J.H. (Ed.). (1992). *The world sport psychology sourcebook,* 2nd ed., Champaign, IL: Human Kinetics.

Schilling, G. (1992). State-of-the-art review of sport psychology. In G. Schilling (Ed.), *Sport Science Review of Sport Psychology* (pp. 1-12). Champaign, IL: Human Kinetics.

Singer, R.N. (1984). What sport psychology can do for the coach and athlete. *International Journal of Sport Psychology,* 15, 52-61.

Singer, R.N. (1989). Presidential address. Sport psychology: International perspectives. In C.K. Giam (Ed.), *Proceedings of the 7th World Congress in Sport Psychology* (pp. 13-15). Singapore: Singapore Sports Council.

Chapter 3

METHODOLOGICAL ISSUES AND MEASURE- MENT PROBLEMS IN SPORT PSYCHOLOGY

Robert W. Schutz

The stated intent of this address is to provide an overview of the "method-ological and measurement problems/issues" in sport psychology. That has proven to be a formidable task! However, the process of trying to identify a small set of measurement and methodological problems and issues has been a challenging and stimulating exercise, and I think it will be informative to start this presentation with an account of that process. Thus, the first part of this paper focuses on an examination of measurement problems from a broad perspective in which I look at the type of issues which researchers in our field, and in the broader field of social science in general, view as being important methodological issues in (sport) psychology. As one would expect, the diversity of issues is great, ranging from very specific concerns about the definition of conjoint measurement to broad-based concerns about how we should measure behavior. In the second part of the paper I take the liberty of identifying eight issues which I view as important methodological problems that should be addressed or acknowledged by sport psychologists. It is a list derived from my own experiences, knowledge and biases, and I make no claim that these issues are the most pressing or important problems facing today's sport psychology researcher.

Measurement Issues and Problems: What the Literature Suggests

Data Bases and Measurement Texts

A search of PsycINFO and of CIJE yielded almost 1,000 articles dealing with methodological problems, methodological issues, measurement problems, and measurement issues. Searching title words only (and thus virtually eliminating duplicate hits) produced approximately 750 articles from the PsycINFO data base. Not surprisingly, the issues identified were extremely diverse, and only a couple of articles were from journals in our field. Although many of the articles were of interest to me, these results did not assist me in identifying any specific methodological problems as no key terms or phrases seemed to emerge. However, I concluded that, across all social science disciplines, a very common set of methodological problems revolves around the definition of constructs and the validity and reliability of the instruments used to measure those constructs. I elaborate on this point later in this paper, but I believe that it may be the most pressing methodological issue in sport psychology today.

Many researchers make use of one or more of the numerous commercial information up-date systems available these days, with Current Contents probably being the most popular one for social scientists in North America. For quantitative methodologists such as myself, the Journal Contents in Quantitative Methods (JCQM) provides the most comprehensive coverage of journals devoted to methodological issues. JCQM covers approximately 150 journals in measurement and statistics, primarily in the behavioral and social sciences. Journals of specific relevance to sport psychologists might be *Applied Psychological Measurement, Behaviormetrika, Multivariate Behavioral Research,* and *Quality & Quantity.* Reviewing the contents of these journals indicates that statistical issues predominate in these fields, specifically; (1) problems (dimensionality, parameter estimation) associated with item-response theory, a methodology which has dominated educational psychometrics in the last number of years, but has had little utilization in our field, and (2) issues related to covariance structural analysis (or structural equation modelling), for example, goodness-of-fit tests, nonnormal data, multi-group analyses. Additionally, there is a continuing interest in problems with traditional procedures such as regression, factor analysis and variance estimation. Although the majority of the methodological issues are statistical in nature, occasionally some very good papers appear which focus on measurement problems. Examples are a paper analyzing a new measurement procedure for attitudinal research (Batista-Fouget & Saris, 1992) and an extensive treatise of statistical models for behavioral observations (Rogasa & Ghandour, 1991). These two papers are excellent examples of the type of research and intellectual inquiry needed if we are to identify, delineate and solve the measurement problems in sport psychology.

Finally, upon examining the textbooks on measurement we see that the measurement theorists have a completely different set of concerns. There (e.g., Berka, 1983) the focus is on the philosophy of measurement, its axiomatic principles and even its definition--issues which tend to have little interest to the applied researcher. However, measurement specialists often provide a valuable service in reminding us that measurement does not necessarily equate with knowledge, nor is it necessarily the best tool of scholarly inquiry. To quote Berka:

> Mathematization in science cannot become a new, or perhaps even the exclusive method of inquiry; it can never replace the dialectico- and-historico-materialist approach to a scientifically founded analysis of the given phenomenon or object of investigation; it is always only a means helping to objectivize the results of inquiries in the social-scientific domain in question (p. 217).

The Sport Psychology Literature

Measurement and methodological papers are rather rare in our field; thus one cannot easily survey the literature with respect to methodological issues. Unlike other fields of study where there are numerous journals solely devoted to methodology (e.g., *Educational and Psychological Measurement, Applied Psychology Measurement, Sociological Methods and Research*), neither sport psychology nor the broader discipline of kinesiology have such specialized journals. Although this may reflect the relatively small size of our field, it also suggests that we do not place high values on the study of measurement or methodology. Rather than develop our own procedures, we borrow those of other disciplines--and, to our credit, we have become quite good at that. Nevertheless, there are a number of references to methodological concerns in the sport psychology literature, some of which I now summarize.

Cox, Qui, and Liu (1993), in their chapter "Overview of Sport Psychology", devote one short paragraph to "methodological concerns". They suggest that the primary (or perhaps only) issue is the need for "methodologically sound sport-specific measurement tools and for well-defined dependent and independent variables" (p. 23). I certainly agree that this is perhaps the most important measurement problem in sport psychology; however, we do not need more tools, only better ones. To be fair, Cox et al. do not explicitly state that we need more instruments. In sport psychology premature publication of measurement tools has led to a proliferation of psychological tests and a considerable amount of research of questionable validity. A quick scan of Ostrow's directory (1990) shows that of the 198 tests reported, only a few can be considered to exhibit sufficient evidence of validity and reliability. Perhaps for every new instrument developed the authors and publishers should agree to remove two existing instruments from the current inventory--and ban them from being used in any and all future publications!

Gessaroli and I put a greater emphasis on statistical issues than on measurement problems in our discussion of the psychometric problems in sport psychology research (Schutz & Gessaroli, 1993). We identified four issues/problems with ANOVA/MANOVA applications: (1) multivariate versus univariate analyses, (2) failure to use the doubly multivariate method for repeated measures designs with multiple dependent variables, (3) failure to adjust p-values in the presence of nonsphericity, and (4) incorrect multiple comparison procedures with repeated measures factors; and we expressed concern over the lack of use of three relatively common (in other fields) statistical procedures: log-linear analysis, hierarchical regression, and structural equation modeling. Additionally, our numerous concerns about inventory development and assessment centered on statistical issues. The identification of misuse and non-use was based on a review of all articles published in 1990 in four journals: *Journal of Sport & Exercise Psychology, Research Quarterly for Exercise and Sport, International Journal of Sport Psychology,* and *The Sport Psychologist.*

Gill (1992) conducted a similar but more comprehensive analysis of the methodologies in all articles submitted to the *Journal of Sport & Exercise Psychology* for the years 1985-1990. Her analyses suggest the following problems: (1) Most studies still use college students as subjects, with very few researchers conducting empirical work on adults over age 25 and even fewer looking at the over-50 population; (2) surveys and lab and field experiments still predominate, and less than 5% of the studies used interpretive or qualitative methodologies; (3) virtually all quantitative studies analyzed the data via traditional ANOVA and regression type procedures, with very few employing newer procedures such as meta-analysis, path analysis, or structural equation modeling; and (4) there is a scarcity of work being done in health-related exercise settings.

What do the North American sport psychologists think are the most important methodological issues in their field? An examination of the 13 chapters in Horn's (1992) edited book, *Advances in Sport Psychology*, clearly identifies a few issues which are acknowledged by most of the authors. Although there are measurement problems unique to each specific area (e.g., imagery, group dynamics, personality), two global problems are evident, namely, lack of theory and excessive adherence to traditional methodologies. In general, it is perceived that we rely too heavily on theories borrowed from psychology or sociology with the result that there exists a lack of theoretical models specific to sport psychology. Personally I'm not sure if I agree with this conclusion. Sport psychology, after all, is the study of sport and exercise from a psychological perspective, and thus the utilization of available psychological theories and methodologies is appropriate and necessary--a point well argued by Landers (1989). "Borrowing" and adapting a psychological theory should be as acceptable as borrowing Newton's theory for biomechanical research. However, I do agree with the assertion made by a few of the chapter authors that sport psychologists have failed to use theory in a systematic way. There are some excellent examples of sport psychologists who have adapted or developed a psychological theory and spent the next 10-15 years testing, refining and extending that theory. Unfortunately, there also far too many short-term research projects being undertaken, as opposed to the more desirable long-term research programs. Perhaps this is due to the nature of the research funding available to most sport psychologists. In Canada, fitness and sport funding is available only for specific projects, whereas the National Science and Engineering Research Council and the Social Science and Humanities Research Council now award research funding to researches on basis of long-term research productivity (or promise thereof) with less than 40% of the research grant evaluation being based on the specific project. If and when such funding becomes more accessible to sport psychologists perhaps we will see a greater number of individuals developing and utilizing theory in a systematic manner.

The second concern raised throughout the Horn text revolved around sport psychologists' reliance on the traditional research methodologies associated with logical positivism. In the last 10 years numerous publications and presentations have extolled and explained the richness available in alternative epistemologies and methodologies such as qualitative research, feminist epistemology, and inclusive ways of knowing, to name only a few descriptors of non-positivist approaches. It was refreshing to see that none of the authors who advocated a move away from hypothesis-testing laboratory experimentation attempted to justify an alternative methodology by unfairly criticizing the traditional methods. The arguments were made, and made well, on the strength of the alternative options now available, and the weaknesses of the traditional approaches in solve all our research questions. There is obviously a strong feeling that sport psychologists need to formulate research questions in additional ways and apply alternative methodological paradigms in their attempts to generate and discover knowledge. How we make this happen is, perhaps, the greatest problem of all.

Measurement & Methodology: A Personal Selection of Eight Pressing Problems

I now propose, and discuss briefly, what I consider to be eight of the most important measurement problems and methodological issues facing sport psychology researchers today. The order of presentation does not necessarily reflect the relative importance of the issues.

1. Heuristic versus Hypothesis Testing Research

There are a number of issues related to this concept and thus I will make only brief comments on each, although all are important topics which deserve extensive discussion.

Martens (1987) applies the term "heuristic" in a very broad context in his plea for the move to alternative ways of knowing in sport psychology. He advocates that we adopt a heuristic paradigm which relies much more heavily on experiential learning and social contextualization. As discussed earlier, the need to include additional methodologies and epistemologies into our scholarly activities is acknowledged by many sport psychologists. However, I doubt if many would support Martens' position that we abandon many of our current "scientific" practices. What we need are multiple ways of understanding and discovery, not just different ways. All methods can contribute.

My concern with the use and misuse of heuristic and hypothesis testing procedures has to do with both the design of studies and the analyses of the data. With respect to design, it is my perception that hypothesis testing in the traditional scientific sense is badly abused in some of the published (and submitted but not published) sport psychology literature. All too often the hypothesis is no more that a wild guess about the outcome of the study, rather than a carefully developed conjecture about the relationship among variables. Failure to adequately develop testable hypothesis, and the generation of untestable hypothesis and/or hypothesis which are established facts, is one of the reasons for the scarcity of supportable theories in sport psychology. On the other side of the coin, the perceived need to frame virtually every research project as an hypothesis testing study is also very stifling as it limits creativity, restricts data snooping, and discourages alternative explanations. Although I do not condone data snooping as a valid method of model testing, it can be a valuable heuristic tool. Unfortunately, academic work as practiced in today's universities, and current publishing practices, rarely reward systematic exploratory research--research which may take years before verifiable relationships are discovered.

Lastly, I am dismayed at the degree to which exploratory/heuristic data analysis procedures are used in hypothesis testing research studies. All too often researchers create well-defined sequential or hierarchical models and then test them with procedures that fail to test the explicit model of interest. Regression procedures can be exploratory (simple multiple regression, stepwise regression) or hypothesis testing (hierarchical regression, path analysis). Factor analysis can search for a structure via the usual principal component or factor analysis techniques, or test a model via confirmatory factor analysis. ANOVA can be followed up with preplanned contrasts to test specific hypothesis or post hoc multiple comparison tests on all possible pairings. Similarly, MANOVA can be followed up with univariate ANOVAs or with sequential stepdown F's to test an a priori ordering of the dependent variables. In each of these cases it is important to distinguish between hypothesis testing and non-hypothesis testing situations. If it is the former, then the more powerful and more specific hypothesis testing analytic procedures must be used.

2. When the Null Hypothesis is the Research Hypothesis

In many cases a researcher wants to test the equality of two means, with the expectation that they will not differ from each other. For example, a new and more efficient test is to be compared to an established test and it is expected that both tests will yield the same results, or theory suggests that there should be no gender differences in reaction time. In such cases the research hypothesis is one of "no differences"; that is, it is equivalent to the usual statistical null hypothesis. Common practice is to test the difference between means using standard procedures (e.g., a t-test) and if the resultant p-value is not less than some predetermined or arbitrary significance level (e.g., .05) then the researcher fails to reject Ho. At this point it is not unusual for the researcher then to accept Ho and conclude that the population means are equal and therefore the two tests or genders are equal. This is obviously an incorrect use of traditional hypothesis testing, and the severity of the violation increases with decreasing sample size (due to the decreased likelihood of obtaining a significant effect). The calculated p-value could be as small as .06 and the researcher would conclude that equality has been established. This is almost like using an alpha level of .94 to show that there is a true difference! Some researchers and methodologists have suggested that we use a much higher alpha level when we are trying to establish equality, say .50. This is certainly better than using .05, and with careful selection of sample size, alpha level and power to detect a substantively important difference while failing to detect a trivial difference, it may be acceptable (such a procedure is called the design-power method). But it is still not the appropriate test for this situation (see Harcum, 1990, for an interesting discussion as to why psychological researchers make this mistake). Although rarely used in the social sciences, an appropriate procedure, the bioequivalence test, has been used in the medical sciences for the last ten years. In this procedure the null hypothesis is that the difference between two means is greater than (or less than) some small difference (d), and the alternate hypothesis is that the difference between the means lies within the interval $[0-d, 0+d]$. The value d is set by the researcher as being the smallest magnitude of the difference between the means which can be considered important and meaningful. Thus if we are expecting no differences, we hope to be able to reject Ho and accept H1, concluding that the difference between the tests or genders is zero, or of a small and trivial (clinically unimportant) magnitude. The procedures for performing a bioequivalence test are somewhat similar to a t-test, but some additional calculations are required to obtain an approximate significance level (see Hauck & Anderson, 1986, for a readable explanation and sample calculations).

3. The Measurement and Analysis of Change

I have had a long-standing interest in the measurement and analysis of change (e.g., Schutz, 1978, 1989a, in press) and still view it as the most fascinating and challenging issue for behavioral scientists. From a measurement point of view, how can we obtain repeated valid and reliable measures on the same individuals such that the measures retain a common metric over behavioral change, and the individuals being measured are not changed differentially as a result of the measurement intervention? From an analysis point of view the problems are endless, varying from How can we obtain a gain score uncontaminated by initial score? to How can we identify interindividual differences in intraindividual change? Psychometricians continue to grapple with these and other problems in this area.

Given that so much of the research in both applied and theoretical sport psychology is dealing with some aspect of learning, stress reduction, change in group dynamics, ageing, etc., one might expect that the measurement and analysis of change would have had a much greater emphasis in our literature than what I perceive to be the case. With only a few exceptions, our researchers ignore the issues and problems and continue to follow the familiar and traditional procedures such as repeated measures ANOVA. In some cases this is appropriate, but there are many other instances where alternative strategies would be preferable. In other fields researchers are taking advantage of recent advances to develop new models of learning and apply new statistical techniques. For example, Embretson (1991) combined item-response theory with latent modeling to formulate a new model for representing learning and change. A series of papers in the American Psychological Association publication, Best Methods for the Analysis of Change (Collins & Horn, 1991), describe a number of new procedures which are directly applicable to sport psychology research (e.g., learning models, growth models, latent variable modeling for assessing change, measuring qualitative transitions). The use of structural equation modeling to analyze change is becoming increasingly popular as researchers realize the advantages of being able to estimate change in the latent constructs (rather than just in observed manifest variables). Aspinwall and Taylor's (1992) longitudinal study of the effects of optimism, psychological control and self-esteem on adjustment to college is a good example of this work. There are very few examples of application of the newer procedures in sport psychology, but

Spray and Newell's (1986) time series analysis of motor learning data and Duncan and Stoolmiller's (1993) analysis of exercise behavior with longitudinal structural equation modeling are two that merit noting.

Procedures such as these permit the researcher to test specific hypothesis, separate measurement error and construct reliability, take into account the dependency in trial-to-trial data, examine more closely the correlates of change, etc. It is past time that sport psychologists made fuller use of these new analytic methods.

4. Evaluating the Magnitude of an Effect

The need to calculate and report a measure of the magnitude of an effect, and not only the statistical significance of that effect, appears to be well understood by researchers in our field. Some of our journals require that authors report Cohen's d or some such effect size indicator; many papers report these values, and the use of meta analyses (an effect size analysis) is becoming relatively common. This is certainly a positive step, and we should encourage the continuation of this practice. However, it is still just a measure of the magnitude of a treatment effect, albeit a relative one. Perhaps it is time we started to evaluate the magnitude of treatment effects, that is, to make a conclusion about the importance of this magnitude. In the fields of clinical psychology and psychotherapy the concept of clinical significance is used to answer questions about the efficacy of a treatment, its impact on the subjects or the extent to which it may change their behaviors and their lives (e.g., see Jacobson & Truax, 1991). Sport psychology has matured to state where some of the more commonly used dependent measures are well developed and understood. Perhaps it is now possible to make situation-specific statements about clinical significance. How much of a reduction in trait anxiety is required before a practically important change in behavior ensues? How many kilograms must a person lose in order to consider a weight loss program a success? There are no definitive answers to these questions, but for each unique situation the researcher (probably in consultation with the subjects) needs to determine this threshold value. For example, in a weight loss program the standard analyses may state that the experimental group lost 4 kg on average, and that this was significantly greater than the 1 kg average loss of the control group. Such information is useful, but it could be supplemented by a statement about the number of subjects in each group that experienced a weight loss of practical or clinical importance (say

2 kg). It may be that there is some minimal value which must be realized if subjects are to continue with the program, and the difference between losing 1 kg and 3 kg is far more important than any additional weight losses above 5 kg. I suggest that clinical significance is a concept which could be applied in some intervention studies in sport psychology--it is certainly not a concept that has universal application.

5. New Statistical Procedures: Clarification or Obfuscation?

Hierarchical linear models, structural equation modeling, log-linear analyses, chaos theory, and item response theory are all relatively new statistical procedures which are viewed as "advances" in statistical theory and application. These and other recently developed techniques are supposed to enable researchers to test complex hypothesis while at the same time assist in understanding the nuances of the data. I agree with these observations and claims, but being an applied statistician I am obviously biased. However, a few years ago I suggested that the complexification of statistical techniques has brought enlightenment in some fields but in others it has directed researchers from a position of univariate clarity to one of multivariate obfuscation. I asked, "Has the increase in sophistication of method brought about a concomitant increase in the depth of understanding of the phenomena being studied?" Or does ".. the complexity of today's statistics serve only to display the analyst's quantitative skills, confuse the readers, and obfuscate the true nature of the research findings (Schutz, 1989b, p. 47)." The answer to both questions is "sometimes yes, sometimes no." As a case in point I relate a personal experience. I recently performed the data analysis for a study (Long, Kahn, & Schutz, 1992) involving 35 observed variables, 10 latent constructs and 3 time periods, and used LISREL to test a full structural equation model. The reviews, and subsequent feedback on the published paper, were very positive with respect to how the analysis aided in providing insight and clarification about the multivariate relationships among a number of constructs. More recently I have been working with similar data, but on the same variables measured repeatedly (6 times), using structural equation modeling (quasi-simplex models) to measure stability and consistency of latent constructs over time. The reviews of our submitted manuscript contain statements like "the way in which the data are presented seems to obscure rather than to illuminate the findings," "the presentation is unnecessarily obscure and technical," and "the reader does not get a good sense of the value of the statistical techniques employed or of what the analyses tell us." I cannot dismiss these comments as stemming from ignorance of the reviewers--I am confident that they are competent and knowledgeable. What it does tell me is that when I use a relatively new and unfamiliar statistical procedure I must (1) be sure that it is a better (i.e., clinically significant) procedure than more common traditional procedures, and (2) be very clear in explaining the procedure and the results in the written document. In general, sport psychology researchers and journal reviewers seem to have been able to maintain high standards with respect to presenting complex analyses in understandable terms--Duncan and Stoolmiller's (1993) presentation of a longitudinal structural equation model and Scanlan, Simons, Carpenter, Schmidt, and Keeler's (1993) confirmatory factor analyses are good examples. However this level of clarity may be primarily due to the fact that very few studies use complex analyses, and the ones that are published are, so far, being written by very competent methodologists. When it becomes just as easy to run a path analysis or confirmatory factor analysis computer program as it is to run a *t*-test computer program, then we may start seeing a proliferation of multivariate obfuscation. It is up to our journal editors to maintain standards of clarity, and not to be overly impressed with sophistication without clarification.

The last three issues I will present are highly interrelated, and could be grouped under one general heading, "The Development and Utilization of Sport Psychology Inventories." However, there are so many issues and problems associated with this topic that it would take a monograph or a complete book to deal with all of them. I have chosen the following three issues as I feel that they are fundamental to the construction, validation and application of tests, inventories and questionnaires in sport psychology research. The issues are certainly not independent and thus there is considerable overlap in the ensuing discussions.

6. The Measurement of Latent Constructs

In the behavioral sciences many of the constructs of interest are not directly observable but are implied from measured behaviors on some task or self-reporting instrument. The unobserved measures are often referred to as latent variables or constructs, and the observed measures called manifest variables. The definition, operationalization and valid measurement of these latent constructs is a very difficult and time-consuming task, when done correctly. However this does not appear to have been a deterrent for sport psychologists, as measures have been developed for a great variety of psychological constructs. Ostrow (1990) identifies 198 psychological tests and categorizes them under 18 construct headings from Achievement Orientation to Cohesion to Sex Roles (he could not classify 29 tests which he listed under the headings "miscellaneous" and "multidimensional"). I address the issue of proliferation of tests in the following section; here I examine some of the problems inherent in trying to measure latent constructs.

Two initial steps in developing a measure of a latent construct are the determination of acceptable conceptual and operational definitions of the construct. The conceptual definition must be based on a sound theoretical foundation and precede the operationalization of the concept. O'Reilly (1988), in an excellent paper on methodological issues in social support research, states that "The continuing lack of a linkage between conceptual definition and operationalization very likely results in the often ambiguous and inconclusive findings obtained in social support research" (p. 868). He suggests that the reason for this lack of linkage is the premature operationalization of a concept before the conceptual definition has been well established. Sport psychologists have expressed similar concerns; for example, Biddle (1988) asserts that the lack of progress in understanding the attribution-emotion links in sport is primarily due to inadequate definition or "conceptual clarity" of the underlying constructs. Fortunately, there are some excellent examples of construct definition and operationalization in the sport psychology literature which can be used as models by researchers who wish to develop new measures of latent constructs (e.g., the "sport commitment" model by Scanlan et al., 1993). Unfortunately, our journals still publish articles with poorly defined and operationalized constructs (e.g., "team psychology" as presented by Partington & Shangi, 1992) which can only lead to inconclusive and inconsistent research findings.

The second issue I wish to raise regarding the measurement of latent structures deals with factor analysis and dimensionality. The measurement of a construct entails the determination of the dimensionality of that construct; that is, is it a unidimensional factor or are there a number of component factors? If there are multicomponents, what is the structure of these constructs: independent, correlated but at the same order, or hierarchical? It is rewarding to see that many sport psychology researchers now use confirmatory factor analysis (CFA) in developing and revising their assessment instruments. This eliminates the "how many factors?" dilemma, as the number of constructs is determined a priori on theoretical grounds. However, we still see far too many articles in which the number of retained factors is determined with a data-driven exploratory factor analysis (EFA), often using the controversial eigen-value-greater-than-one rule (see Cliff, 1988, for a discussion of potential problems in applying this procedure). Ford, MacCallum, and Tait (1986) reviewed 152 EFA studies reported in 4 psychology journals over the ten-year period 1975 to 1984. They concluded that researchers made poor choices with respect to retention criteria, rotation and interpretation of factor structures, and that little improvement was apparent from 1975-1979 to 1980-1984. I would expect that we would find similar results with an analysis of the sport psychology literature, with some, but not a lot, of improvement from 1985 to 1993. What is needed is a more careful application of EFA computer programs (i.e., don't use the default options unless that is really what you want) in those research situations where EFA is justifiable, but use CFA in most cases. Assuming the researcher has decided on the number of factors that underlie the construct of interest, the next step is to determine the organizational structure of those constructs. In most instances this decision seems to be one of deciding if the factors should be correlated or not. If we are measuring something like team cohesion, motivation or aggression, and there are a number of sub-factors, it is highly unlikely that these factors are independent. The practice of forcing pseudo independence (with an orthogonal rotation like Varimax in EFA, or setting the phi matrix as diagonal in a LISREL CFA) so that the resultant factor scores are "independent," which they won't be in reality, has very little if any theoretical justification. Thus I agree with most psychometricians in recommending correlated factors in many applications. Once it has been decided to allow for correlated factors, the next step is to decide on the organizational structure of the factors. With only a few exceptions, researchers accept without question a "group-factor" model, in which all factors exist within the same grouping or level. In many cases this may be appropriate, but there are numerous situations where some sort of second-order structure or hierarchical structure may be theoretically justifiable. A good example in the sport psychology literature is McAuley, Duncan, and Tammen's (1989) psychometric analysis of the Intrinsic Motivation Inventory. They showed that the best fitting theoretically justifiable model was one which contained four first-order factors and one general second-order factor. Rindskopf and Rose (1988) provide a good explanation of possible second-order CFA models, and show how such models can also be used to separate reliability and validity estimates.

7. The Proliferation of Sport Psychology Questionnaires

As I noted above, Ostrow (1990) listed 199 sport psychology "tests", and supposedly he included only those tests for which there was some evidence of reliability and/or validity. A cursory glance through the 1990-1993 sport psychology journals suggests that there now must be more than 220 instruments available to assess constructs related to sport psychology. Do we really need any more? My answer to this question is "NO", not unless it can be clearly shown that (1) there is a need for the test, (2) the conceptual definition of the construct is well developed and theoretically sound, and (3) the developer of the questionnaire/test/inventory has followed careful procedures and adhered to rigorous standards in constructing the items and in establishing the reliability and validity of the test. A presentation of guidelines for test construction is beyond the scope of this paper, but I would like to refer the reader to three relevant publications. Phillips (1992), in his "Reinventing the wheel ..." paper, questions the need for constructing new psychological measures and gives a clear description of the expectations and pitfalls in creating such measures. Dawis (1987) provides a succinct overview of what is necessary in order to design, develop and evaluate valid counseling psychology scales. Finally, Angleitner and Wiggins' (1986) edited volume on personality assessment is a must read for anyone developing a measure of psychological traits. As the editors state, it is a thorough treatment of the "theoretical and methodological issues that have arisen in the context of the construction and evaluation of personality questionnaires over a period of more than half a century" (p.1). Especially useful are the chapters dealing with the application of structural equation modeling to evaluate convergent and discriminant validity.

8. The Validity, Reliability and Stability of Factor Structures

This issue is closely related to the problems in measuring latent constructs and my concern over the proliferation of sport psychology tests, but the focus here is on the mechanics of how we can go about validating our measures and weeding out the psychometrically unacceptable instruments that exist in our literature. It is my view that no test is sacred--just because an instrument like the POMS has been around for years and used in dozens of published studies does not necessarily mean it is a valid and reliable instrument. In other fields even the most venerable of tests are constantly being re-evaluated and questioned; Cattell is still defending the need for 16 factors to describe human personality (Cattell & Krug, 1986), and the factor structure of the Stanford-Binet Intelligence Scale is continually under investigation (e.g., Boyle, 1990). Many of the sport psychology tests in common use today were developed before CFA and other sophisticated psychometric procedures were readily available, and thus they may have not been subjected to the careful scrutiny required these days. In particular, the assumed factor structure was probably data-driven, the result of an exploratory factor analysis of some type. It is well known that the use of EFA frequently results in arbitrary solutions and misplaced substantive insights or, as Hendrickson and Jones (1987) state, are no better than "an undisciplined romp through a correlation matrix" (p. 105). Often, when CFA psychometric analyses are conducted, the assumed structure of the construct cannot be supported. Recently Ford and Summers (1992) tested the factorial validity of the Test of Attentional and Interpersonal Style (TAIS), and Chartrand, Jowdy, and Danish (1992) examined the psychometric characteristics of the Psychological Skills Inventory for Sports (PSIS R-5). Both studies employed CFA procedures and both studies failed to find support for the hypothesized factor structures. Such evidence certainly does not necessarily invalidate the factor structures of the TAIS and the PSIS R-5 as hypothesized by the original test developers; however, it does shed doubt on these structures and suggests that further investigations are required before utilizing either of these instruments.

Advances in psychometric theory are such that sport psychologists must venture well beyond current practice. Not only must we use CFA to test the claimed or hypothesized factorial validity of new and existing sport psychology constructs, but we need to take advantage of the techniques which enable us to make valid comparisons of the factor structures between groups and over time. LISREL and other covariance structure analyses programs can be used to test for scale invariance over time and scale invariance over groups. It is no longer sufficient to assume that males and females exhibit the same factor structure, nor is it acceptable to perform separate analyses and "eyeball" the results to see if they are the same. Fleishman and Benson (1987) provide a succinct methodological explanation scale invariance using LISREL, and Usala and Hertzog's (1991) study assessing the differential longitudinal stability of trait and state anxiety is a good empirical example.

Although it is much easier said than done, it is time sport psychologists used these psychometric procedures as a matter of course.

Conclusion

I have presented what I consider to be eight of the most important methodological issues and measurement problems in sport psychology research. The list is certainly not exhaustive, and I would expect that others would delete some of my items and add some of their own (e.g., I have omitted the important and often troublesome areas of self-reports and self-monitoring). I do not profess to have the answers to all these problems; for some there are no answers available, for others there are undoubtedly solutions available of which I am unaware, and for others I may have suggested the most appropriate solutions--but how to get the practicing sport psychology researchers to adopt these solutions is yet another problem. It is difficult enough for methodologists such as myself to try to keep abreast of new techniques, methodologies and philosophies of knowledge. It is even more difficult to maintain the level of expertise required in order to be able to perform the analyses and provide valid and lucid explanations of the results. For the researcher who must conduct the empirical research and keep abreast of developments in the substantive area, it is virtually impossible to acquire and maintain the methodological sophistication I am suggesting here. The solution, in my opinion, is to adopt the model often used in medicine and occasionally in other fields. There, every research project involves a methodologist at all stages--from the development of the research grant to the publication of the paper. However, this type of collaboration can be successful only if (1) there is a competent methodologist available, (2) there is sufficient funding to support the methodologist's graduate students as well as the principal investigator's assistants, (3) the principal investigator places high value on the contributions of the methodologist and accepts him/her as an integral part of the research and publication team, (4) the methodologist takes the responsibility to publish methodological papers using the researcher's data and includes the researcher in the writing and publishing of these papers, and (5) the tenure and promotion committees of academic institutions acknowledge and reward the creative and substantive contributions of researchers who call upon others for methodological support, and of the methodologists who use others' data to solve methodological problems. This situation would require that every department have at least one faculty member who is, essentially, a full-time measurement specialist or applied statistician. Although this does happen it is rare (to my knowledge I am the only such person in physical education in Canada), and it is unlikely to change in the near future, given the economic climate at most universities. So what does one do? Well, just do the best we can, which, as I have noted throughout this paper, is really very good in some sport psychology research.

References

Angleitner, A., & Wiggins, J.S. (Eds.). (1986). *Personality assessment via questionnaires: Current issues in theory and measurement.* Berlin: Springer-Verlag.

Aspinwall, L.G., & Taylor, S.E. (1992). Modeling cognitive adaptation: A longitudinal investigation of the impact of individual differences and coping on college adjustment and performance. *Journal of Personality and Social Psychology, 63,* 989-1003.

Batista-Fouget, J.M., & Saris, W.E. (1992). A new measurement procedure for attitude research: Analysis of its psychometric and informational properties. *Quality & Quantity, 26,* 127-146.

Berka, K. (1983). *Measurement: Its concepts, theories and problems.* London: Reidel Publishing Co.

Biddle, S.J.H. (1988). Methodological issues in the researching of attribution-emotion links in sport. *International Journal of Sport Psychology, 19,* 264-280.

Boyle, G.J. (1990). Stanford-Binet IV Intelligence Scale: Is its structure supported by LISREL congeneric factor analyses? *Personality and Individual Differences, 11,* 1175-1181.

Cattell, R.B., & Krug, S.E. (1986). The number of factors in the 16PF: A review of the evidence with special emphasis on methodological problems. *Educational and Psychological Measurement, 46,* 509-522.

Chartrand, J.M., Jowdy, D.P., & Danish, S.J. (1992). The Psychological Skills Inventory for Sports: Psychometric characteristics and applied implications. *Journal of Sport & Exercise Psychology, 14,* 405-413.

Cliff, N. (1988). The eigenvalues-greater-than-one rule and the reliability of components. *Psychological Bulletin, 103,* 276-279.

Collins, L.M., & Horn, J.L. (Eds.). (1991). *Best methods for the analysis of change.* Washington, D.C.: American Psychological Association.

Cox, H.R., Qui, Y., & Liu, Z. (1993). Overview of sport psychology. In R. N. Singer, M. Murphy & L. K. Tennant (Eds.), *Handbook of Research on Sport Psychology* (pp. 3-31). New York: Macmillan.

Dawis, R.V. (1987). Scale construction. *Journal of Counseling Psychology, 34,* 481-489.

Duncan, T.E., & Stoolmiller, M. (1993). Modeling social and psychological determinants of exercise behaviors via structural equation systems. *Research Quarterly for Exercise and Sport, 64,* 1-16.

Embretson, S.E. (1991). A multidimensional latent trait model for measuring learning and change. *Psychometrika, 56,* 495-515.

Fleishman, J., & Benson, J. (1987). Using LISREL to evaluate measurement models and scale reliability. *Educational and Psychological Measurement, 47,* 925-939.

Ford, J.K., MacCallum, R.C., & Tait, M. (1986). The application of exploratory factor analysis in applied psychology: A critical review and analysis. *Personnel Psychology, 39,* 291-314.

Ford, S.K., & Summers, J.J. (1992). The factorial validity of the TAIS attentional-style subscales. *Journal of Sport & Exercise Psychology, 14,* 283-297.

Gill, D. L. (1992). Status of the *Journal of Sport & Exercise Psychology,* 1985-1990. *Journal of Sport & Exercise Psychology, 14,* 1-12.

Harcum, E.R. (1990). Deficiency of education concerning the methodological issues in accepting null hypothesis. *Contemporary Educational Psychology, 15,* 199-211.

Hauck, W.W., & Anderson, S. (1986). A proposal for interpreting and reporting negative studies. *Statistics in Medicine, 5,* 203-209.

Hendrickson, L., & Jones, B. (1987). A study of longitudinal causal models comparing gain score analysis with structural equation approaches. In P. Cuttance & R. Ecob (Eds.), *Structural modeling by example: Applications in educational, sociological, and behavioural research* (pp. 86-107). New York: Cambridge.

Horn, T.S. (Ed.). (1992). *Advances in sport psychology.* Champaign, IL: Human Kinetics.

Jacobson, N.S., & Truax, P. (1991). Clinical significance: A statistical approach to defining meaningful change in psychotherapy research. *Journal of Consulting and Clinical Psychology, 59,* 12-19.

Landers, D.M. (1989). Sport psychology: A commentary. In J. S. Skinner, C. B. Corbin, D. M. Landers, P. E. Martin & C. L. Wells (Eds.), *Future directions in exercise and sport science research* (pp. 475-486). Champaign, IL: Human Kinetics.

Long, B.C., Kahn, S.E., & Schutz, R.W. (1992). A causal model of stress and coping: Women in management. *Journal of Counseling Psychology, 39*, 227-239.

Martens, R. (1987). Science, knowledge, and sport psychology. *Sport Psychologist, 1*, 29-55.

McAuley, E., Duncan, T., & Tammen, V.V. (1989). Psychometric properties of the intrinsic motivation inventory in a competitive sport setting: A confirmatory factor analysis. *Research Quarterly for Exercise & Sport, 60*, 48-58.

O'Reilly, P. (1988). Methodological issues in social support and social network research. *Social Science in Medicine, 26*, 863-873.

Ostrow, A.C. (1990). *Directory of psychological tests in the sport and exercise sciences.* Morgantown, WV: Fitness Information Technology Inc.

Partington, J.T., & Shangi, G.M. (1992). Developing and understanding of team psychology. *International Journal of Sport Psychology, 23*, 28-47.

Phillips, R.D. (1992). Reinventing the wheel?: On the wisdom of constructing new measures in psychosocial research. *Children's Health Care, 21*, 140-147.

Rindskopf, D., & Rose, T. (1988). Some theory and applications of confirmatory second-order factor analysis. *Multivariate Behavioral Research, 23*, 51-67.

Rogosa, D., & Ghandour, G. (1991). Statistical models for behavioral observations. *Journal of Educational Statistics, 16*, 157-252.

Scanlan, T.K., Simons, J.P., Carpenter, P.J., Schmidt, G.W., & Keeler, B. (1993). The sport commitment model: Measurement development for the youth-sport domain. *Journal of Sport & Exercise Psychology, 15*, 16-38.

Schutz, R.W. (1978). Specific problems in the measurement of change: Longitudinal studies, difference scores, and multivariate analyses. In D. Landers & R. Christina (Eds.), *Psychology of motor behavior and sport - 1977* (pp. 151-175). Champaign, IL: Human Kinetics.

Schutz, R.W. (1989a). Analyzing change. In J. Safrit & T. Wood (Eds.), *Measurement concepts in physical education and exercise science* (pp. 206-228). Champaign, IL: Human Kinetics.

Schutz, R.W. (1989b). "Advances" in statistics: From univariate clarity to multivariate obfuscation. In J. Safrit (Ed.), *Measurement theory and practice in exercise and sport science* (pp. 47-61). Madison: University of Wisconsin.

Schutz, R.W. (in press). The measurement, modelling and analysis of change: Somecomments on Embretson's paper. In D. Laveault, B. D. Zumbo, M. E. Gessaroli & M. W. Boss (Eds.) *Modern theories of measurement: Problems and issues.* Ottawa: Edumetric Research Group, U. of Ottawa.

Schutz, R.W., & Gessaroli, M.E. (1993). Use, misuse, and disuse of psychometrics in sport psychology research. In R. N. Singer, M. Murphy & L. K. Tennant (Eds.), *Handbook of Research on Sport Psychology* (pp. 901-917). New York: Macmillan.

Spray, J.A., & Newell, K.M. (1986). Time series analysis of motor learning: KR versus no-KR. *Human Movement Science, 5,* 59-74.

Usala, P.D., & Hertzog, C. (1991). Evidence of differential stability of state and trait anxiety in adults. *Journal of Personality and Social Psychology, 60,* 471-479.

Chapter 4

THE NATURE OF EXPERTISE IN SPORT

Bruce Abernethy

Why Study Sport Expertise?

Understanding the nature of expert performance in sport is important in both theoretical and practical terms for the sport psychologist. Theoretically, studying the expert is valuable in providing an insight into the processes underlying the acquisition of perceptual-motor skills, in determining the explanatory power of theories and models of expertise developed in other domains (such as the cognitive models developed to describe chess expertise), and, in concert with information from other sub-disciplines of the exercise sciences, in providing insight into the limiting factors to sport performance. The exquisite skills of the sport expert come about only as a result of literally millions of trials of specific, goal-oriented practice. As a consequence, studying the expert can provide a wealth of information on skill acquisition which simply cannot be gleaned from conventional laboratory-based learning studies in which the subjects are untrained. At the practical level, knowledge generated from studying the expert has the promise of immediate relevance to the key questions of training, testing and talent identification routinely faced by sports coaches and athletes. Isolating the source of the expert advantage in a particular sport can provide the coach with an informed basis for the development of practice routines to facilitate the acquisition of skill (expertise) and for the development of test batteries for the identification of talent and the monitoring of skill development.

Historical Trends in the Study of Sport Expertise

Despite the strong arguments that can be made for the study of sport expertise being a central focus for sport psychology, historically expertise has not been a favored topic for sport psychology research. It is only in the past decade that the development of a systematic, concentrated body of sport expertise research can be identified, with its origins clearly linked to the testing in sport settings of paradigms, such as the pattern-recognition paradigm of de Groot (1966) and Chase and Simon (1973) and the knowledge-based paradigms of Chi (1981) and Anderson (1982), developed to explain expertise in cognitive tasks. The delayed emergence of expertise as a focal point for sport psychology research was due primarily to the dominance, throughout the 1960s and 1970s, of laboratory-based research, especially in the motor control and learning field. Traditionally the bulk of the research in the motor control and learning field has sought to identify the fundamental limitations and capacities of putative processing stages and has sought to do so by studying untrained subjects performing simple, but novel tasks. Fortunately renewed concern for ecological validity (e.g., Neisser, 1976), the emergence of a branch of psychology (ecological psychology) specifically concerned with the functional couplings which develop between perception and action in natural tasks (e.g., Gibson, 1979), the continued growth in expertise as a focal concern for cognitive psychology, and the burgeoning interest of computational (cognitive) scientists in the artificial simulation of expert systems has collectively fuelled significant contemporary interest in expertise generally and in sport expertise in particular. Interest in the nature of sport expertise, at least as can be gauged by examining published research on the topic, has grown progressively since the early 1980s to the point where it is now a major area of genuinely international focus for sport psychology research.

In the remainder of this paper I will attempt to provide a necessarily brief overview of the existing research on sport expertise, highlighting key findings as well as limitations within the existing knowledge base and with existing methodological approaches. An attempt will also be made, within the constraints of existing knowledge, to draw practical implications for the design of practice and skill enhancement and to make some speculation on future directions for sport expertise research.

Key Observations on the Nature of Sport Expertise

1. Expertise Is Task-Specific

Despite its intuitive appeal, there is very little evidence of sport expertise being a generalizable characteristic. Expertise in motor skills, as in cognitive skills, is extremely task (domain)-specific, there being little or no correlation in performance from one sport task to the next and apparently little or no transfer of training (either positive or negative) from one sport to the next (e.g., Lotter, 1960). As is the case with cognitive tasks (e.g., see Voss & Post, 1988) experts from other domains typically behave much more like novices than experts when given tasks which fall outside their domain of familiarity and established expertise.

2. Expertise Does Not Emerge on Generalized Measures

A corollary to the observation that expertise is task-specific is the finding that expert-novice differences do not systematically emerge on general measures, lacking sport-specificity. For example, reviews of studies which compare the performance of expert and novice performers from a wide range of different sports reveal that experts are not systematically superior to novices on standardized visual tests, such as those for reaction time, acuity, depth perception and ocular muscle balance. Systematic expert-novice differences emerge, however, when the processing of sport-specific visual information is assessed (Abernethy, 1987; Starkes & Deakin, 1984).

3. Expertise Is Context-Sensitive

As Chase & Simon (1973) have clearly demonstrated in their studies of pattern-recognition in chess, and Starkes (1987) has also demonstrated most clearly in her studies of the sport of field hockey, the normal performance context must be preserved in test protocols if expertise-related differences are to be demonstrated. Changes as subtle as disruption to the patterns of play normally exhibited in the sport (even if sport-specific stimuli are used) or alteration to the normal time-constraints for decision-making can apparently negate the expert advantage. In short, it appears that the test context must match as precisely as possible the normal information processing requirements of the sport task if expertise effects are to be demonstrated. Studies demonstrating expert advantages in different facets of information processing have typically done so by creating tasks in which the preservation of ecological validity has been an imperative.

4. Experts Are Faster at Detecting and Locating Objects of Relevance

While experts appear no faster than novices in the processing of briefly presented visual information which is non-domain-specific (e.g., alphanumeric characters presented tachistoscopically) there is some evidence that expert ball sport players (e.g., volleyballers) are faster than less skilled players in detecting the location of a ball from slides depicting typical game situations (Allard & Starkes, 1980). This finding is not always replicated however and appears sensitive to the exposure durations used and the type of sport examined (Abernethy & Neal, 1990).

5. Experts Are Faster and More Accurate in Recognising Patterns From Within Their   Domain of Expertise

A robust observation from the study of chess experts (de Groot, 1966; Chase & Simon, 1973), which holds equally consistently with sport experts (e.g., Allard, Graham & Paarsulu, 1980; Starkes, 1987), is that experts outperform novices in the recall of briefly presented stimulus information for displays which have the structure typical of the domain of expertise (e.g., briefly presented slides of basketball offences) but not for displays lacking normal structure (e.g., a slide of the same basketball players in purely random positions). Such observations have given rise to a view of perceptual expertise that posits that experts have both a larger store of domain-specific patterns in long-term memory and a superior discrimination process for making comparisons between observed patterns and previously encoded ones (Simon & Gilmartin, 1973). Recognising complex displays in terms of patterns rather than a compilation of individual items (e.g., individual player positions) both speeds up the processing rate and facilitates a deeper level of processing (Craik & Lockhart, 1972), an action which in turn facilitates subsequent recall as well as recognition (e.g., Abernethy & Neal, 1990).

6. Experts Have Superior Knowledge

A number of researchers on chess (e.g., Holding & Reynolds, 1982; Pfau & Murphy, 1988) have argued that the selective superiority of experts in recognising and recalling structured display information is not so much a function of differences in pattern recognition capability as it is a reflection of expert-novice differences in knowledge. In the sports tasks of basketball (French & Thomas, 1987) and tennis (McPherson & Thomas, 1989), as in cognitive tasks, experts can be shown to have greater knowledge than novices both in terms of knowing specific facts about their sport (*declarative knowledge*) and, more importantly, knowing how to select correct courses of action in their sport (*procedural knowledge*). Indeed across the duration of a playing season improvements in performance, in young players at least, may be more attributable to knowledge development than to improvement in technique, fitness or strength (French & Thomas, 1987).

7. Experts' Knowledge Is Organized in a Deeper, More Structured Form Than That of Novices

Not only do experts appear to have more knowledge than novices, their knowledge is organized in a fundamentally different way. Studies of sport experts using approaches such as re-sequencing tasks (e.g., Vickers, 1986) and categorisation tasks (e.g. Russell, 1990) have shown experts, consistent with findings on experts from cognitive tasks (e.g., Glaser & Chi, 1988), to see and represent problems at a deeper, more principled level than novices, using abstract principles rather than superficial, literal features as the basis for problem solving and knowledge structure.

8. Experts Have a Better Knowledge of Situational Probabilities

A priori knowledge of event probabilities can impact directly on the time taken to respond in multi-choice tasks of the type presented in many sports. Any prior knowledge a player has that one option is more probable than another can directly reduce the reaction time to the more probable stimulus. Despite methodological difficulties in measuring the subjective probabilities athletes assign to different events there is some evidence (Cohen & Dearnaley, 1962) that the subjective estimates held by expert players match more closely actual event probabilities than the estimates made by less successful performers.

9. Experts Are Better Able to Plan Their Own Actions

In cognitive activities such as playing board games and solving mental problems thinking-aloud protocols have been used to demonstrate that experts consider more alternatives, are more forward looking and evaluate available options more fully yet more rapidly than novices (e.g., Holding & Reynolds, 1982). Similar characteristics also emerge for sport tasks, such as billiards and snooker and perhaps golf, which afford the performer response selection decisions in the absence of severe time-constraints (Abernethy & Neal, 1990).

10. Experts Are Superior in Anticipating the Actions of an Opponent

In time-constrained activities, such as the ball sports, experts are able to alleviate the time constraints and plan their own actions through being able to reliably anticipate the actions of an opponent from advance information. Naturalistic observations of expert racquet sport players show that their responses are initiated earlier in the event sequence than are the responses of less skilled players (Howarth, Walsh, Abernethy, & Snyder, 1984). Companion evidence from film-based studies using occlusion of the display of the opposing player prior to racquet-ball contact confirms expert superiority in the anticipation of event outcomes from information available from the opponent's action prior to the onset of ball flight (e.g., Jones & Miles, 1979).

11. Experts Are Superior Perceivers of Essential Kinematic Information

A series of studies from our own laboratory (see Abernethy, 1992 for a summary) indicates a direct link between perceptual expertise in racquet sports and the kinematics of the action being viewed. Evidence for this notion comes from three convergent sources, namely (i) the observation based on temporal and spatial occlusion paradigms that experts are able to pick up earlier occurring, more proximal sources of information in the opponent's action (Abernethy & Russell, 1987a), (ii) the observation that expert-novice differences in anticipation occur earlier in time for the sport of squash than badminton--the heavier racquet causing essential kinematic changes to occur earlier in squash (cf. Abernethy, 1990) and (iii) the observation that the same time course of information pick-up and expert-novice differences holds with degraded, point-light displays as normal, full-colour, high-texture displays.

12. Experts May Have Similar Visual Search Patterns to Novices

The evidence regarding expert-novice differences in visual search strategy is equivocal. Although some evidence has been presented to suggest experts search the display at a slower rate than novices, using fixations which are distributed to different display features and are of longer average duration than those used by novices, much of this evidence is methodologically flawed (see Abernethy, 1988a for a review). Our own data demonstrate that expert-novice differences in anticipatory performance are possible in situations where the visual search strategies are indistinguishable (Abernethy & Russell, 1987b).

13. Expert Performance Is Less Effortful and More Automatic

An essential adjunct to (or perhaps cause of) expertise is the development of automaticity. Unlike the novice, the expert is able to perceive essential information, select correct responses, or initiate and control well-learned actions apparently automatically, with a minimum of attention or effort. The expert's superiority in this regard surfaces especially in dual-task performance where expert sports performers consistently outperform less skilled performers on secondary tasks, even when expertise effects are not apparent on the primary task itself (e.g., see Parker, 1981). Automaticity in movement control can create the impression of expert superiority in functional visual field size even though this may simply be a consequence of the greater amount of free processing resources which can be allocated to concurrent perception.

14. Experts Cannot Accurately Self-Report on Many Aspects of Their Own Expertise

One of the trade-offs in the attainment of increased automaticity is a decreased capability to introspect on the operation of those processes which are under automatic control. Expert performers are demonstrably inaccurate in their self-reporting of some aspects of their own performance (e.g., in reporting watching the ball onto the bat or racquet [Bahill & La Ritz, 1984] or in reporting on their anticipatory cue usage [Abernethy, 1990]) although undoubtedly self-report data can be insightful with respect to some of the more conscious, strategic decisions made by athletes in many sports.

15. Experts Possess Superior Self-Monitoring Skills

Like experts in cognitive tasks, sport experts appear more aware than novices of when they have produced an error, even before the error becomes apparent. Expert cyclists, for instance, are able to reliably monitor personal work output from intrinsic sources of information without reliance on extrinsic information sources whereas the same is not true of novices (Lynagh, 1987).

Limitations in the Existing Knowledge on Sport Expertise

In examining what is currently a quite limited knowledge base on sport expertise it is apparent that there are a number of needs which must be addressed if the field is to advance. Foremost among these are the needs to:
- recognise the mediating effect of task type on the mechanisms through which expertise is obtained
- recognise the limitations in adopting paradigms developed to study expertise in other domains (e.g., a number of the key paradigms imported from cognitive psychology make assumptions about knowledge structure, about the rule-based nature of expertise and about the fidelity of self- report data which may be untenable).
- preserve situation-specificity and ecological validity in the investigative paradigm
-link studies of sport expertise to contemporary theories of motor control and learn to move the field beyond description and towards explanation
- examine alternatives to one-off studies using cross-sectional research designs
- develop more universal criteria as to what constitutes an expert
- discriminate, through the use of appropriate control groups, the effect of inexperience from the effects of persistent poor performance
- recognise the essential multi-dimensional nature of expertise through the use of multiple dependent measures.

Abernethy, Thomas & Thomas (1993) provide a detailed examination of each of these needs and how they might be satisfied.

Applications of Existing Knowledge to the Design of Practice

How might our (currently rudimentary) knowledge of the nature of expert-novice differences in sport be used to design practice in a way which might facilitate the acquisition of skill? The speculations which follow are directed specifically at the acquisition of anticipation skills for ball sport players. A useful starting point for these speculations is to note the existence of evidence (Abernethy, 1988b) indicating that task-specific practice is essentially for the improvement of anticipatory skill with age--in the racquet sports children do not improve in their ability to use advance sources of information unless they are actively involved in playing and practising their sport. Knowing what aspects of performance differentiate and equally importantly do not differentiate experts from novices provides an informed basis as to where practice efforts might best be directed. Training of the type advocated by many sports optometrists which attempts to improve general visual skills, for example, is unlikely to be effective because (i) it does not train a limiting factor to expert performance and (ii) improvement in general visual skills with practice may not necessarily translate into improved sports performance. Recent visual training experiments from our laboratory confirm this expectation. Likewise approaches which seek to have learners mimic the visual search patterns of expert performance are unlikely to be effective as they do not guarantee concomitant acquisition of information pick-up skills. More likely to be beneficial are approaches which provide players with the opportunity to learn the linkage between early information and ultimate event outcome (e.g., through the use of paused video sequences), which direct player's attention to the location of relevant information sources, and which provide players with essential knowledge related to the biomechanics of the action being viewed. Training programs which incorporate practice of this type have recently been shown to be significantly more effective than other types of generalised training in improving the anticipatory performance of racquet sport players (Abernethy & Wood, 1992). One can speculate that the effectiveness of such approaches might be facilitated further by (i) the use of point-light displays which minimise distraction and reduce the display to essential information only and by (ii) the provision of a priori event probability information to supplement the existing knowledge base of the subjects.

Rapid technological developments such as those from cognitive science underlying virtual reality applications ensure an exciting future for both the examination and training of expertise in simulated sport settings.

References

Abernethy, B. (1987). Selective attention in fast ball sports. II: Expert-novice differences. *Australian Journal of Science and Medicine in Sport, 19* (4), 7-16.

Abernethy, B. (1988a). Visual search in sport and ergonomics: Its relationship to selective attention and performer expertise. *Human Performance, 1,* 205-235.

Aberneth, B. (1988b). The effects of age and expertise upon perceptual skill development in a racquet sport. *Research Quarterly for Exercise and Sport, 59,* 210-221.

Abernethy, B. (1990). Anticipation in squash: Differences in advance cue utilization between expert and novice players. *Journal of Sport Sciences, 8,* 17-34.

Abernethy, B. (1992). Visual search strategies and decision-making in sport. *International Journal of Sport Psychology, 22,* 189-210.

Abernethy, B. & Neal, R.J. (1990). Perceptual-motor characteristics of elite performers in aiming sports. *Research report to the Australian Sports Commission.* Canberra, Australia. 180 p.

Abernethy, B., & Russell, D.G. (1987a). Expert-novice differences in an applied selective attention task. *Journal of Sport Psychology, 9,* 326-345.

Abernethy, B., & Russell, D.G. (1987b). The relationship between expertise and visual search strategiy in a racquet sport. *Human Movement Science, 6,* 283-319.

Abernethy, B., Thomas, K.T., & Thomas, J.R. (1993). Strategies for improving understanding of motor expertise. In J.L. Starkes & F. Allard (Eds.), *Cognitive issues in motor expertise.* (pp. 317-356). Amsterdam: Elsevier.

Abernethy, B., & Wood, J. (1992). An assessment of the effectiveness of selected visual training programs in enhancing sports performance. *Research Report to the Australian Sports Commission.* Canberra, Australia. 180 pp.

Allard, F., Graham, S., & Paarsalu, M.E. (1980). Perception in sport: Basketball. *Journal of Sport Psychology, 2*, 14-21.

Allard, F., & Starkes, J.L. (1980). Perception in sport: Volleyball. *Journal of Sport Psychology, 2*, 22-33.

Anderson, J.R. (1982). Acquisition of cognitive skill. *Psychological Review, 89*, 369-406.

Bahill, A.T., & La Ritz, T. (1984). Why can't batters keep their eyes on the ball? *American Scientist, 72*, 249-253.

Chase, W.G., & Simon, H.A. (1973). Perception in chess. *Cognitive Psychology, 4*, 55-81.

Chi, M.T.H. (1981). Knowledge development and memory performance. In M.P. Friedman, J.P. Das, & N. O'Connor (Eds.), *Intelligence and learning* (pp. 221-229). New York: Plenum Press.

Cohen, J., & Dearnaley, E.J. (1962). Skill and judgement of footballers in attempting to score goals. *British Journal of Psychology, 53*, 71-88.

Craik, F.I.M., & Lockhart, R.S. (1972). Levels of processing: A framework for memory research. *Journal of Verbal Learning and Verbal Behavior, 11*, 671-684.

De Groot, A.D. (1966). Perception and memory versus thought. In B. Kleinmuntz (Ed.), *Problem solving research, methods and theory* (pp. 19-50). New York: Wiley.

French, K.E., & Thomas, J.R. (1987). The relation of knowledge development to children's basketball performance. *Journal of Sport Psychology, 9*, 15-32.

Gibson, J.J. (1979). *The ecological approach to visual perception.* Boston, MA: Houghton-Mifflin.

Glaser, R., & Chi, M.T.H. (1988). Overview. In M.T.H. Chi, R. Glaser, & M.J. Farr (Eds.), *The nature of expertise* (pp. xv-xxviii). Hillsdale, NJ: Erlbaum.

Holding, D.H., & Reynolds, R.A. (1982). Recall or evaluation of chess positions as determinants of chess skill. *Memory and Cognition, 10*, 237-242.

Howarth, C., Walsh, W.D., Abernethy, B., & Snyder, C.W., Jr. (1984). A field examination of anticipation in squash: Some preliminary data. *Australian Journal of Science and Medicine in Sport, 16* (3), 7-11

Jones, C.M., & Miles, T.r. (1978). Use of advance cues in predicting the flight of a lawn tennis ball. *Journal of Human Movement Studies, 4*, 231-235.

Lotter, W.S. (1960). Interrelationships among reaction times and speeds of movement in different limbs. *Research Quarterly, 31*, 147-155.

Lynagh, M. (1987). *The role of internal and external sensory cues in the perception of effort.* Unpublished Honours thesis, The University of Queensland.

McPherson, S.l., & Thomas, J.R. (1989). Relation of knowledge and performance in boys' tennis: Age and expertise. *Journal of Experimental Child Psychology, 48*, 190-211.

Neisser, V. (1976). *Cognition and reality.* San Francisco: Freeman.

Parker, H. (1981). Visual detection and perception in netball. In l.M. Cockerill & W.W. MacGillivary (Eds.), *Vision and sport* (pp. 42-53). London: Stanley Thornes.

Pfau, H.D., & Murphy, M.D. (1988). The role of verbal knowledge in chess skill. *American Journal of Psychology, 101*, 73-86.

Russell, S.J. (1990). Athletes' knowledge in task perception, definition and classification. *International Journal of Sport Psychology, 21*, 85-101.

Simon, H.A., & Gilmartin, K. (1973). A simulation of memory for chess positions. *Cognitive Psychology, 8*, 165-190.

Starkes, J.L. (1987). Skill in field hockey: The nature of the cognitive advantage. *Journal of Sport Psychology, 9*, 146-160.

Starkes, J.L., & Deakin, J. (1984). Perception in sport: A cognitive approach to skilled performance. In W.F. Straub, & J.M. Williams (Eds.), *Cognitive sport psychology* (pp. 115-128). Lansing, N.Y.: Sport Science Assoc.

Vickers, J.N. (1986). The resequencing task: Determining expert-novice differences in the organization of a movement sequence. *Research Quarterly for Exercise and Sport, 57*, 260-264.

Voss, J.F., & Post, T.A. (1988). On the solving of ill-structured problems. In M.T.H. Chi, R. Glaser, & M.J. Farr (Eds.), *The nature of expertise* (pp. 261-285). Hillsdale, NJ: Erlbaum.

ACKNOWLEDGMENTS

Appreciation is expressed to Australian Sports Commission and to the Australian Research Council for supporting a number of the research projects described in this paper.

Chapter 5

COGNITION AND DECISION MAKING IN SPORT

Hubert Ripoll

Position of the Problem

The idea according to which decision making depends on underlying cognitive processing implies that logic operations subtend human complex behaviors. The cognitive, or computo-symbolic, approach considers a very strong analogy between computer functioning and the human modes of functioning. According to this approach, the subject is assimilated to a system that processes information with respect to the following principles: The capacity of the system is limited. It results that information has to be selected, that is to say filtered. Data processing is processed by stages in which specific processings occur. Different systems of memories are used; these memories depend directly on immediate relationship with the physical and human environment--short-term memory--or result on past experience--long-term memory. The subject uses representations by manipulating symbols and makes inferences on events to be occurred. These representations and computations serve to the elaboration of formal logical operations. Finally, following these operations, the subjects takes the more appropriate decisions to fit with the situation. The concept of decision making refers to the concept of strategy. In general, a decision has to be made each time a situation is ambiguous, that is to say when only a specific response, among multiple possible responses, is adequate to solve the problem. So, this concept cannot be dissociated from the notion of choice and from the concept of problem solving. A possible approach of this problem is furnished by the mathematical signal detection theory developed by Tanner and Sweets (1954). This theory, developed at first in the domain of transmission, has been extended with a strong pertinency in the field of sport psychology by Alain and Proteau (1980). In this perspective, complex sport situations, such as those in which decision making intervenes, could be assimilated to a signal detection task in which subjects would have to extract pertinent cues, assimilated to signals, and to ignore non-pertinent cues, assimilated to noises. However, athletes are not only confronted with the objective processing of information that is related to the legibility of events, to the task uncertainty and to the signal/ noise ratio which derives from it, but also with their own subjective expectations and the level of risk they accept to take. This subjective expectation can finally modulate the objective information displayed by the opponent or conveyed by the environment. The interest of this model lies in its capacity to discriminate between the sensitivity of the system, which reflects the physical properties of the receptor, and the decisional processes, which reflect the subject's strategy.

The state of the question about cognition and decision making:

There are different ways to address the question of cognition and decision making. These ones have been differently developed in sport research, and we will present at the following, the main line of research.

Formal operations subtending logical processing and reasoning:

Paradoxically, while identification of formal and logic operations subtending reasoning constitutes the main objective of research in cognitive psychology, little specific research has been developed in sport psychology. Consequently, if we are able to describe specific operations underlying different aspects of processing, such as attention, memory, preparation, inference, we know very little about the elaboration of appropriate formal logic operations, either throughout the stages of development or as a consequence of practice. These questions have to be clarified, mainly in team sports, in which player has to coordinate his strategy with the teammates' and opponents' individual and collective tactics. It has been demonstrated (Parlebas, 1981) that collective games have in common universal principles of structural organization. These universals, which can be formalized by mathematical descriptions, result from the common basic structure of collective games. Each game has these universals in common and specific features depending upon its own characteristics. Then, universals and specific features determine an internal logic. It is clear that communication between players depends on the knowledge of the internal logic of the game characterized, as for formal language, by syntactic and semantic rules. Then, using these common structures, players can apply conventional production rules of the type if (condition) then (action) and take their decision. An important question consists in how a player passes from a schemata, which consists in a static and abstract representation of relationship between elements of the structure, to a dynamic structure, which consists in transformations of the basic schemata by using specific formal rules. In these situations, the pertinency of the decision-making process has to be considered as being determined by this underlying formal logic.

Description of specific operations involved in the classical model of information processing:

The development of computer sciences has furnished a conceptual framework to study cognitive processes. By analogy to computer systems, it is hypothesized that the human operator processes information, manipulates symbols, organizes memories under the effect of practice, activates a situation problem in long-term memory which is analogous to the one being processed, then takes his decision. Different models, generally assimilated to models working in sequential stages (Atkinson & Shiffrin, 1968), have been proposed to describe how the information is processed between the input and the output. This type of research has been largely explored in sport psychology and it mainly concerns studies on visual processing, attention, and memory. Our knowledge of these mechanisms is important and we have now a large and complete understanding of this problem (see Tenenbaum & Bar-Eli, 1992 for a recent and complete overview). The comparison between athletes from different levels of experience shows that experts develop cognitive skills compatible with the informational demand of the task and of which the aim is to increase the speed and the capacity of processing. For instance, this has been particularly well demonstrated in visual search activity or in the study of visual attention. Results show that expertise is dependent on the transformation of the software that concerns both the structural functioning of the system, concerning the nature of the processing at different stages, and the elaboration of appropriate strategies, concerning the modalities of the processing (Ripoll, 1991). These mechanisms can be considered as being adapted to the nature of each type of situation. They result from intensive sport practice, and they are automatically driven, in the perspective of Schneider & Shiffrin (1977). These operations do not play directly on the decision making process but facilitate the treatment of the information used in the elaboration strategy.

Cognition then action or cognition and action in decision making?

Although sport practitioners and sport researchers share the opinion according to which an evident and strong relationship exists between cognition and decision making, there is little evidence of an effective link between experimental results and practical applications. In reality, it is not evident that practitioners and researchers speak about the same thing when they address the question of cognition and decision making. The main difference concerns the fact that experimental research considers cognition and motor behavior separately. This results from different factors. First, from the Greek philosophy to the philosophy of the nineteenth century and now with the contemporary philosophy and the dominant model of cognitive psychology, there has always been a gap between thinking and acting. This conception still exists and psychological contemporary approaches consider the cognitive processes and the motor behavior separately. Consequently, we know many things about cognition and decisional processes but all that we know is provided from results examining this question in laboratory task. Indeed, there is little research, excepted that from Sarrazin, Lacombe, Alain, and July (1983) in squash games, and ours presented at the following, that addresses this question in ecological situations. Indeed, the major problem posed by ecological situation is to separate what results from cognitive limitation from what results from motor limitation. To solve this problem we have adopted an experimental procedure by varying different levels of the situation complexity related either to the event complexity or to the motor complexity or to the combination of the two. Then, the behavioral variations, corresponding to the situations' degree of complexity, allowed us to isolate each component of the behavior (cognitive or sensorimotor) in order to describe the relationship between the semantic and the sensorimotor processing. This research has been carried out in two open situations examining the visual and the motor behavior of athletes from different level of expertise.

Cognition, action and decision making in internally paced sport situations:

These situations concern open sports, such as skiing, canoeing, rock climbing, in which uncertainty is not manipulated by the opponent but "conveyed" by the topography of the environment. The quantity of information is "closed" in the sense that no new information is added while the subject is performing the task. Another characteristic is that the behavior is self-paced. Rock-climbing furnishes a good example of such a situation in which we have studied the visual (Dupuy & Ripoll, 1989) and the motor behavior (Dupuy & Ripoll, 1991; Dupuy, Flahaut & Ripoll, 1992) of climbers from different levels of expertise. The characteristic of this activity is that the climbers have to analyze the general topography, to select the route, to identify and to select the handholds, then to use these handholds and to climb. The problem here is to select the appropriate handles--considered as signals--among inappropriate ones--considered as noises. Each passage can be characterized by the motor complexity, determined by the level of difficulty, and the semantic complexity, determined by the legibility of the rock and by the ratio between signals and noises. We have shown (Dupuy & Ripoll, 1991) that experts are unaffected by the increase of the semantic complexity, which means that they use efficient decision- making strategies. If we analyze the evolution of the visual and motor behavior in successive climbing of the same passage, we can see that expert climbers use immediately the correct motor behavior contrarily to less expert climbers whose motor behavior is progressively adapted throughout the different passages. A good indicator of the evolution of the motor behavior is, for instance, furnished by the analysis of the kinematic of the trajectory and a mathematical analysis (entropy and fractal dimension) of the curves. These mathematical functions, which can be considered as the dynamic transition from disorder to order (Cordier & al., 1993) indicates the quantity of information necessary to the specification of the curve and the quantity of information processed. Results confirm that experts' motor behavior is unchanged throughout successive passages while less experts' behavior is progressively adapted. This means, in the perspective of the theory of information, that experts are able to process more efficiently and more completely the information conveyed by the environment. If we ask the expert climbers to describe, before climbing and by using an emitting laser lamp, the route, the handles and the behavior that they think of using, we can see that their description perfectly fits with the motor behavior subsequently carried out. This is not the case for the less expert. This means that expert climbers have an accurate mental representation of their motor behaviors related to the characteristic of the task. This behavior constitutes a kind of cognitive "affordance", that is to say a process for which an organism can directly extract the relationship between physical and event properties of the environment and properties of its own action. It is because expert climbers have a perfect functional representation of their motor capacity than they can immediately chose the appropriate trajectory and subsequently adopt the appropriate motor behavior. This signifies that a perfect link exists between cognition, which includes the strategy resulting from the properties of the organism, and motor behavior. The practical consequence of this is that a larger place should be given to mental imagery and representation in this type of activity.

Cognition and action in externally paced sport situations:

These situations, which are characterized by the presence of opponents, high-stress pressure and high level of uncertainty, are different from internally paced situations in the sense that these factors are manipulated by the opponent. The method used to examine the relationship between the semantic and the sensorimotor mechanisms consists of analyzing situations with varying degrees of complexity. For instance, we compare drill situations, presenting no uncertainty and fixed stress pressure, to match situations. Match situations require the player to predict the forthcoming action of the opponent before the strike. Results, from research on visual and motor behavior, show that time-stress and uncertainty caused antagonistic effects between the identification stage during which the semantic process occurs and the execution stage during which the sensorimotor process is carried out. The greater the uncertainty, the more complex the visual strategy and the longer the motor response takes. This confirms that motor behavior (using sensorimotor visual information) occurs once the semantic process is carried out and when the situation is identified. The relationship between the level of performance of the sensorimotor system and the nature of the strategy can be artificially analyzed by preventing the player from preparing himself/ herself to act by using cognitive operations. This has been done by Ripoll

(1989a) in studying situations in which the ball could be (or not) deviated at the bounce. Comparison of players from different levels of expertise (research in progress) shows that the higher speed of processing of expert contributes to determine a specific strategy. This shows that strategy used in match has to be considered taking into account both cognitive operations and motor efficiency. In this perspective, decision making results from interactions between operations involved in understanding the situation and sensorimotor mechanisms involved in acting. In conclusion, the comparison of internal and external-paced situations shows that the nature of cognitive operations depends on the nature of the task, its motor and event complexity, and on the characteristic of the speed-accuracy trade-off determined by the nature of the stress pressure.

Decision making and level of cognition associated with expertise:

An important question concerns the condition necessary to reach a high level in sport and the underlying operations subtending its evolution. It is well admitted that the "hardware" components which underlie a skilled performance fall short of explaining the level of expertise and that the difference between experts and nonexperts should be only dependent on cognitive "software" dimension (Starkes & Deakin, 1984; Keele, 1986, Glencross, 1989; Ripoll, 1991). Here again, it is necessary to precise what is the exact meaning of the term cognitive. We (Ripoll, 1990, 1991) have proposed to consider different levels of cognition characterized by different modalities of relationship between cognition and action. A first, noncognitive, level concerns the execution of pure sensorimotor mechanisms. We have shown that constraints of sport situations generally overflow the basic performances of the system--this has been demonstrated for instance in visuomotor coordination of experts' ball skills (Ripoll & Fleurance, 1988) or in rapid- fire pistol shooting (Ripoll, 1986). These noncognitive transformations result from a sensorimotor auto-adaptation of the basic performances of the system. An important question consists of knowing why certain athletes (that is the case for experts) develop these auto-adaptations, while others do not. A second, cognitive level concerns the strategies used in the preparation of the motor behavior and the planning of the action. Here cognition works on the physical characteristics of the body-environment relationship, such as in operations involved in coincidence-anticipation. A third, cognitive level concerns the semantic level involved in the determination of the meaning of the situation.

Here, cognition works on the event characteristic of the situation in order to extract its logic and to plan the strategy. In complex sport situations, these different levels interact and the quality of the performance depends on the efficiency of this interaction.

To conclude, the question of the relationship of cognition and decision making has not to be considered in itself but including the condition of the production of the action, that is to say by studying the relationship between decision making, underlying basic sensorimotor organization and different level of cognition.

References

Alain, C., & Proteau, L. (1980). Decision making in sport. In C. Nadeau, W.R. Halliwell, K.M. Newell, G.C. Roberts (Eds.), *Psychology of motor behavior and sports* (pp. 465-477). Champaign, IL: Human Kinetics.

Atkinson, R.C., & Shiffrin, R.M. (1968). Human memory: a proposed system and its control process. In K. W. Spence & J.T. Spence (Eds.), *The psychology of learning and motivation. (Vol. 2).* New York: Academic Press.

Cordier, P., Mendès France, M., Bolon, P., & Pailhous, J. (1993). Entropy, degrees of freedom, and free climbing: A thermodynamic study of a complex behavior based on trajectory analysis. *International Journal of Sport Psychology, 24* (4), 370-378.

Dupuy, C., & Ripoll, H. (1989). Analyse des stratégies visuomotrices en escalade sportive. *Science et Motricité 7,* 19-26.

Dupuy, C., & Ripoll, H. (1991). Analyse des stratégies d'organisation motrice en escalade. In C. Dupuy (Ed.), *Actes du congrès international d'escalade* (pp. 174-188). Paris : Bazina.

Dupuy, C., Ripoll, H., & Flahaut, J.J. (1992). Organisation spatio-temporelle de la motricité• en escalade sportive. In M. Laurent & P. Therme (Eds.), *Recherches en A.P.S. 4* (pp. 233-253). Marseille : Presses de l'Université, d'Aix-Marseille 2.

Glencross, D. (1989). Cognitive science, human performance and sports psychology. In C.K. Giam, K.K. Chook, and K. C. Teh (Eds.), *Proceedings of the 7th world congress in sport psychology* (pp. 83-85). Singapore: Singapore Sport Council.

Keele, S.W. (1986). Motor control. In L. Kaufman, J. Thomas, & K. Boff (Eds.), *Handbook of perception and performance: Sec. 5. Information processing* Vol 2) (pp. 1-60). New York: Willey.

Parlebas, P. (1981). *Contribution à un lexique comment en sciences de l'action motrice.* Paris: INSEP.

Ripoll, H. (1986). The study of visuo-manual coordination in rapid fire pistol. In D. Landers (Ed), *Sport and elite performers.* (Vol 3) (pp. 153-162) Champaign, IL: Human Kinetics Publishers.

Ripoll, H. (1989a). How are the visual and the motor behaviors modified when a ball is unpredictably deviated just before hitting? In C.K. Giam, K.K. Chook, and K.C. Teh (Eds.), *Proceedings of the 7th world congress in sport psychology* (pp. 236). Singapore: Singapore Sport Council.

Ripoll, H. (1989b). Uncertainty and visual strategies in table tennis. *Perceptual and Motor Skill, 68,* 507-512.

Ripoll, H. (1990). De l'observation du comportement moteur... la description des processus centraux. In V. Nougier & J.P. Bianchi (Eds.), *Pratiques sportives et modélisation du geste* (pp. 131-142). Grenoble : Collection Sciences.

Ripoll, H. (1991). The understanding-acting process in sport: The relationship between the semantic and the sensorimotor visual function. *International Journal of Sport Psychology, 22* (3/4), 221-250.

Ripoll, H., & Fleurance, P. (1988). What does keeping one's eye on the ball mean? *Ergonomics, 31,* 1647-1654.

Sarrazin, C., Lacombe, D., Alain, C., & Joly, J. (1983). Simulation study of a decision making model of squash competition, phase 1: The analysis of the protocol. *Human Movement Science, 2,* 279-306.

Schneider, W., & Shiffrin, R.M. (1977). Controlled and automatic human information processing. 1. Detection, search, and attention. *Psychological Review, 84,* 1-66.

Starkes, J.L., & Deakin, J. (1984). Perception in sport: a cognitive approach to skilled performance. In W.F. Straub & J.M. Williams (Eds.), *Cognitive sport psychology* (pp. 115-129). New York : Lansing. Sport Science Associates.

Tanner, W.P.J., & Sweets, J.A. (1954). A decision making theory of visual detection. *Psychological Review, 61,* 401-409.

Tenenbaum, G., & Bar-Eli, M. (1992). Decision making in sport: a cognitive perspective. In R.N. Singer, M. Murphey, & L.K. Tenant (Eds.), *Handbook of research on sport psychology* (pp. 171-192). New York: Macmillan Publishing Company.

Chapter 6

GROUP DYNAMICS IN SPORT

Albert V. Carron

Group Dynamics in Sport

Cartwright and Zander (1968) aptly pointed out 25 years ago that if we wish to understand or improve human behavior we need to know a great deal about the nature and operation of groups, how individuals relate to groups, and how groups relate to a larger society. This perspective can be readily extended to sport and exercise groups. In order to understand or to improve behavior in the specific domain of sport and exercise, we need to know a great deal about the nature and operation of sport and exercise groups, how participants relate to sport and exercise groups, and how sport and exercise groups relate to the larger society.

Over the past 15 years, my interest has been focused in the general area of group dynamics in sport and exercise settings. The overall purpose of the present discussion is to provide an overview of the research undertaken by me in collaboration with my students and colleagues. Specifically, the objectives of the present paper include (1) to provide a definition for the term "group" in the context of sport, (2) to outline a conceptual model that We've used to examine the phenomena associated with group dynamics in sport teams, (3) to present the research We've carried out relative to this conceptual model, and (4) to suggest some potential areas for future research.

The Sport Team Defined

Integral to the study of sport groups is definitional clarity; it is important to insure that there is consensus among researchers concerning the phenomenon under consideration. This certainly holds true in the area of group dynamics in general. And yet, even a cursory examination of the general group dynamics literature shows that there is wide diversity in what researchers consider to constitute a group. Undoubtedly this is a reflection of the fact that in different groups—families, fraternities, encounter groups, social groups, and sport teams—different processes are preeminent. That is, the dynamics in group formation, group development, group performance, and group dissolution seem to vary markedly. It is not possible to simply adopt a definition and transfer it to the context of sport.

Thus, I would define a sport team as a collection of individuals who possess a collective identity, have common goals and objectives, share a common fate, develop structured patterns of interaction and modes of communication, exhibit personal and task interdependence, reciprocate interpersonal attraction, and consider themselves to be a group·

This is highly similar to a definition I provided in an earlier article (cf. Carron, 1981). The major difference is in the addition of two elements. One is the acknowledgment that the members of a group share a common fate. However, since the two strangers shooting baskets would share the common fate of eviction if the gymnasium were to close, this factor is not sufficient by itself. A second addition is that the collective considers itself to be a group. It is unlikely, for example, that strangers waiting for a bus, shooting baskets over the course of an afternoon, or competing against one another would consider themselves to constitute a group—even though they might possess many of the characteristics listed in the definitions presented above. Thus, this last criterion is essential in order to define a group.

A Conceptual Model to Study Group Dynamics

Also integral to the process of understanding sport teams is the need to develop and use a conceptual framework. As McGrath (1984) pointed out, conceptual (theoretical) perspectives are as important as data. Theories provide strength to data because they serve (a) to identify problems for investigation; (b) as a bridge or connection between problems or pieces of evidence (even those with different labels); (c) as a basis for hypothesizing or predicting the interrelationships among variables not yet examined; (d) as a basis for anticipating those aspects of a situation most likely to be important (McGrath, 1984).

A useful conceptual framework (model) I have proposed to examine the group dynamics of sport teams is illustrated in Figure 1 (Carron, 1988). This conceptual model provides a starting point for the four processes highlighted by McGrath (1984)—namely, to identify problems for research, to connect information about sport groups, to provide a basis for hypotheses about group-related phenomena in sport, and to identify problems that might become important.

As Figure 1 illustrates, the two types of outcomes emanating from group involvement can be categorized as either *individual products* or *group products*. Insofar as the former is concerned, for example, membership in sport groups can contribute to individual feelings of satisfaction, greater personal conformity to behavioral norms, reduced anxiety, reduced independence, greater participation and adherence, and so on. Similarly, sport teams produce group (or collective) products such as team success, heightened morale, and so on.

As Figure 1 illustrates, the various factors contributing to group and individual products can be categorized under the labels *member attributes* (or *group composition*), *group environment, group structure, group cohesion,* and *group processes.* As indicated earlier, a purpose of the present paper is

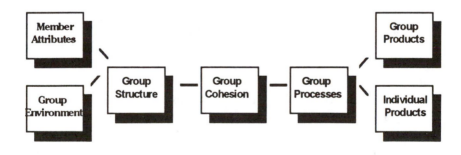

Figure 1. A conceptual framework to examine group dynamics in sport teams (from Carron, 1988. Used with permission)

to discuss research my colleagues, students, and I have carried out with sport groups. This discussion is presented within the framework of the categories illustrated in Figure 1.

Group Composition

Group composition refers to "the relationship among the characteristics of individuals who compose the group" (Shaw, 1981, p. 454). These characteristics can include the group members' physical size and body type, mental and motor abilities, attitudes, aptitudes, motives, needs, personality traits, and such social identifiers as age, education, religion, occupation, race, sex, and social status.

The effects of group composition can be examined in terms of (1) the quantity of resources in the group; (2) the degree of heterogeneity in the resources in the group; and (3) the complementarity or fit in the resources in the group. The research questions I have focused on in collaboration with my students and colleagues have been related to the quantity of resources and the complementarity of resources.

Quantity of team resources. The principal question in research on the quantity of resources is whether the presence of more of a specific attribute in group members (e.g., motivation) is associated with a better group product (e.g., success). Our research has led us to conclude that

(i) *group composition—considered from the perspective of the quantity of resources—is associated with the cohesiveness of a team* (Ball & Carron, 1976; Durand, Danylchuk, & Carron, 1992).

Durand et al. (1992), for example, reported that cohesiveness as manifested in individual attractions to the team was associated with members' extrinsic (instrumental) motivations. On the other hand, cohesiveness as manifested in group integration was associated with both the extrinsic (instrumental) and intrinsic (autotelic) motivations of team members.

Compatibility of resources. The principal concern of research relating to the complementarity of resources is whether the fit (i.e., compatibility) between members in terms of the attributes they bring to the group is associated with improved individual or group products. Our research in this area has focused on the causes and correlates of compatibility/incompatibility between coaches and athletes (Carron, 1978; Carron & Bennett, 1977; Carron & Chelladurai, 1978, 1981; Carron & Garvie, 1978; Horne & Carron, 1985). That research contributes to a conclusion that

(ii) *the major interpersonal (social) need associated with coach-athlete incompatibility is the need for inclusion* (Carron and Bennett, 1977).

Coaches and their athletes are dyads; these dyads may be more or less socially compatible on the fundamental interpersonal needs of control (i.e., to dominate), affection (i.e., to affiliate), and inclusion (i.e., to manifest personal significance). When Carron and Bennett (1977) had coaches identify those athletes with whom they felt the most and the least compatible, the most important interpersonal need which discriminated between the compatible and incompatible coach-athlete dyads was inclusion (Carron & Bennett, 1977).

In a follow-up study, Horne and Carron (1985) had athletes identify the coaches with whom they felt the most and the least compatible. This research led us to conclude that

(iii) *the most important predictor of coach-athlete compatibility is the discrepancy between the athlete's preferences for training and instruction from his/her coach and the athlete's perceptions of the degree to which this is provided.*

The greater the discrepancy between the athlete's preference and perception, the greater the incompatibility (Horne & Carron, 1985).

Our research has also led us to conclude that

(iv) *coach-athlete compatibility is associated with the amount of group cohesiveness present* (Carron & Chelladurai, 1981).

(v) *coach-athlete compatibility is unrelated to athlete performance.*
(Carron & Garvie,1978)

In this regard, Carron and Chelladurai (1981) found that when compatibility in the need for control was greatest between basketball coaches and their athletes, the athletes' perceptions of cohesiveness were also highest. Also, Carron and Garvie (1978) reported that coach-athlete compatibility was not associated with the performance success of elite wrestlers.

Group Environment

As Figure 1 illustrates, the group environment also has an impact on the group's collective outputs as well as each group member's outputs. Group environment represents the situational, physical, climate and/or geographical conditions which surround the group. These environmental conditions can be described from either an objective or subjective perspective. Thus, for example, the density of a room (i. e., the number of people present per unit of space) would be an objective environmental factor whereas individual perceptions of crowding would be a subjective environmental factor.

The environmental factors that I have focused on in collaboration with my colleagues and students have been territoriality (specifically, the home advantage) and group size. The latter area of research has been undertaken with both sport teams and exercise groups.

The home advantage. Early classic research by Schwartz and Barsky (1977) served as a catalyst for my students, colleagues, and me to undertake a number of research studies pertaining to the nature and extent of the home advantage in sport (Agnew & Carron, In press; Bray & Carron, 1992; Courneya & Carron, 1990, 1991, 1992; Hobbs, Carron & Courneya, 1992; McGuire, Courneya, Widmeyer, & Carron, 1992; Pace & Carron, 1992). As a result of the work in this area, Kerry Courneya and I recently (1) proposed a model for the study of the home advantage phenomenon, (2) provided a comprehensive overview of home advantage research carried out prior to 1991, and (3) presented a series of research-based generalizations emanating from that research (Courneya & Carron, 1992).

The model is founded on the assumption that game location (i.e., competing at home versus away) contributes to a differential set of situational conditions for the two teams. These situational conditions include crowd factors (e.g., degree of support from fans), learning factors (e.g., familiarity with the playing surface), rule factors (e.g., batting last in baseball), and travel factors (e.g., an intercontinental flight to the competition site). In turn, these influence critical psychological states (e.g., anxiousness, pride) in the principals involved in the competition—the coaches, competitors, and officials. The psychological states, in turn, impact on critical behavioral states (e.g., effort, types of decisions made) of the coaches, officials, and competitors. Finally, performance outcomes can be influenced by game location at three levels: The primary level represents the most fundamental skill level (e.g., batting average, free throw percentage); the secondary level represents the measures used to determine the competition's outcome (e.g., goals scored, runs batted in); and the tertiary level is the traditional outcome measures used (i.e., win/loss).

As indicated above, our comprehensive overview of available research led us to propose a number of generalizations. One of these is that

(vi) *the home advantage exists in all the major team sports,* and

(vii) *the home advantage is virtually identical in both college and professional sport* (Courneya & Carron, 1992).

The extent of the home advantage has been found to vary across sports: baseball, 53.5%; football, 57.3%; ice hockey, 61.1%, basketball, 64.4%; and soccer, 69.0%.

Subsequent to the publication of the Courneya & Carron review, an investigation was carried out in the individual sport of Alpine skiing by Bray & Carron (in press). On the basis of this research, it can be concluded that

(viii) *the home advantage is also present in the individual sport of alpine skiing.*

The extent of the advantage for skiers competing in their home country varied from discipline to discipline, between males and females, and between top-level and second- level skiers. Overall, however, a 9.86% and a 10.32% home advantage were observed for top-and second-level skiers respectively.

Our literature review in combination with our research also led us to a number of conclusions pertaining to the impact of the game location factors. These are:

(ix) *the influence of travel factors on the home advantage is minimal* (cf. Courneya & Carron, 1991, 1992; Pace & Carron, 1992).

(x) *the influence of the rule factors on the home advantage is also minimal* (cf. Courneya & Carron, 1990, 1992).

(xi) *absolute crowd size does not appear to be a contributing factor to the home advantage but crowd density does* (cf. Courneya & Carron, 1992, Agnew & Carron, In press).

Finally, our literature review and research associated with the "critical psychological states" and "critical behavioral states" components of our model contributes to two conclusions:

(xii) *no differences exist between home and visiting teams in aggressive behavior* (cf. Courneya & Carron, 1992; McGuire et al., 1992), and

(xiii) *the psychological states of competitors is different in competitions at home versus away* (cf. Courneya & Carron, 1992; Hobbs et al., 1992).

Hobbs et al. found that basketball teams competing at home had greater somatic anxiety than visiting teams. In light of the fact that (a) the somatic anxiety scores for both home and visiting teams were below the 50th percentile on the norms and (b) the home team somatic anxiety scores were greater, Hobbs et al. suggested that the home teams might be psychologically more prepared for competition.

Group size in sport. The impact of group size in sport teams is another situational factor we have examined. Group size may be considered from the perspective of the size of the (1) action unit, that is, number of team members competing at any given time; (2) dress roster, that is, the number of team members in uniform for a competition; (3) team roster, that is, the total number of team members who practice and/or are retained on the team; and, (4) general social system, that is, the number of people associated with the team including coaches, trainers, physicians, and so on (Carron, 1990).

One of the conclusions our research has led us to is that

(xiv) *both dress roster size and action unit size are related to the athlete's perceptions of cohesiveness.*

In one study (Widmeyer, Brawley, & Carron, 1990, Study 1), we varied the size of the dress roster in a 3-on-3 basketball league from 3 to 6 and 9 members. Task cohesion was highest in the 3-person groups and lowest in the 9-person groups. Conversely, social cohesion was highest in the 6-person groups and lowest in the 9-person groups.

In a second study, (Widmeyer et al., 1990, Study 2), we varied the size of the action unit in intramural volleyball teams from 3 to 6 and 12 members. Both cohesion and enjoyment were lowest in the 12-person groups.

Sport teams retain a particular roster for practices and games. Athletes develop perceptions about what is ideal, and too large or too small in terms of the size of their team's roster. One of the conclusions our research has led us to is that

(xv) *there is no systematic relationship between the size of the action unit and athletes' perceptions of what is an ideal team roster* (Carron, Widmeyer, & Brawley, 1989).

In basketball, for example, where the action unit is 5, the ideal size was perceived to be 12 athletes. In soccer and hockey, however, where the action units are 11 and 6 respectively, the ideal sizes in both sports were perceived to be 16.

Another conclusion this research has led us to, however, is that

(xvi) *there is a systematic pattern across sports in athlete's perceptions of what can be considered "too large" and "too small"* (Carron et al., 1989).

Across all sports examined, a team roster 25% greater than the ideal was perceived to be too large and a team roster 25% less than the ideal was perceived to be too small.

Group size in exercise classes. Group size has an influence in exercise classes as well. On the basis of our research, we would conclude that

(xvii) *adherence—as assessed by both attendance and withdrawal behavior—is greater in small and large classes than in intermediate-sized classes* (Carron, Brawley, & Widmeyer, 1990, Study 1).

(xviii) *exercise class size is related to the attitudes of participants* (Carron, Brawley, & Widmeyer, 1990, Study 2).

Carron et al. (1990, Study 2) found that participants in the smallest exercise classes expressed the greatest satisfaction, perceived the least crowding and density, and held the most favorable perception of their instructor. Participants in medium-sized classes perceived that they had the greatest opportunities for social interactions with other class members.

Group Structure

According to Shaw (1981), there are four components which reflect the emergence of group structure: (1) group position, that is, the geographical place or location of group members; (2) status, that is, the differences in power, prestige and importance among group members; (3) roles, that is, personal responsibilities within the group about which members have shared expectations; and (4) norms, that is, collective standards for behavior for which members have shared expectations. Within the broad rubric of group structure, my colleagues, students and I have carried out research investigating the concomitants of group position and status, and group roles.

Athlete position and individual rewards. Early research by Grusky (1963a, 1963b) and Loy and his students (Loy, Theberge, Kjeldsen, & Donnelly, 1975) served as a catalyst for my colleague, Chella Chelladurai, and me to undertake research on the relationship between the specific position an athlete occupies and the status and rewards he/she receives within the team (Chelladurai & Carron, 1977).

Chelladurai and I proposed that the positions athletes occupy in sport teams vary in the degree to which they provide the occupant with observability (i.e., knowledge of ongoing events), visibility (i.e., prominence in terms of being seen), and task interdependent responsibilities (i.e., tasks requiring cooperation with other group members). Our analyses of available data led us to the conclusion that

(xix) *occupants of positions high in visibility, observability, and task interdependence have greater status, rewards, and leadership opportunities.*

Roles within the sport team. Role clarity and role acceptance—the cognitive and the affective aspects respectively of individual role performance—are essential for effective group functioning. Athletes must clearly understand the nature of their role within the team and then be accepting of it. Our research has shown that

(xx) *role clarity and acceptance are related—when understanding is higher, acceptance is greater* (Grand & Carron, 1982).

(xxi) *team cohesion is an antecedent of role clarity and role acceptance.* (Dawe & Carron, 1990)

Dawe & Carron (1990) assessed the cohesiveness and role perceptions of high school hockey teams in early, mid-and post-season. Regression analyses showed that early measures of task cohesion were more strongly related to role clarity (R = .535) and role acceptance assessed later in the season (R = .595) than the opposite scenario of early role clarity and acceptance and later cohesiveness (R = .420 and .525 respectively). When group cohesion is higher, there is an increased tendency for team members to better understand and accept their role responsibilities.

One of the more important group roles in sport teams is leadership. My colleague Chella Chelladurai has made major contributions in this area and I have been associated with some of his research (Chelladurai & Carron, 1978, 1981, 1982, 1983). On the basis of our work, it can be concluded that

(xxii) *athlete maturity is related to preferences for leadership behavior from coaches* (Chelladurai & Carron, 1983).

The Leadership Scale for Sport was administered by Chelladurai & Carron (1983) to high school midget, junior and senior and university basketball players and two significant results were noted. One was that the athletes' preferences for training and instruction from coaches progressively decreased from midget to junior to senior but then increased in university. The second was that athletes' preferences for social support increased progressively from the high school midget level to the university level.

Group Cohesion

The overwhelming emphasis in my research interests in group dynamics over the past 15 years has been on group cohesiveness. My colleagues, Larry Brawley and Neil Widmeyer, and I initially developed an instrument to assess cohesiveness, the Group Environment Questionnaire (GEQ), (Brawley, Carron & Widmeyer, 1987; Carron, Widmeyer, & Brawley, 1985;

Widmeyer, Brawley, & Carron, 1985). The GEQ is based on a conceptual model where cohesiveness is viewed as a multidimensional construct composed of perceptions of the group as a totality (a dimension called *group integration*) and perceptions of the personal attractiveness of the group (a dimension called *individual attractions to the group*). Each of these is considered to be manifested in *task* and a *social* orientation. As a result, the GEQ consists of four scales: Group Integration-Task (GI-T), Group Integration-Social (GI-S), Individual Attractions to the Group-Task (ATG-T), and Individual attractions to the Group-Social (ATG-S).

The GEQ has been used to examine a number of issues associated with group cohesiveness in sport and exercise classes. In the present paper, I have only presented the research with which I have been directly involved.

Exercise classes. Table 1 contains a summary of the cohesion-related research we have carried out with exercise classes. Exercise classes are likely minimal groups — collectives that members perceive as groups because of an individual need for a collective identity. When we developed the GEQ, it was for sport groups, not exercise classes. Thus, in an early investigation, small modifications were made the wording of items to shift the focus for the respondents from sport groups to exercise classes (Carron, Widmeyer, & Brawley, 1988). In a subsequent investigation, we computed Cronbach alpha values and found them to be virtually identical for sport groups and exercise classes (cf. Carron et al., 1985; Carron & Spink, 1991).

Two generalizations emanating from our research with exercise classes are that:

(xxiii) *participants in more cohesive classes hold stronger perceptions that their class is able to withstand the negative impact of disruptive events* (Brawley, Carron, & Widmeyer, 1988, Study 2), and

(xxiv) *perceptions of cohesiveness are strongly associated with improved adherence behavior* (Spink & Carron, 1992, 1994; Carron et al., 1988, Study 1; Spink & Carron, 1992).

In short, participants who perceive their exercise class to be more cohesive have more confidence in their class's ability to overcome adversity. They also demonstrate greater adherence in respect to three measures: absenteeism, punctuality, and drop-out behavior .

A third generalization resulting from our research with exercise classes is that:

(xxv) *a team building intervention program introduced into an*

**Table 1. Research on the Correlates of Cohesiveness in
Exercise Classes**

Authors	Group Context	Group Variable	Cohesion Variables
Carron, Widmeyer, & Brawley (Study 1 1988)	Exercise Classes	Drop Out Behavior	ATG-Task
Brawley, Carron, & Widmeyer (1988, Study 2)	Exercise Classes	Resistance to Disruptive forces	GI-Task
Carron & Spink (1992)	Exercise Class	Absenteeism Punctuality	ATG-Social ATG-Task
Spink & Carron (1992)	Exercise Classes in a University	Adherence	ATG-Task GI-Task
	Exercise Classes in a Club Setting	Adherence	ATG-Social GI-Social
Carron & Spink (in press)	Exercise Class	Team Building Intervention Program	ATG-Task
Spink & Carron (in press)	Exercise Class	Team Building Intervention Program	ATG-Task

*exercise class setting serves to enhance perceptions of cohesiveness
and facilitate adherence.*
In two independent research projects (Carron & Spink, 1993; Spink & Carron, 1993), we held a workshop for fitness instructors in which we (a) outlined the relationship of cohesion to adherence, (b) identified critical elements associated with the development of cohesiveness, and then (c) provided the fitness instructors with an opportunity to suggest strategies for team building in their own classes. The instructors then developed lists of team-building strategies and subsequently introduced them into their classes. The result was enhanced cohesiveness and improved adherence.

Sport teams. Table 2 provides a summary of my research with colleagues and students which has focused on the correlates of cohesiveness in sport teams (some of this research has been discussed in previous sections of the present paper so it is not reexamined here). One generalization resulting from our research is that

(xxvi) *members of more cohesive sport teams hold stronger percep-tions that their team will be able to withstand the negative impact of disruptive events* (Brawley et al., 1988, Study 1).

As was the case with exercise classes, we have also found a strong rela-tionship between group cohesiveness and athlete adherence. In short,

(xxvii) *there is more stability and fewer drop outs in more cohesive sport teams* (Carron et al., 1988, Studies 1 and 2; Robinson & Carron, 1982).

Our research efforts with both the GEQ and the Sport Cohesiveness Ques-tionnaire (Martens, Landers & Loy (1972) support three conclusions related to the cohesion-performance relationship (Carron & Ball, 1977; Carron & Chelladurai, 1981; Dawe and Carron, 1990; Kinal & Carron, 1987; Shangi & Carron, 1987):

(xxviii) *cohesion in sport teams is positively associated with perfor-mance success,*

(xxix) *the performance-cohesion relationship is stronger than the co-hesion-performance relationship,* and

(xxx) *immediate game outcome does not produce changes in cohesive-ness. Cohesion remains unchanged in athletes tested prior to and following a win and a loss in competition.*

Table 2. Research on the Correlates of Cohesiveness in Sport Groups

Authors	Group Context	Group Variable	Cohesion Variables
Kinal & Carron (1987)	Intercollegiate Basketball	Immediate game outcome	No relationship to cohesion
Shanghi & Carron (1987)	High School Basketball	Performance, satisfaction	ATG-Task ATG-Social GI-Task GI-Social

Table 2. Research on the Correlates of Cohesiveness in Sport Groups (cont).

Authors	Group Context	Group Variable	Cohesion Variables
Brawley, Carron, & Widmeyer (1988, Study 1)	Elite Sport Groups in General	Resistance to disruptive forces	ATG-Task GI-Task
Brawley, Carron, & Widmeyer (1988, Study 2)	Recreational Sport Groups in General	Resistance to disruptive forces	ATG-Task GI-Task GI-Social
Brawley, Carron, & Widmeyer (1987, Study 2)	Sport Groups in General	Team vs individual sport athletes	ATG-Task GI-Task
		New vs long-standing team members	ATG-Social GI-Social
Brawley, Carron, & Widmeyer (1987, Study 3)	Sport Groups in General	Attributions for success/failure	ATG-Task GI-Task
Carron, Widmeyer, & Brawley (Study 1 1988)	Sport Participants	Adherence	ATG-Task ATG-Social GI-Task
Carron, Widmeyer, & Brawley (Study 2 1988)	Recreation Softball	Adherence Behavior	GI-Social
Widmeyer, Brawley, Carron (1990)	3-on-3 Basketball	Size: 6-Persons performance Size: 3-Persons	ATG-Social GI-Social ATG-Task
Dawe & Carron (1990)	High School Hockey	Role clarity, role acceptance, Performance Success	ATG-Task ATG-Social GI-Task GI-Social
Huntley & Carron (1992)	High School Basketball	Screens, Passes, Claps, Task & Social Communications	No relationship to cohesion

**Table 2. Research on the Correlates of
Cohesiveness in Sport Groups** (cont).

Authors	Group Context	Group Variable	Cohesion Variables
Durand, Danylchuk, & Carron (1992)	Sport Groups in General	Intrinsic and extrinsic motives for participation	ATG-Task ATG-Social GI-Task GI-Social
Robinson & Carron (1982)	High School Football	Adherence	Sense of Belonging Enjoyment, Closeness
Carron & Ball (1976)	Intercollegiate Ice Hockey	Performance success	Teamwork, Closeness, Enjoyment
Carron & Chelladurai (1981)	High School Wrestling	Performance success	Sense of belonging, Value of membership, Enjoyment
	High School Basketball	Performance success	Sense of belonging, Value of Membership

Group Processes

Group processes (see Figure 1 again) reflect the dynamic vital interactions associated with membership in mature groups. Team members communicate relative to task and social concerns, establish collective and personal goals, experience performance successes and failures, make causal explanations in an attempt to explain group events (including success and failure), develop personal and collective confidence (i.e., efficacy), and so on. Under the broad rubric of group processes, my colleagues, students and I have carried out research focusing on collective efficacy, group goal setting, and causal attributions for team success and failure.

Collective efficacy. In a laboratory study, Hodges and Carron (1992) used a pretest manipulation involving bogus feedback about strength to obtain groups that differed in their collective efficacy. These high and low collective efficacy groups were then placed in a competitive situation against a confederate group where they experienced failure. One generalization from that research is that:

(xxxi) *collective efficacy has an impact on the group's response to failure. Groups with high collective efficacy increase their effort while groups with low collective efficacy diminish their effort.*

Hodges and Carron (1992) found that the groups that possessed high collective efficacy showed an improvement in endurance performance following failure whereas the groups with low collective efficacy showed a decrement.

Team goal setting. Individual goal setting has been frequently linked to athletic success. With this as a frame of reference, we undertook a program of research which focused on team goal setting. In one of the studies (Brawley, Carron & Widmeyer, 1992), our purpose was to identify and describe the nature of collective goals for practices and competitions in intact sport teams. We came to three conclusions on the basis of the results from that research:

(xxxii) *the overwhelming majority of team goals are general (>.70%) rather than specific in nature,*

(xxxiii) *in practice situations, process goals predominate (89.9%) whereas in competitions, the emphasis on process and outcome goals is approximately equal,* and

(xxxiv) *the majority (66.1%) of team goals for practice are related to skill/strategy development. For competition, an approximately equal emphasis is place on skill/strategy (43.5%) and outcomes (41.5%).*

In another study (Brawley, Carron, & Widmeyer, 1993), we examined the psychological consequences of athlete involvement in team goal setting. On the basis of this research, we came to two conclusions:

(xxxv) *with greater participation in team goal setting, team cohesion is greater,* and

(xxxvi) *when cohesion is high, athletes are more satisfied with their team's goals for practice and competition.*

Attributions for responsibility. Individuals in social, athletic, and academic situations are self-serving in their tendency to enhance personal responsibility for successes and reduce personal responsibility for failures. This has been linked to a need to maintain self-esteem. However, our research has shown that the dynamics of the group can help to moderate this effect. Specifically, our research has led to the conclusion that:

(xxxvii) *athletes on teams perceived to be high in task cohesiveness readily accept more personal responsibility for team failure than athletes on teams perceived to be low in task cohesiveness* (Brawley, et al., 1987).

Potential Areas for Research

It should be pointed out by way of summary that despite the importance of groups, all evidence indicates that the level of research interest is minimal (Brawley, 1989, 1990; Carron, 1988; Widmeyer, Brawley, & Carron, 1992). For example, in the *Journal of Sport and Exercise Psychology* (JESP), only 8% of the articles published in its initial seven-year period were concerned with group dynamics (Landers, Boutcher, & Wang, 1986). Furthermore, the majority of these either focused on leadership or group cohesion. As another example, at the North American Society for the Psychology of Sport and Physical Activity Conferences, an identical pattern has emerged; less than 15% of the papers presented over the past nine years have focused on group dynamics topics. And, again, the majority of these have been concerned with either leadership or group cohesion. And as yet another example, a content analysis of major sport psychology textbooks published between 1984 and 1989 showed that 87% of the content dealt with individual issues; 13% with group issues. What this means is that at the present time we know very little about the how, why, and what of effective sport groups.

Four years ago, I suggested some avenues for future research (Carron, 1988). That discussion is reproduced here.

One seemingly obvious suggestion is that research in sport psychology must try to take into account the impact of group factors—even when the group is not the primary focus of the research. Sherif and Sherif (1969) have pointed out, for example, that intergroup conflict can be looked at from three levels of interaction—from an individual perspective, from an intragroup perspective, and from an intergroup perspective. They emphasized that it is a mistake to try to extrapolate from the individual's motivations, frustrations, and attitudes and make assumptions about the relations which exist within the group. They also emphasized that it would be equally erroneous to extrapolate from the pattern of interactions which occur within a group to make assumptions about the relations between groups. The nature of motivation, goal setting, and attributional explanations to name but a few are different for individuals and for groups. Thus, one essential first step in gaining a better understanding of behavior and performance in sport and physical activity is to increase the amount of attention paid to the group.

Second, the focus of research in sport group dynamics topics must be expanded. The focus to date has largely been on leadership and cohesion. These are important topics, as indicated by the fact that they are also among the most extensively examined in the general group dynamics literature. Nonetheless, they are not sufficient by themselves to account for the dynamics of effective sport groups. It is necessary to improve our understanding of the impact of member resources, environmental factors, structural parameters, and group processes.

Third, group dynamics research in sport has primarily been concerned with the relationship of various team or individual factors to team success. Certainly, performance outcome is an important issue. But group dynamics researchers in other fields have identified a host of equally meaningful outcomes of group involvement—adherence, conflict, aggression, satisfaction, conformity, and self-deception, for example. Any science or area of science which focuses primarily on one outcome only has limited utility.

Fourth, care must be taken in sport research to examine group dynamics problems in a wide cross-section of research settings—field studies, field experiments, laboratory experiments, and real life situations. Landers (1983) was particularly persuasive on this point in an article in which he argued for the need for theory testing in sport psychology. He noted that field studies are useful in the initial stages when very little is known about a phenomenon. Research with intact, natural groups can help to identify more important variables for further analysis. Then the relationships among these variables can be examined in field experiments and laboratory experiments where greater control is possible. Theories can be refined in this context and then validated in real-life situations.

A fifth, related point is that research in sport on group dynamics must go beyond simple description—a suggestion that can be directed toward much of the research in sport psychology generally. According to Zanna and Fazio (1982), there are three generations of research questions. The first is descriptive in nature; it addresses the question what is it? The concern here is with issues such as "What is the relationship of x to y?" "What are the characteristics of x?" The second generation of research question focuses on the question when does it? The concern here is with issues such as "When does x influence y?" In the third generation, the researcher attempts to answer the question why? Thus, for example, it might be interesting to know that groups composed of female athletes score higher on task cohesion than groups composed of males (Widmeyer, et al., 1985). But why is this the case?

Sport psychology is still an infant science. And group dynamics is one of the youngest members in the family. In order for it to grow and make a meaningful contribution to the psychology of sport and physical activity, it needs a large number of researchers pursuing a wide variety of topics with a broad cross section of methodologies.

References

Agnew, G., & Carron, A.V. (In press). Crowd effects and the home advantage. *International Journal of Sport Psychology.*

Ball, J.R., & Carron, A.V. (1976). The influence of team cohesion and participation motivation upon performance success in intercollegiate ice hockey. *Canadian Journal of Applied Sport Sciences, 1,* 271-275.

Brawley, L.R. (1989, June). *Group size in physical activity: Psychological and behavioral impacts.* Paper presented at the North American Society for the Psychology of Sport and Physical Activity Conference. Kent, O.

Brawley, L.R. (1990). Group cohesion: Status, problems and future directions. *International Journal of Sport Psychology, 21,* 355-379.

Brawley, L.R., Carron, A.V., & Widmeyer, W.N. (1987). Assessing the cohesion of teams: Validity of the Group Environment Questionnaire. *Journal of Sport Psychology, 9,* 275-294.

Brawley, L.R., Carron, A.V., & Widmeyer, W.N. (1988). Exploring the relationship between cohesion and group resistance to disruption. *Journal of Sport and Exercise Psychology, 10,* 199-213.

Brawley, L.R., Carron, A.V., & Widmeyer, W.N. (1992). The nature of group goals in sport teams: A phenomenological analysis. *The Sport Psychologist. 6,* 323 - 333.

Brawley, L.R., Carron, A.V., & Widmeyer, W.N. (1993). The influence of the group and its cohesiveness on perceptions of group goal-related variables. *The Journal of Sport and Exercise Psychology. 15,* 245 - 260.

Bray, S., & Carron, A.V. (in press). The home advantage in Alpine skiing. *Australian Journal of Science and Medicine in Sport.*

Carron, A.V. (1978). Role behavior and coach-athlete interaction. *International Review of Sport Sociology, 13,* 51-65.

Carron, A.V. (1981). Processes of group interaction in sport teams. *Quest, 33,* 245-270.

Carron, A.V.(1988). *Group dynamics in sport.* London, Ont.: Spodym Publishers.

Carron, A.V. (1990). Group size in sport and physical activity: Social psychological and performance consequences. *International Journal of Sport Psychology, 21,* 286-304.

Carron, A.V., & Ball, J.R. (1977). Cause-effect characteristics of cohesiveness and participation motivation in intercollegiate hockey. *International Review of Sport Sociology, 12,* 49-60.

Carron, A.V., & Bennett, B.B. (1977). Compatibility in the coach-athlete dyad. *Research Quarterly, 48,* 671-679.

Carron, A.V., Brawley, L.R., & Widmeyer, W.N. (1990). The impact of group size in an exercise setting. *Journal of Sport and Exercise Psychology, 12,* 376-387.

Carron, A.V., & Chelladurai, P. (1978). Psychological factors and athletic success: An analysis of coach-athlete interpersonal behavior. *Canadian Journal of Applied Sport Sciences, 3,* 43-50.

Carron, A.V., & Chelladurai, P. (1981). The dynamics of group cohesion in sport. *Journal of Sport Psychology, 3,* 123-139.

Carron, A.V., & Garvie, G.T. (1978). Compatibility and successful performance. *Perceptual and Motor Skills, 46,* 1121-1122.

Carron, A.V., & Spink, K.S. (1991). Internal consistency of the Group Environment Questionnaire modified for an exercise setting. *Perceptual and Motor Skills, 74,* 1-3, 1992.

Carron, A.V., & Spink, K.S. (1993). Team building in an exercise setting. *The Sport Psychologist, 7,* 8 - 18.

Carron, A.V., Widmeyer, L.R., & Brawley, L.R. (1985). The development of an instrument to assess cohesion in sport teams: The group environment questionnaire. *Journal of Sport Psychology, 7,* 244-266.

Carron, A.V., Widmeyer, W.N., & Brawley, L.R. (1988). Group cohesion and individual adherence to physical activity. *Journal of Sport and Exercise Psychology, 10,* 119-126.

Carron, A.V., Widmeyer, W.N., & Brawley, L.R. (1989). Perceptions of ideal group size in sport teams. *Perceptual and Motor Skills, 69,* 1368-1370.

Cartwright, D., & Zander, A. (1968). *Group dynamics: Research and theory* (3rd ed.). New York: Harper & Row.

Chelladurai, P., & Carron, A.V. (1977). A reanalysis of formal structure in sport. *Canadian Journal of Applied Sport Sciences, 2,* 9-14.

Chelladurai, P., & Carron, A.V. (1978). *Leadership.* Ottawa, Ont. CAHPER Sociology of Sport Monograph Series.

Chelladurai, P., & Carron, A.V. (1981). Applicability to youth sports of the Leadership Scale for Sport. *Perceptual and Motor Skills, 53,* 361-362.

Chelladurai, P., & Carron, A.V. (1982). Task characteristics and individual differences and their relationship to preferred leadership in sports. *Psychology of motor behavior and sport - 1982: Abstracts*. North American Society for the Psychology of Sport and Physical Activity, College Park, MD.

Chelladurai, P., & Carron, A.V. (1983). Athletic maturity and preferred leadership. *Journal of Sport Psychology, 5*, 371-380.

Courneya, K.S., & Carron, A.V. (1990). Batting first vs. last: Implications for the home advantage. *Journal of Sport and Exercise Psychology, 12*, 312-316.

Courneya, K.S., & Carron, A.V. (1991). The home advantage: Effects of travel and length of the home stand/road trip. *Journal of Sport and Exercise Psychology, 13*, 42-49.

Courneya, K.S., & Carron, A.V. (1992). The home advantage in sport competitions: A literature review. *Journal of Sport and Exercise Psychology, 14*, 28-39.

Dawe, S., & Carron, A.V. (October, 1990). *Interrelationships among role acceptance, role clarity, task cohesion, and social cohesion.* Paper presented at the Canadian Psychomotor Learning and Sport Psychology Conference, Windsor, Ontario.

Durand, M.C., Danylchuk, K.E., & Carron, A.V. (October, 1992). *Relationship of intrinsic-extrinsic motives for participation & perceptions of cohesiveness.* Paper presented at the Canadian Psychomotor Learning and Sport Psychology Conference, Saskatoon, Saskatchewan.

Grand, R.R., & Carron, A.V. (1982). Development of a team climate questionnaire. In L.M. Wankel & R.B. Wilberg (Eds.), *Psychology of sport and motor behavior: Research and practice. Proceedings of the Annual Conference of the Canadian Society for Psychomotor Learning and Sport Psychology,* Edmonton, Alberta. (pp. 217 - 229).

Grusky, O. (1963a). Managerial succession and organizational effectiveness. *American Journal of Sociology, 69*, 21-31.

Grusky, O. (1963b). The effects of formal structure on managerial recruitment: A study of baseball organization. *Sociometry, 26*, 345-353.

Hobbs, M., Carron, A.V., & Courneya, K.S. (1992, October). *Competitor's psychological states and game location*. Paper presented at the Canadian Psychomotor Learning and Sport Psychology Conference, Saskatoon, Saskatchewan.

Hodges, L., & Carron, A.V. (1992). Collective efficacy and group performance. *International Journal of Sport Psychology, 23*, 48-59.

Horne, T., & Carron, A.V. (1985). Compatibility in coach-athlete relationships. *Journal of Sport Psychology, 7*, 137-149.

Kinal, S., & Carron, A.V. (1987). Effects of game outcome on cohesion in male and female intercollegiate teams. *Canadian Journal of Sport Sciences, 12*, p. 12.

Landers, D.M. (1983). Whatever happened to theory testing in sport psychology? *Journal of Sport Psychology, 5*, 135-151.

Landers, D.M., Boutcher, S.H., & Wang, M.Q. (1986). The history and status of the *Journal of Sport Psychology*: 1979-1985. *Journal of Sport Psychology, 8*, 149-163.

Loy, J.W., Theberge, N., Kjeldsen, E. & Donnelly, P. (1975). *An examination of hypothesized correlates of replacement processes in sport organizations*. Paper prepared for presentation at the International Seminar for the Sociology of Sport, University of Heidelberg.

Martens, R., Landers, D.M., & Loy, J.W. (1972). *Sport cohesiveness questionnaire*. Washington, DC: AAHPERD Publications.

McGrath, J.E. (1984). *Groups: Interaction and performance*. Englewood Cliffs, NJ: Prentice-Hall.

McGuire, E.J., Courneya, K.S., Widmeyer, W.N., & Carron, A.V. (1992). Aggression as a potential mediator of the home advantage in professional ice hockey. *Journal of Sport and Exercise Psychology, 14*, 148-158.

Pace, A., & Carron, A.V. (1992). Travel and the home advantage. *Canadian Journal of Sport Sciences, 17*, 60-64.

Robinson, T.T., & Carron, A.V. (1982). Personal and situational factors associated with dropping out versus maintaining participation in competitive sport. *Journal of Sport Psychology, 4*, 364-378.

Schwartz, B. & Barsky, S.F. (1977). The home advantage. *Social Forces, 55*, 641 - 666.

Shangi, G., & Carron, A.V. (1987). Group cohesion and its relationship with performance and satisfaction among high school basketball players. *Canadian Journal of Sport Sciences, 12*, p. 20.

Shaw, M.E. (1981). *Group dynamics: The psychology of small group behavior* (3rd ed.). New York: McGraw-Hill.

Sherif, M., & Sherif, C. (1969). *Social psychology* (Rev. ed.). New York: Harper & Row.

Spink, K.S., & Carron, A.V. (1992). Group cohesion and adherence in exercise classes. *Journal of Sport and Exercise Psychology, 14,* 78-86.

Spink, K.S. & Carron, A.V. (1993). The effects of team building on the adherence patterns of female exercise participants. *Journal of Sport and Exercise Psychology, 15,* 39 - 49.

Spink, K.S. & Carron, A.V. (1994). Group cohesion effects in exercise classes. *Small Group Research, 25,* 26 - 42.

Widmeyer, W.N., Brawley, L.R., & Carron, A.V. (1985) *The measurement of cohesion in sport teams: The Group Environment Questionnaire.* London, Ont.: Sports Dynamics.

Widmeyer, W.N., Brawley, W.N., & Carron, A.V. (1990). The effects of group size in sport. *Journal of Sport and Exercise Psychology, 12,* 177-190.

Widmeyer, W.N., Brawley, L.R., & Carron, A.V. (1992). *Group dynamics in sport,* In T.S. Horn (Ed.), *Advances in sport psychology* (pp. 163-180). Champaign, IL: Human Kinetics.

Zanna, M.P., & Fazio, R.H. (1982) The attitude-behavior relation: Moving toward a third generation of research. In M.P. Zanna, E.T. Higgins, & C.P. Herman (Eds.), *Consistency in social behavior: The Ontario symposium* (vol. 2) (pp. 282 - 301). Hillsdale, NJ: Erlbaum.

Chapter 7

MOTIVATION AND PARTICIPATION IN EXERCISE AND SPORT[1]

Stuart Biddle

Introduction

The importance of motivation is recognised by people in all aspects of physical activity. Similarly, it spans different areas of our field—sport psychology, exercise psychology, motor learning, and motor development. The motivation to perform well is evident in many people who play sport at varying levels of ability. Also, the recreational jogger interested in exercise for health is all too aware of the motivation required to maintain participation. Similarly, sport psychologists, as will be demonstrated later, think that motivation is an important topic for research as well as applied interventions through such techniques as goal-setting. The relatively new and expanding field of exercise psychology devotes a large proportion of its literature to the motivational factors thought to be associated with starting and maintaining participation in exercise. In addition, those interested in motor development and learning recognise the importance of motivation in their quest to understand underlying mechanisms of human development and movement.

The recognition of the importance of motivation hides the fact that there has been a great diversity of opinion on a number of issues related to motivation. Historically, perspectives on the study of human motivation have shifted considerably. Also, contemporary motivational research has a number of 'frameworks' in use which, one might argue, form the basis for different 'theories' of motivation. Whether one theory is possible or desirable is, of course, open to debate.

The purpose of this chapter is to analyse the contemporary situation in exercise and sport motivation. To do this I will analyse trends identified in the literature. These have been obtained by a detailed analysis of two key journals. The main perspectives in motivation research currently being adopted in exercise and sport psychology (E&SP) will be discussed in more detail. Finally, the chapter will conclude with a discussion of key issues and future directions.

The title of this chapter refers to motivation in exercise *and* sport. Why the distinction? Historically, it has been the case that the psychology of physical activity has focussed primarily on either sport behaviours or those associated with motor learning. The former emphasis is reflected in studies on motivation that attempt to shed light on why people play sport, why they drop out, and what can motivate them to perform better. However, more recently, researchers have recognised the importance of physical activity for health promotion. Structured physical activity, usually with the intent to maintain or improve fitness, has been labelled exercise (Caspersen, Powell & Christenson, 1985) and has now been studied in its own right. One reason for the distinction between sport and exercise, therefore, is that sometimes they could be two quite different behaviours from the point of view of psychology. For the purposes of this paper, exercise will be defined in the same way as that used by Caspersen et al. (1985) whereas sport will be defined as physical activity that is generally rule governed and structured, involves gross motor movement, and takes place in competitive or competition-related (e.g., training for competition) contexts.

Finally, this chapter refers to motivation and *participation*. By this I mean all aspects of behaviour in sport and exercise rather than just motivation to perform well. As such it combines both the process and product orientations of sport and exercise.

Human Motivation: Definitional and Historical Trends

The study of human motivation has been central to psychology since its earliest days (see Weiner, 1992) and has developed through different perspectives originating from both Europeans (e.g., Freud, Lorenz, Heider) and North Americans (e.g., Bandura, Weiner). Maehr and Braskamp (1986) stated that "most motivational talk arises from observations about variation in five behavioral patterns, which we label direction, persistence, continuing motivation, intensity, and performance" (p. 3). These five areas mean that motivation can be a complex phenomenon to study and understand since it can be manifested in many different ways.

Historically, human motivation has been viewed from several different, yet overlapping, perspectives such as 'people as machines' (Weiner, 1992; e.g., drive theory), personality (e.g., some achievement motivation theories), and social cognition (e.g., attribution theories, self-efficacy, achievement goals). Contemporary motivation research is no longer based on drive or instinct perspectives but more on social perception and cognitive perspectives. Weiner (1992) talks of psychology moving from 'the machine metaphor' to 'God-like metaphors' in its paradigmatic shift in human motivation research. The 'people as machines' metaphor summarised the early approaches to motivation by emphasising that behaviours were involuntary and predetermined, fixed and routine, and where energy is transmitted. Should the 'machine' get out of balance there is a movement towards change to restore balance. Under this heading, Weiner (1992) discusses psychoanalytic, ethological, sociobiological, drive, and gestalt theories of motivation and human action and suggests that these dominated psychology up to about 1955.

The God-like metaphor, according to Weiner (1992), suggests that humans are fully informed about possible behavioural options, have complete rationality, and are able to calculate "their most hedonic course of action" (p. 159). Such theories include those using expectancy-value approaches, such as Atkinson's theory of achievement motivation (see Atkinson, 1964) and theories of attribution and control. This paradigmatic shift is clear to see in the E&SP literature, as will be discussed later. However, Weiner (1992) also says that humans are not quite rational decision makers and that their information processing capacities are more limited than such theories sometimes suggest. These theories, therefore, paint a picture of humans that is a little unrealistic and rather too positive. Consequently, Weiner proposes that the God-like metaphor be modified so that it "relies more on emotionality and less on rationality, more on evaluation and less on decision-making and choice, and is more focused on the external social world and less on the self and hedonic maximization" (p. 299).

'Person as judge' is a label used by Weiner to describe this metaphor, and this reflects more recent research in human motivation sometimes referred to as utilising a 'social cognitive' perspective. Social cognition is defined by Fiske and Taylor (1991) as the study of "how people make sense of other people and themselves" and, regardless of the specific topic, share the basic features of "unabashed mentalism, orientation toward process, cross-fertilization between cognitive and social psychologies, and at least some concern with real-world social issues" (p. 14).

This short historical perspective provides a background against which we are able to view motivation research in exercise and sport. Certainly the literature in E&SP has tended to follow quite closely the developments and shifts in emphasis in other areas of psychology. For example, some of the textbooks written at the time of rapid expansion in sport psychology (e.g., Alderman, 1974; Butt, 1976) reflect a strong emphasis on drive theory and early expectancy-value theory approaches. More recent chapters and books (e.g., Roberts, 1992a; Singer, Murphey, & Tennant, 1993; Weiss & Chaumeton, 1992) reflect the trend towards more social cognitive approaches. Indeed, Roberts (1992b) is quite clear about this when he says in his edited volume that "this book is firmly placed within the present zeitgeist of social cognitive perspectives on motivation" (p. vii).

Research Trends in Exercise and Sport Motivation

The historical background described so far helps to locate E&SP research on motivation in a broader framework. However, what have been the trends *within* E&SP where motivation is concerned? To help answer this, a content analysis was undertaken of two key E&SP journals—the *International Journal of Sport Psychology* (IJSP) and the *Journal of Sport (and Exercise) Psychology* (JSEP). *IJSP* was chosen for its international focus and *JSEP* (the word exercise was added to the title of the journal in 1988) for its reputation as a leading research journal in the field. However, the analysis of trends through these two journals means that research published elsewhere, and particularly in a language other than English, has been missed and may reflect different trends to those reported here. I claim no more than a summary of trends from two key journals that *may* reflect a wider picture.

Method

JSEP was first published in 1979 and *IJSP* in 1970. To reflect trends using both journals, 1979-1991 was chosen as the period of study. This accounted for a total of 104 single issues.

Each issue was scrutinised and articles on any aspect of motivation were selected. There is no clear-cut agreement on what should or should not be included. However, topics were included if they were primarily motivational in orientation and if agreement was reached by two researchers.[2] I did omit personality research that focussed only on trait profiles, although traits overtly associated with motivation (e.g., achievement motivation; self-motivation) were included.

Selected details were entered into a computer database (PC-File+ V2.0), including journal title, date, main topic, other topics, research design, and sample characteristics. The data were analysed by sorting the various fields of interest, either singly or in combination.

Results

A total of 224 entries were used in the analysis, with more being published in *JSEP* (60.9%) in comparison with *IJSP* (39.1%).

Topics

The topics listed as the main focus of investigation in the studies are listed in Table 1. This shows that the most frequently researched topics were attributions, self-confidence, and achievement motivation. Table 1 gives a breakdown of the different topics considered to fall under each main heading.

Of the five most frequently studied topics, all but group cohesion showed a clear change in the number of studies across the years when the figures were analysed for the two time periods of 1980-1985, 1986-1991 (see Figure 1). Specifically, the study of attribution declined whereas confidence, achievement motivation and goal-setting increased.

Sample Characteristics

The subjects investigated in these studies were categorised by type (e.g., student, elite athlete), gender, and age. Very few studies provided cultural,

Table 1. Frequency of Main Topics in Rank Order.

Main Topic Category (f) (%)	Topics Included
ATTRIBUTION (29) (12.9%)	attributions attributions and emotion
SELF-CONFIDENCE (27) (12)	self-confidence self-efficacy
ACHIEVEMENT MOTIVATION (20) (8.9)	achievement motivation competitive orientation goal orientations
GROUP COHESION (12) (5.4)	group cohesion group size
GOAL-SETTING (11) (4.9)	
ADHERENCE (9) (4.0)	adherence to: exercise, mental training, rehabilitation, and sport
SELF-ESTEEM (8) (3.6)	self-concept self-esteem self-image body-image
INTRINSIC MOTIVATION (7) (3.0)	intrinsic motivation intrinsic/extrinsic motivational orientations
PARTICIPATION MOTIVES (7) (3.0)	
ATTITUDE (6) (2.7)	
PSYCH-UP STRATEGIES (6) (2.7)	psych-up cognitive strategies mental preparation strategies

Table 1. Frequency of Main Topics in Rank Order (cont).

Main Topic Category (f) (%)	Topics Included
ENJOYMENT (5) (2.2)	
EXPECTANCY (5) (2.2)	
PERCEIVED COMPETENCE (5) (2.2)	
EMOTION (4) (1.8)	emotions emotion and RPE emotive imagery
LEADERSHIP (4) (1.8)	
SELF-MOTIVATION (4) (1.8)	self-motivation commitment

OTHERS (each <4, including aggression, behavior modification, burnout, exercise addiction, home advantage, locus of control, perfectionism, psychological momentum, social facilitation).

ethnic or nationality background so these could not be analysed.

The samples used in the studies were usually comprised of both men and women (62.9%), with about one-third being single-sex (only men 20%; only women 15.2%). Gender was not specified in 1.9% of the studies.

Surprisingly, it was found that in 44.8% of the studies, the age of the subjects was not specified exactly, although in many of these cases it appeared to be assumed that age could be inferred from other characteristics, such as stating that subjects were 'college students' or 'high school students'. Predictably, most of the other studies investigated younger subjects: children and youth (up to 18 years of age) 23.7%, students and adults (18-50 years) 25.4%, and older adults (over 50 years) 6%. Clearly there is a need to specify the exact age of subjects and to investigate older adults.

The subjects were also categorised by type of involvement (e.g., referee, teacher), or by other characteristics (e.g., student). The details in many

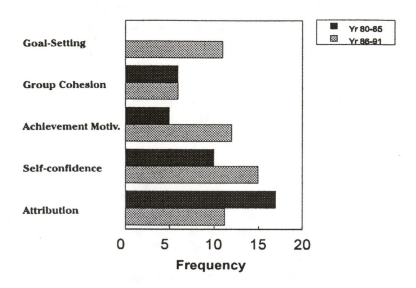

Figure 1. Chronological trends for the five most frequently studied topics identified in the content analysis.

studies were insufficient to provide a clear classification. Nevertheless, some trends could be detected, as shown in Figure 2. Again this shows the bias towards younger subjects, and, in this case, towards what are probably convenience samples of students. It is also recommended that samples are described in more detail so that subject groups can be identified more clearly. Interestingly, coaches were rarely studied, referees comprised one sample only, and physical education teachers were not studied at all. There were no detectable trends across time for sample characteristics, with the exception of a small increase in the study of children in the latter part of the 1980s.

Research Design

Figure 3 shows the types of research designs used in the study of motivation from the two journals sampled. This shows that survey research (50%) and experimental designs (30.8%) were the most favoured methods. Very few studies were longitudinal (1.3%) or qualitative (0.89%). There were no clear trends in these data over time.

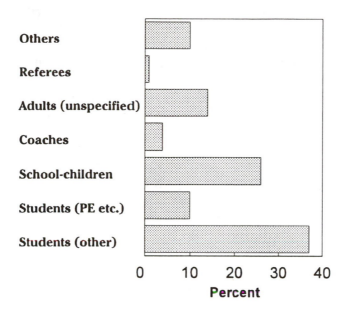

Figure 2. Sample characteristics of studies identified in the content analysis.

Theory Testing

Finally, the articles were analysed to see if they tested psychological theory. A liberal interpretation of theory testing was adopted. The research paper was categorised as 'theory testing' in its focus if, first and most obviously, it was a direct test of a known theory, or alternatively, if it used a theory as its main focus of analysis. In the latter case, it might not have tested the theory in full. Results showed that 56.7% of the studies tested known theory.

Conclusions From the Content Analysis

The content analysis allows us to see indications of research trends in motivation, at least as reflected in two main journals. Whilst a more detailed discussion of the major motivational issues appears later in this chapter, the content analysis can be summarised as follows:

a). The most frequently studied areas of motivation research are attributions, self-confidence, and achievement motivation, with the latter two
showing an increased frequency over the years of study. Attribution research declined slightly, although the overlap with goal orientations research
may mean that the focus of interest in attributions shifted rather than
declined *per se*. This is discussed in more detail later.
b). The types of individual studied tended to be children, youth or younger
adults. This does not allow for much confidence in the generalisability of
the findings of these studies to older adults.
c). Many of the studies investigated students and players, with very few
studies using other populations, such as officials, coaches or teachers.
d). The research designs were predominantly survey or experimental, with
only two adopting qualitative/interpretative paradigms.
e). Just over half the studies attempted to test all or part of a psychological
theory.
Overall, these results show that while the knowledge base is accumulat-
ing in some areas where the frequency of publications is quite high, the
studies have tended to adopt restricted research paradigms and use a narrow
range of subjects.

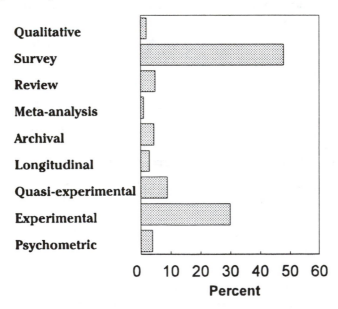

**Figure 3. Research methods used in studies identified in the
content analysis.**

The Big 3: Attributions, Self-Confidence and Achievement Motivation

The most frequently addressed topics of motivation in the content analysis of *IJSP* and *JSEP* reflected the social cognitive trend in psychology in general. This section of the paper will discuss key issues in each of these popular areas: attributions, self-confidence, and achievement motivation. It is not intended to review each area in detail. This has been done elsewhere (see Biddle, 1993; Biddle & Mutrie, 1991; Duda, 1992, 1993; McAuley, 1992a; McAuley & Duncan, 1990; Roberts, 1992a). It is also important to note that the three areas overlap each other conceptually, although this has not always been addressed in individual research studies. An overlap exists between attributions and achievement motivation. Historically, the development of achievement attribution theory by Weiner and others has its roots in expectancy-value theories such as the achievement motivation perspectives of Atkinson (1964; see also Weiner, 1992). In addition, contemporary perspectives on achievement motivation focus on goals and goal orientations which, in turn, have been shown to have clear links with attributional thought (Duda, 1992).

Similarly, McAuley (1992a) has pointed out that the commonality between the theoretical perspectives of self-efficacy and attribution is 'self-referent thought' and the capability of the individual to exercise control over cognitions, motivation and behaviour. However, he also suggests that such links have not been manifested a great deal in individual research studies, with the two themes often being addressed independently.

Attributions

The topic of attributions has been a dominant force in social psychology throughout the 1970s and 1980s, and is set to continue to feature prominently in the 1990s as well. Although attributions was first ranked in frequency in the content analysis, it showed a slight decline across the time period studied. The early 1980s saw a great deal of interest in analysing the attributions made after sports events. However, the focus of many studies was narrow and this may have led to a decline in interest. I have expressed my disappointment before at the narrow approach to attribution research in sport and exercise (see Biddle, 1993). Investigations into attribution-emotion links in sport have been published, but very little investigation has taken place in physical activity contexts in areas such as actor-observer differences in attributions, learned helplessness, attribution re-training, or using theoretical perspectives other than Bernard Weiner's (see Weiner, 1986).

Similarly, some researchers (e.g., Roberts, 1984) have argued for a perspective that is oriented towards perceptions of ability rather than attributions *per se*. This has led to the increased interest observed in the current perspective adopted in the study of achievement motivation—that of goal orientations (see later). However, the link between goal orientations and attributions is strong and, as such, the two topics are not mutually exclusive.

In my review of attribution theory in sport (Biddle, 1993), I summarised our current state of knowledge as follows:

a). Although ability and effort appear to be dominant attributions made in sport contexts, the adoption of the original model by Weiner using the four attributions of ability, effort, luck and difficulty of the task is clearly too restrictive for sport;

b). Winners in sport tend to make attributions to internal and controllable factors more than losers;

c). A self-serving bias has been shown to exist in sport;

d). Attributions are more likely to be made after unexpected events or goal nonattainment;

e). Few gender differences have been found, but age differences in information processing are thought to account for differences between some age groups;

f). Ability and effort attributions are associated with ego and task (mastery) goal orientations respectively;

g). The perceived stability of attributions is associated with the prediction of expectancy change;

h). Both attribution elements and dimensions are associated with emotional feelings after sports contests;

i). Appraisal of performance is thought to be more strongly associated with sport emotion than attributions.

In addition, I summarised what I thought we needed to know in attribution research if we are to progress. I highlight some of the key points here. In sport and exercise, we need to know:

a). The applicability of different theoretical perspectives on attributions;

b). Differences in attributions made for performance and outcome;

c). The role of individual and team attributions in team sports;

d). The nature of actor-observer differences;

e). The nature and importance of attributional style;

f). Developmental trends;

g). Cultural influences and cross-cultural differences;

h). Nature, type and predictability of attribution-emotion relationships;

i). Behavioural consequences of attributions and emotions;

j). The nature and extent of learned helplessness in sport;

k). The utility and effectiveness of attribution re-training;

l). The role of attributions in spectators, officials and coaches;

m). The nature and content of attributions in health-related exercise contexts.

We have moved on from the early descriptive studies of attributions for winners and losers. However, the orientation is still narrow and an adoption of other theoretical perspectives found elsewhere in attribution research in the social psychology literature might be helpful for the understanding of sport and exercise motivation.

Self-Confidence

The study of self-confidence in E&SP has tended to focus on self-efficacy (SE) theory, although other perspectives have been adopted, such as performance expectancies, estimation and gender (Corbin, 1981; Lirgg, 1991), movement confidence (Griffin & Keogh, 1982), and sport confidence (Vealey, 1986). Several reviews of sport and exercise confidence now exist [see Feltz (1988) on sport confidence; Feltz (1992) and McAuley (1992a) on self-efficacy in sport; Biddle & Mutrie (1991) and McAuley (1992b) on self-confidence and efficacy in exercise].

Research suggests that Bandura's (1977, 1986) theory of self-efficacy is an important milestone for cognitive motivational research in sport and exercise. In the sport context, it has been shown that SE is associated strongly with past behaviours and perceived success but less so with vicarious experiences. The other sources of efficacy information suggested by Bandura (persuasion and physiological states) have received less support. In addition, research has shown that SE can be an important predictor of sport performance (see Feltz, 1992).

We undertook a detailed review of self-confidence in exercise settings and identified nine studies (see Biddle & Mutrie, 1991). This number has since increased as the study of health-related exercise has developed. Much of the early work was with male patients using exercise in coronary heart disease (CHD) rehabilitation contexts. Some evidence has been shown that

SE generalises from one exercise mode to another, but this is rather limited. Also, it has been shown that generalised measures of efficacy are less effective predictors of behaviour than specific efficacy expectations, as predicted by Bandura (1986).

In evaluating the literature in both sport and exercise, further issues require study. Specifically, Feltz (1992) identified the following factors for study in sport psychology:

a). Team efficacy;

b). The influence of SE on motivation rather than just behaviour or skill;

c). The resilience of SE beliefs;

d). The extent to which SE beliefs generalise across situations;

e). The relationships between SE and future thought patterns.

In exercise, Biddle and Mutrie (1991) identified the following key issues:

a). How does SE influence behaviour in diverse exercise settings, such as habitual 'free-living' activity?

b). The need for more integration between theories of efficacy and attribution;

c). Further research on the nature and extent of gender differences in SE;

d). The need to study SE in situations of prolonged effort;

e). The longevity of SE; can it be studied in the context of child-to-adulthood 'carry-over' effects?

f). What is the role of SE alongside other theoretical constructs? This has started to be addressed in attitude models, for example, and efficacy beliefs have been shown to particularly important constructs (see Biddle, Goudas & Page, in press; Dzewaltowski, 1989).

Achievement Motivation

The approaches adopted in the study of achievement motivation have changed a great deal in E&SP in recent years. In the content analysis, even with relatively little detail coded on recorded topics, it was possible to see reference to 'achievement motivation' in the first half of the survey period more than the latter, whereas this was reversed for 'goal orientations' and 'competitive orientations'. These latter topics typify the change in direction in achievement motivation.

Early research in this field in E&SP followed the theoretical perspectives associated with 'need for achievement' and expectancy-value theories (see Weiner, 1992). Sport psychologists adopted similar positions by attempting to identify differences in dispositional achievement motivation in sport and non-sport groups (e.g., McElroy & Willis, 1979). However, a major change of direction in the study of achievement motivation can be traced to the work of Maehr and Nicholls. Their chapter on achievement motivation in 1980 has been cited widely and probably signals a 'landmark' for sport psychologists outside of North America (Maehr & Nicholls, 1980). However, Maehr addressed the North American Society for the Psychology of Sport and Physical Activity (NASPSPA) some years before and discussed many ideas that led to the adoption of a change in emphasis in achievement motivation in sport psychology (Maehr, 1974).

Maehr and Nicholls (1980) influenced the thinking of many people interested in achievement-related constructs and behaviour, and in particular in education. Such an approach was readily adopted by those in sport psychology. In rejecting many of the assumptions of Atkinsonian achievement motivation theory, Maehr and Nicholls (1980) argued that "success and failure are not concrete events. They are psychological states consequent on perception of reaching or not reaching goals....It follows that, if there is cultural variation in the personal qualities that are seen to be desirable, success and failure will be viewed differently in different cultures" (p. 228).

Maehr and Nicholls (1980) went on to suggest that achievement motivation should not be defined as a unitary concept, but rather three types could be defined: ability-orientated motivation, task-orientated motivation, and social approval-orientated motivation. Ability-orientated motivation was when "the goal of the behavior is to maximize the subjective probability of attributing high ability to oneself" (Maehr & Nicholls, 1980, p. 237). This has been modified in sport psychology to refer to 'ego' (Duda, 1992) or 'competitive' (Roberts & Balague, 1989) goal orientations whereby success is defined as the demonstration of superiority over others.

In task-orientated motivation, according to Maehr and Nicholls (1980), "the primary goal is to produce an adequate product or to solve a problem for its own sake rather than to demonstrate ability" (p. 239). This has become known as 'task' (Duda, 1992) or 'mastery' (Roberts & Balague, 1989) goal orientation. Finally, the social approval-orientated motivation identified by Maehr and Nicholls, although discussed in sport psychology (see Roberts, 1984), has been investigated less than the other two goals (see Whitehead, 1992). This dimension of achievement motivation was defined by Maehr and Nicholls (1980) in terms of demonstration of "conformity to norms or virtuous intent rather than superior talent" (pp. 241-242). This requires further study in E&SP. Maehr (Maehr & Braskamp, 1986) has now developed notions of goals into a more comprehensive social cognitive theory of motivation ('theory of personal investment'), and this has started to be used in E&SP research (see Duda, 1992).

The adoption of a 'goal orientations' perspective in achievement motivation is now clear to see (for reviews see Duda, 1992, 1993). Indeed, Joan Duda's paper in this volume, and her other reviews, give comprehensive coverage of such perspectives. For this reason I will not attempt a summary of the research findings. However, I will point out a number of issues that I feel are important for future work in this area.

Goal Orientations: Key Issues

Nature of Goals

Several issues arise under this heading. First, the claim by Nicholls, Duda and others that the two main achievement goal orientations of ego and task are largely uncorrelated has been supported in many studies (e.g., Duda, Fox, Biddle, & Armstrong, 1992). On this basis, it would appear more useful to investigate goal profiles rather than individual goals *per se*. In other words, rather than research the correlates of ego and task orientations separately, investigations need to account for different profiles such as individuals scoring high in both orientations, low in both, or a combination of high/low across the two goals. Initial research using this approach looks promising (Fox, Goudas, Biddle, Duda & Armstrong, in press; Goudas, Biddle & Fox, in press).

Similarly, research is required on the influence of different profiles on different types of task. For example, Fox et al. (in press) found that the motivationally most positive group when looking at a measure of sport participation was the group high in both ego and task orientation. However, Goudas et al. (in press) found that for a specific endurance run task it was the group favouring task over ego orientation that was motivationally most adaptive, particularly for those in the lower performance group.

Another important issue on the nature of achievement goals relates to the longevity and generalisability of such goals. Researchers so far have readily adopted labels such as 'ego oriented', yet have not demonstrated whether this applies across time, and whether this is a relatively enduring trait. In addition, research has shown that goals and associated beliefs may have some generalisability, at least across sport and classroom domains, but this is not always the case (Duda & Nicholls, 1992).

Beyond Task and Ego Goals

Several related perspectives on achievement goals and orientations have appeared in the recent E&SP literature. In addition to the ego/task perspective of Duda and co-workers, adopted in both theory and measurement (Task and Ego Orientation in Sport Questionnaire; TEOSQ; see Duda, 1992), Roberts has adopted a measure of 'perceived sport success' and labelled the two dimensions 'competitive' and 'mastery' (Roberts & Balague, 1989), Gill and Deeter (1988) have developed the 'Sport Orientation Questionnaire', and Vealey (1986) presents a 'Competitive Orientation Inventory'. The conceptual overlap between such instruments and constructs requires further investigation (see Duda, 1992).

Similarly, to what extent do other goals exist in sport and exercise and are they 'achievement' goals? Whitehead (1992) has identified three main clusters of goals in children's sport, each with two factors. She has labelled these 'personal progress' (breakthrough, mastery), 'beating others' (victory, ability), and 'pleasing others' (social approval, teamwork). Further work is required to see if additional goals, whether truly 'achievement-related' or not, exist in sport and exercise for different populations.

Goals: Where do they come from?

An important issue is to investigate how and why different goal orientations or profiles are developed. Dweck and Leggett (1988), for example, suggest that academic goals are related to underlying beliefs about the nature of intelligence. For example, those believing that intelligence is relatively fixed are more likely to adopt a 'performance' (ego) goal whereas others who believe that intelligence is more changeable will be predisposed to a 'learning' (task) goal. This has some intuitive appeal, but little evidence has been produced beyond some exploratory data (Dweck & Leggett, 1988; Elliott & Dweck, 1988). Initial efforts to find parallels in sport have met with weak or mixed results (Biddle & Fox, 1992; Durant & Cailton, 1992). Nevertheless, the identification of socialisation influences, or precursors, of goal orientations is an important research issue.

Finally, consideration needs to be given to the interaction between individual goal orientations and the goals that appear to be dominant in the social situation. Ames (1992; Ames & Archer, 1988) refers to a 'motivational climate' in school classrooms. Using perspectives of goal orientation, physical education (PE) classes or sport teams might be perceived by participants to be, say, mastery or competitive in their orientation. The interaction of climate and individual goals remains an important area of investigation to be developed. Although group climate is likely to be important, it may be difficult in establishing a consistently strong climate to assess its impact on the motivation of individuals. Recent research by Papaioannou, with Greek adolescents, found that both individual goals and class climate in PE interacted to affect perceptions and motivation in physical education (see Papaioannou, in press). Similarly, we have found that PE class climate dimensions of mastery and performance differentially affect intrinsic motivation (Goudas & Biddle, in press). Mastery class climate scores were shown to significantly enhance intrinsic motivation beyond that accounted for by perceived competence, whereas performance climate did not. In addition, we found that children perceiving their PE class to be high in both mastery and performance climate reported greater intrinsic motivation and perceived competence.

Conclusions

In concluding, I wish to draw attention to three main issues as I highlight future directions for the study of motivation in E&SP.

Physical Activity Contexts

The title of this paper includes both sport and exercise. I have already stated that these two contexts may be substantially different from the point of view of psychological factors, including motivation. For example, the motivation associated with elite sports training is likely to be quite different from that of the health club participant. The implications of such differences are important for the promotion of motivational strategies and the education of coaches and exercise leaders.

However, the motivational issues in physical activity are not restricted to sport and exercise. Two other important contexts require identification: physical education and recreational (leisure) sport. The latter has a substantial overlap, at least potentially, with participants in health-related exercise. However, we need to know about the motivational processes involved in those who take part in sport at a more 'casual' or recreative level and who have little or no ambitions to be high level performers (see Ashford, Biddle & Goudas, 1993).

In addition, the important arena of the physical education class seems to have been forgotten in contemporary E&SP. The content analysis reported here substantiates the claim that children are often the focus of attention in sport motivation research. However, most of these studies involve children in volunteer sport programmes. We now require a much greater research effort in the motivation of children in physical education contexts, or at least using samples that are representative of all ability and interest levels (see Fox et al., 1993). Similarly, research on the motivation of the physical education teacher would appear to be important for the future (see Goudas & Biddle, 1993). In short, we are too narrow in our focus in motivation research.

Methodological Issues

The content analysis has highlighted a number of problems associated with methodology in sport and exercise motivation research. If the two journals sampled are representative of other journals in this field, we are currently relying on research that is too restrictive methodologically. For example, Figure 3 shows the domination of survey and experimental methods. Similarly, very few qualitative studies are reported. Although the research questions should determine the method, one cannot help feeling that the bias shown in Figure 3 is due to a reluctance to adopt different methods and to explore alternative paradigms. E&SP, in this respect, has much to learn from research in other disciplines (see Fahlberg, Fahlberg & Gates, 1992; Sparkes, 1991, 1992).

In addition to paradigmatic bias, research in exercise and sport motivation is essentially ethnocentric. Although *IJSP*, predictably, publishes research from all over the world, the E&SP literature has a poor record in true cross-cultural research. Greater collaboration between countries and cultures is recommended.

Descriptive and Theoretical Research

The content analysis showed that about half of the studies sampled tested psychological theory in full or in part. This is probably a slight overestimation of true 'theory testing'. E&SP, it is often claimed, merely follows the lead given by the parent discipline of psychology. This is not altogether a bad thing since one would not expect sport or exercise contexts to be so unique that they require different theoretical perspectives. However, we must avoid a simple blind allegiance to known theories, adopted when they are fashionable and rejected some time later as a new and more fashionable perspective appears. Similarly, it would be informative to test some theories in sport and exercise *alongside* other contexts, such as school classrooms, to see if some overlap exists (see Duda & Nicholls, 1992). Given the importance of some personal and situational cues in physical activity settings which may not appear in other contexts, such as physical effort and physical self-disclosure, a comparison across settings might be informative.

Finally, the example of participation motives research illustrates the importance of descriptive research. Just describing what participants or nonparticipants feel or think is an important first step in theory building (but should not be the last). Much of the descriptive motives research in E&SP has been informative and should be recognised as such.

In closing, I hope that the currently buoyant research efforts in sport and exercise motivation continue, but, at the same time, we consider alterative perspectives and issues in our quest for a greater understanding of human motivation in physical activity.

References

Alderman, R.B. (1974). *Psychological behavior in sport.* Philadelpia: W.B. Saunders.

Ames, C. (1992). Achievement goals, motivational climate, and motivational processes. In G. C. Roberts (Ed.), *Motivation in sport and exercise* (pp. 161 - 176).   Champaign, IL: Human Kinetics.

Ames, C. & Archer, J. (1988). Achievement goals in the classroom: Students' learning strategies and motivational processes. *Journal of Educational Psychology, 80,* 260 - 267.

Ashford, B., Biddle, S.J.H., & Goudas, M. (1993). Participation in community sports centres: Motives and predictors of enjoyment. *Journal of Sports Sciences, 11,* 249-256.

Atkinson, J. W. (1964). *An introduction to motivation.* Princeton, NJ: Van Nostrand

Bandura, A. (1977). Self-efficacy: Toward a unifying theory of behavioral change. *Psychological Review, 84,* 191-215.

Bandura, A. (1986). *Social foundations of thought and action: A social cognitive theory.* Englewood Cliffs, NJ: Prentice-Hall.

Biddle, S.J.H. (1993). Attribution research and sport psychology. In R.N. Singer, M. Murphey, & L.K.Tennant (Eds.), *Handbook of research on sport psychology* (pp. 437-464). New York: Macmillan.

Biddle, S.J.H., & Fox, K.R. (1992). Goal orientations and children's beliefs about sport ability. *Journal of Sports Sciences, 10,* 607-608. [abstract]

Biddle, S.J.H., Goudas, M., & Page, A. (in press). Social-psychological predictors of self-reported actual and intended physical activity in a university workforce sample. *British Journal of Sports Medicine.*

Biddle, S.J.H., & Mutrie, N. (1991). *Psychology of physical activity and exercise: A health-related perspective.* London: Springer.

Butt, D.S. (1976). *Psychology of sport.* New York: Van Nostrand Reinhold.

Caspersen, C.J., Powell, K.E., & Christenson, G.M. (1985). Physical activity, exercise and physical fitness: Definitions and distinctions for health-related research. *Public Health Reports, 100,* 126-131.

Corbin, C.B. (1981). Sex of subject, sex of opponent and opponent ability as factors affecting self-confidence in a competitive situation. *Journal of Sport Psychology, 3,* 265-270.

Duda, J.L. (1992). Motivation in sport settings: A goal perspective approach. In G.C. Roberts (Ed.), *Motivation in sport and exercise* (pp. 57-91). Champaign, IL: Human Kinetics.

Duda, J.L. (1993). Goals: A social-cognitive approach to the study of achievement motivation in sport. In R.N. Singer, M. Murphey, & L.K. Tennant (Eds.), *Handbook of research on sport psychology.* New York: Macmillan.

Duda, J.L., Fox, K.R., Biddle, S.J.H., & Armstrong, N. (1992). Children's achievement goals and beliefs about success in sport. *British Journal of Educational Psychology, 62,* 313-323.

Duda, J.L., & Nicholls, J.G. (1992). Dimensions of achievement motivation in schoolwork and sport. *Journal of Educational Psychology, 84,* 290-299.

Durant, M., & Cailton, A-I. (1992). Developpement des conceptions de la competence physique chez des sujets de 7 a 18 ans. In M. Laurent, J-F. Marini, R. Pfister, & P. Therme (Eds.), *Recherches en A.P.S. - 3* (pp. 319-325). Paris: Actio/Université Aix-Marseille II (UFR STAPS).

Dweck, C.S., & Leggett, E.L. (1988). A social-cognitive approach to motivation and personality. *Psychological Review, 95,* 256-273.

Dzewaltowski, D.A. (1989). Toward a model of exercise motivation. *Journal of Sport and Exercise Psychology, 11,* 251-269.

Elliott, E.S., & Dweck, C.S. (1988). Goals: An approach to motivation and achievement. *Journal of Personality and Social Psychology, 54*, 5-12.

Fahlberg, L.L., Fahlberg, L.A., & Gates, W.K. (1992). Exercise and existence: Exercise behavior from an existential-phenomenological perspective. *The Sport Psychologist, 6*, 172-191.

Feltz, D.L. (1988). Self-confidence and sports performance. *Exercise and Sport Sciences Reviews, 16*, 423-457.

Feltz, D.L. (1992). Understanding motivation in sport: A self-efficacy perspective. In G.C. Roberts (Ed.), *Motivation in sport and exercise* (pp. 93-105). Champaign, IL: Human Kinetics.

Fiske, S.T., & Taylor, S.E. (1991). *Social cognition* (2d ed.). New York: McGraw-Hill.

Fox, K.R., Goudas, M., Biddle, S.J.H., Duda, J.L., & Armstrong, N. (in press). Children's task and ego goal profiles in sport. *British Journal of Educational Psychology.*

Gill, D.L., & Deeter, T.E. (1988). Development of the Sport Orientation Questionnaire. *Research Quarterly for Exercise and Sport, 59*, 191-202.

Goudas, M., & Biddle, S.J.H. (in press). Perceived motivational climate and intrinsic motivation in school physical education classes. *European Journal of Psychology of Education.*

Goudas, M. & Biddle, S.J.H. (1993). *Physical education teacher efficacy: Scale development and relationship with teacher goals.* Manuscript under review.

Goudas, M., Biddle, S.J.H. & Fox, K.R. (in press). Achievement goal orientations and intrinsic motivation in physical fitness testing with children. *Pediatric Exercise Science.*

Griffin, N.S., & Keogh, J.F. (1982). A model of movement confidence. In J.A.S. Kelso & J.E. Clark (Eds.), *The development of movement control and co-ordination.* New York: Wiley.

Lirgg, C.D. (1991). Gender differences in self-confidence in physical activity: A meta-analysis of recent studies. *Journal of Sport and Exercise Psychology, 13*, 294-310.

Maehr, M.L. (1974). Toward a framework for the cross-cultural study of achievement motivation: McClelland reconsidered and redirected. In M.G. Wade & R. Martens (Eds.), *Psychology of motor behavior and sport* (pp. 146-163). Champaign, IL: Human Kinetics.

Maehr, M.L., & Braskamp, L.A. (1986). *The motivation factor: A theory of personal investment.* Lexington, MA: Lexington Books.

Maehr, M.L. & Nicholls, J.G. (1980). Culture and achievement motivation: A second look. In N. Warren (Ed.), *Studies in cross-cultural psychology* (Vol. 2)(pp. 221-267). London: Academic Press.

McAuley, E. (1992a). Self-referent thought in sport and physical activity. In T.S. Horn (Ed.), *Advances in sport psychology* (pp. 101-118). Champaign, IL: Human Kinetics.

McAuley, E. (1992b). Understanding exercise behavior: A self-efficacy perspective. In G.C. Roberts (Ed.), *Motivation in sport and exercise* (pp. 107-127). Champaign, IL: Human Kinetics.

McAuley, E., & Duncan, T.E. (1990). The causal attribution process in sport and physical activity. In S. Graham & V.S. Folkes (Eds.), *Attribution theory: Applications to achievement, mental health, and interpersonal conflict* (pp. 37-52). Hillsdale, NJ: Erlbaum.

Papaioannou, A. (in press). Motivation and goal perspectives in children's physical education. In S.J.H. Biddle (Ed.), *Exercise and sport psychology: A European perspective.* Champaign, IL: Human Kinetics.

Roberts, G.C. (1984). Toward a new theory of motivation in sport: The role of perceived ability. In J.M. Silva & R.S. Weinberg (Eds.), *Psychological foundations of sport* (pp. 214-228). Champaign, IL: Human Kinetics.

Roberts, G.C. (1992a)(Ed.), *Motivation in sport and exercise.* Champaign, IL: Human Kinetics.

Roberts, G.C. (1992b). Introduction. In G.C. Roberts (Ed.), *Motivation in sport and exercise* (pp. vii-xii). Champaign, IL: Human Kinetics.

Roberts, G.C., & Balague, G. (1989). *The development of a social cognitive scale of motivation.* Paper presented at 7th World Congress of Sport Psychology, Singapore.

Singer, R.N., Murphey, M., & Tennant, L.K. (1993)(Eds). *Handbook of research on sport psychology.* New York: Macmillan.

Sparkes, A.C. (1991). Toward understanding, dialogue and polyvocality in the research community: Extending the boundaries of the paradigms debate. *Journal of Teaching in Physical Education, 10,* 103-133.

Sparkes, A.C. (1992). The paradigms debate: An extended review and celebration of difference. In A.C. Sparkes (Ed.), *Research in physical education and sport: Exploring alternative visions* (pp. 9-60). London: Falmer Press.

Vealey, R.S. (1986). Conceptualization of sport-confidence and competitive orientation: Preliminary investigation and instrument development. *Journal of Sport Psychology, 8,* 221-246.

Weiner, B. (1986). *An attribution theory of motivation and emotion.* New York: Springer.

Weiner, B. (1992). *Human motivation: Metaphors, theories and research.* Newbury Park, CA: Sage.

Weiss, M.R., & Chaumeton, N. (1992). Motivational orientations in sport. In T.S. Horn (Ed). *Advances in sport psychology* (pp. 61-99). Champaign, IL: Human Kinetics.

Whitehead, J. (1992). *Toward the assessment of multiple goal perspectives in children's sport.* Paper presented at Olympic Scientific Congress, Benalmadena, Malaga, Spain.

Author Notes

1. Thanks are extended to Dr Ken Fox and Marios Goudas (University of Exeter) for their helpful comments on an earlier version of this paper.

2. I am grateful to Marios Goudas (University of Exeter) for his assistance with the content analysis.

Chapter 8

A GOAL PERSPECTIVE THEORY OF MEANING AND MOTIVATION IN SPORT

Joan L. Duda

One social cognitive model of achievement motivation which has laid the basis for recent classroom (Dweck, 1986; Ames, 1984, 1992; Nicholls, 1989) and sport (Duda, 1992, 1993; Roberts, 1992) research is goal perspective theory. This theoretical framework assumes that there are two predominant goal perspectives operating in achievement settings which relate to how people define success and judge how competent they are at activities. These two goal perspectives are termed task and ego involvement (Nicholls, 1989).

When in a state of task involvement, the experience of learning, task mastery and/or personal improvement occasions a sense of success. Perceptions of competence are personally referenced in this case and are intimately linked to trying one's best. If a person is ego-involved, subjective success entails that she/he has shown her/his ability to be superior. Performing similarly to others with less effort also results in feelings of success when in a state of ego involvement. When focused on this goal perspective, perceptions of competence are dependent on comparison of one's own personal performance outcomes and exerted effort with what has been demonstrated by others.

Goal perspective theory predicts that task involvement will correspond to desirable achievement patterns regardless of whether an individual thinks that she/he is competent or incompetent at the activity at hand. That is, a task-involved person is expected to work hard, choose challenging tasks, perform optimally (given her/his level of ability), and persevere when faced with obstacles and frustrations. Moreover, task involvement is presumed to reduce the chance of feeling incompetent in achievement situations.

In contrast, maladaptive achievement patterns are hypothesized to relate to ego involvement when a person is not confident in her/his ability. An ego-involved individual who has low perceived ability is expected to experience performance impairment, withhold effort or report a lack of interest when it appears that she/he will appear incompetent, select tasks which are either too easy or too difficult, and/or quit when the possibility of repeated failure exists. This negative constellation of achievement behaviors is not predicted for ego-involved persons who have high perceived ability. They are expected to exhibit adaptive achievement strivings. However, perceptions of high competence are held to be especially at risk when ego involvement prevails. Consequently, even among the currently confident, an emphasis on ego-involved goals is hypothesized to lay the basis for forthcoming achievement-related difficulties.

Dispositional Goal Perspectives and Motivational Responses

There are individual differences in pronenesses for task- and ego-involved goal states in achievement situations. Several years ago, my colleagues and I developed a measure to assess these dispositional tendencies in the athletic domain (Duda, 1989; Duda & Nicholls, 1992). To date, we have conducted a number of investigations examining the validity and reliability of the Task and Ego Orientation in Sport Questionnaire or TEOSQ. The TEOSQ, which is comprised of two orthogonal scales, has been found to possess strong psychometric properties in studies of American youth and adults (Chi & Duda, 1993; Duda, 1992). Further support for this instrument has been accrued in research on British (Duda, Fox, Biddle, & Armstrong, 1992), Greek (Papaoiunnou & Duda, 1992), and German (Rethorst & Duda, 1993) children and adolescents.

Drawing from Nicholls' work in the educational setting (Nicholls, 1989), one line of research that we have pursued over the past five years has centered on examining the motivation-related correlates of task and ego orientations in sport. In particular, this series of studies has been concerned with identifying variations in dimensions of the meaning of sport in relation to differences in the endorsement of task- and ego-oriented goal perspectives. The indices of meaning which have been addressed include (1) beliefs about the causes of sport success, (2) perceptions of the functions of athletic involvement, (3) views concerning illegitimate/aggressive behaviors, (4) intrinsic interest and enjoyment, and (5) strategy use.

Beliefs About the Causes of Success

One dimension of the meaning of the activity relates to individuals' ideas about how that activity works or the perceived causes of accomplishment in that context. Nicholls (1989) has suggested that there is a conceptually consistent relationship between goal orientations (or how people tend to define success) and their views concerning the determinants of success in achievement activities. This proposition has been supported in classroom-based research. Task-oriented students tend to believe that working hard, trying to understand what one is learning rather than memorizing the material, and cooperation with other students lead to academic achievement. Ego orientation is linked to the views that trying to outdo others and being smart result in classroom success.

Duda and Nicholls (1992) were the first to investigate the interdependencies between goals and beliefs in the sport context. The subjects in our study were high school athletes and non-athletes. Consistent to what has been observed in the educational domain, task orientation corresponded to the beliefs that trying hard and collaborative efforts "get one ahead" in athletic settings. An ego-oriented goal perspective was associated with the view that possessing high ability causes success in sport. The perception that deceptive and/or illicit tactics are antecedents to athletic accomplishment was negatively correlated with task orientation and positively related to ego orientation.

In general, this pattern of findings has emerged in research on young athletes (Hom, Duda, & Miller, 1993; Lochbaum & Roberts, 1993; Newton & Duda, 1993a), British children and youth (Duda et al., 1992; Treasure, Roberts, & Hall, 1992), disabled adolescent athletes (White & Duda, 1993a), and elite college-age competitors (Duda & White, 1992). Similar goal-belief dimensions have been found as well in the context of physical education (Walling & Duda, in press).

Nicholls (1989) argues that the belief system corresponding to a task orientation in sport should set the stage for maximal investment. The constellation of beliefs which have emerged as correlates of ego orientation in the athletic setting, however, is expected to lead to motivational (as well as ethical and health-related) difficulties (Duda, 1992, 1993; Nicholls, 1989).

Perceptions of the Purposes of Sport

A second facet of the meaning of achievement activities is a person's ideas about what should result as a consequence of participation in the activity. This dimension is reflective of the values of people or their views about what should be the socialization outcomes of achievement endeavors. Nicholls (1989) has proposed that there should be a logical congruence between one's goals in an achievement situation and her/his perceptions of the functions of that experience. Educational research has revealed that task orientation is coupled with the views that school should foster students' commitment to society, understanding of the world, and love of learning. Ego orientation, on the other hand, is associated with the perception that education should lead to wealth and status.

In a study of high school athletes and non-athletes, I examined the interrelationships between goal orientations and perceptions of the purposes of sport (Duda, 1989). As can be seen in Figure 1, a positive association between task orientation and the views that sport should teach individuals the importance of always working hard, how to cooperate with others, and the way to become good citizens was revealed. Ego orientation was connected with the perceptions that sport should result in greater popularity, self-importance, and competitiveness (Figure 2).

The overall results of the Duda (1989) investigation have been replicated in subsequent studies of youth and interscholastic sport participants (McNamara & Duda, in press; White, Duda, & Keller, 1993). Conceptually consistent associations between goal orientations and values have also been observed in research conducted in physical education classes (Walling & Duda, in press). In total, these studies suggest that task-oriented individuals perceive sport and physical activity as an experience which brings intrinsic benefits and the opportunity to work hard and work with others. Ego-oriented persons view athletics as a vehicle to extrinsic gains and personal glory.

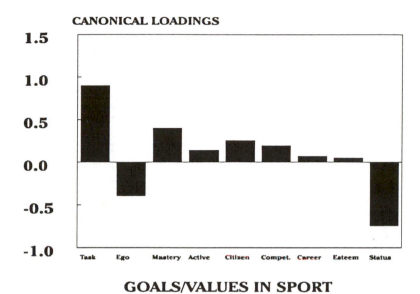

Figure 1. Canonical loadings for the task orientation/purposes
of sport function.

Attitudes Toward Sportsmanship and Aggressive Acts

A third component of the meaning of an activity are people's conceptions
about what are the appropriate means to accomplishment. An awareness of
individual differences in goal orientation has been found to provide insight
into views about what is legitimate to do within the confines of sport competition. In a study of high school basketball players, Duda, Olson, and
Templin (1991) reported a positive relationship between the emphasis placed
on task-oriented goals and sportsmanship attitudes. Ego orientation was
positively associated with an endorsement of "cheating" behaviors. Moreover, athletes who were high in ego orientation were more likely to agree
with intentionally injurious acts than those low in ego orientation.

Results of a recent study by Stephens and Bredemeier (1992) involving
young female soccer players were compatible with the Duda et al. (1991)
investigation. Research on high school and college football players also
replicated this initial work (Huston & Duda, 1992). Further, the Huston
and Duda study revealed that perceptions of the legitimacy of aggressive

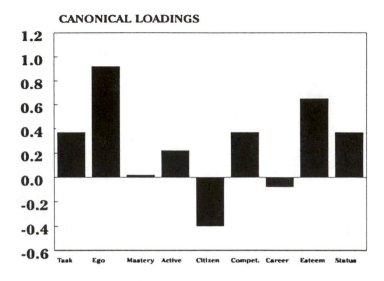

CANONICAL LOADINGS

GOALS/VALUES IN SPORT

**Figure 2. Canonical loadings for the ego orientation/puposes
of sport function.**

acts were best predicted by variations in goal orientations rather than differences in competitive level.

Intrinsic Interest and Enjoyment

The degree to which individuals find activities enjoyable and interesting is another facet of the meaning of our endeavors. From a motivational standpoint, people tend to persevere and invest in activities which are fun and inherently interesting. A consistent result in the goal perspective literature has been the positive association between task orientation and the enjoyment of, satisfaction with, and intrinsic interest in achievement domains such as school and sport. This positive relationship has emerged in studies of youth sport participants (Hom et al., 1993), British children (Duda, et al., 1992), high school students (Duda & Nicholls, 1992), and college students (Duda, Chi, Newton, Walling, & Catley, in press). In research on youngsters involved in a sport competition, participants who were high in task orientation tended to report greater enjoyment and interest both pre- and post-game regardless of their competence level or whether they won or lost (Walling, Duda, & Crawford, 1992).

Strategy Use

Whether people are willing to problem solve in and work at achievement activities also reflects the meaning of such an enterprise. At the very least, this aspect of our actions tells us something about whether the focus is on the process or outcome of the achievement experience. Ames (1992) and others (Dweck, 1986; Nicholls, 1989) have suggested that goals may influence achievement behaviors by impacting the use of effective or ineffective performance strategies. In the physical domain, task-oriented college students have been found to stress the relevance of practice as a vehicle to learning and improvement (Roberts, Hall, Jackson, Kimiecik, & Tonymon, 1990). In a study of students enrolled in bowling classes, individuals high in task orientation (and low in ego orientation) reported greater employment of diverse strategies during play (Newton & Duda, 1993b).

Lochbaum and Roberts (1993) examined the links between goal orientations and competition and practice strategies among male and female interscholastic sport participants. While engaged in competition, athletes high in task orientation reported that they listened to the coach and kept trying new skills even if they were having trouble mastering those skills. Task-oriented athletes were also more likely to see the benefits of regular practice while ego-oriented competitors tended to view practice as an ineffective strategy.

In a study conducted in college-level tennis classes, Solomon and Boone (1993) found that students who were higher in task orientation selected more challenging tasks to work on throughout the semester (as reflected in a class contract grading system). These task-oriented students also reported that they engaged in more adaptive cognitive strategies during the class (e.g., making sure that they understood what the instructor was telling them; asking themselves what they may have done wrong on a particular shot). Controlling for initial differences in tennis ability, the selection of challenging tasks and reported engagement in adaptive cognitive processes significantly and positively predicted skill improvement.

Situationally Induced Goal Perspectives

Whether an individual is in a state of task or ego involvement is also assumed to be impacted by situational factors (Nicholls, 1989). A second line of research in the sport goal perspective literature has focused on the motivational correlates of the perceived psychological climate. Drawing from the work of Ames (1992; Ames & Archer, 1988; Ames & Maehr, 1989), this work is concerned with the influence of perceived situationally-induced goals on people's cognitive and affective responses in athletic settings.

The initial study in this area involved male high school basketball players (Seifriz, Duda, & Chi, 1992). During the mid-point of the season, players were administered the Perceived Motivational Climate In Sport Questionnaire or PMCSQ as well as the TEOSQ. The PMCSQ was developed for this investigation and support for the factor validity, predictive validity, and internal reliability of this measure was found.

The PMCSQ is comprised of two scales assessing the degree to which the coach is viewed as creating a task-involving (i.e., he/she emphasizes hard work and personal improvement, treats mistakes as part of the learning process, and has all players feel like they make a contribution to the team) and ego-involving (i.e., he/she has players focus on outperforming each other, makes his players fear making mistakes, and rewards/recognizes only the outstanding players) goal structure on the team.

In our investigation, the basketball players who perceived that their coach fostered a task-involving atmosphere reported greater enjoyment of basketball and believed that exerting effort and cooperation lead to success. Perceptions of an ego-involving climate were linked to the belief that superior ability is needed if one is to be successful in basketball. Low correlations were observed between dispositional goal orientation and the basketball players' perceptions of the motivational climate.

Subsequent research by Walling, Duda, and Chi (1993) provided further evidence for the validity and reliability of the PMCSQ. The subjects in this investigation were boys and girls who were participants in an amateur international competition. Congruent with theoretical predictions, athletes who perceived that the goal structure prevailing on their team was task-involving were more satisfied with being part of the team. They also were lower in performance worry. Perceptions of an ego-involving environment were negatively related to team satisfaction and positively associated with concerns about one's performance. In a study of high school and college female basketball and volleyball players, Newton (1993) also found a positive relationship between scores on the ego-involving climate scale and performance-related anxiety.

Treasure (1993) investigated the associations between perceptions of the goal structure operating in their physical education class and select motivational indices. In this study, children were assigned to soccer skills lessons which were manipulated to be either task- or ego-involving. At the conclusion of the intervention, they were asked to respond to an adapted version of the Perceived Motivational Climate in Sport Questionnaire. Consistent with the Seifriz et al. study (1992), perceptions of the motivational climate were not related to dispositional goal orientation in Treasure's research. Perceptions of a task-involving class climate positively related to attitudes toward the class, preference for challenging soccer tasks, satisfaction/interest, perceived ability, and the belief that motivation and effort lead to success in soccer. Perceptions of a task-involving environment were negatively associated with boredom experienced in the class.

The children who perceived a pronounced ego-involving climate reported a less positive class attitude, greater preference for easy soccer tasks, less satisfaction with and interest in the soccer class, and greater boredom. Perceptions of an ego-involving situation were positively linked to the view tht external factors are precursors to soccer success and negatively related to the belief that motivation and effort get one ahead in this sport.

Combined with the efforts of Seifriz and his colleagues (1992), Walling et al. (1993), and Newton (1993), Treasure's study demonstrates that coaches/teachers can have a pronounced influence on the motivation of young sport participants. Whether individuals perceive that the coach/teacher is stressing task versus ego goals predicts their beliefs, cognitions, and affective responses in the athletic context.

Recently, White and colleagues have begun to examine the psychometric characteristics of a measure of the perceived motivational climate created by parents in the physical domain (White, Duda, & Hart, 1992; White & Duda, 1993). The Parent-Initiated Motivational Climate Questionnaire assesses the degree to which youngsters feel that their parents value personal improvement and the learning of skills and success without effort. Also measured is the degree to which children perceive that their parents are concerned when they make a mistake while learning physical skills. Subsequent work will ascertain the motivational correlates of the goal structure perceived to be emphasized by mothers and fathers in terms of their children.

Experimental Work

The two lines of research discussed above are correlational in design. Several experimental studies have been conducted to date, however, which have tested the tenets of goal perspective theory in physical activity settings.

Duda and Chi (1989) determined the impact of pregame perceived competence, task- and ego-involving game conditions, and objective outcome on performance attributions and post-performance ratings of perceived ability. College-age males were requested to play a one-on-one basketball game against an opponent of equal skill. In the ego-involving condition, the men participated in a competitive game where the outcome was reported to a class instructor. In the task-involving situation, the players were requested to play one-on-one basketball and work on a specific offensive and defensive weakness. Although the score was inobstrusively recorded by an observer, the subjects were told to try their best and that there would be no winner or loser.

We found a significant effect for the situational goal structure on the effort attributions of objective winners and losers. Losers in the ego-involving condition were less likely to attribute their performance to the amount of effort exerted when compared to losers in the task-involving game or winners in general. Further, regardless of objective outcome, low perceived competence subjects who participated in the task-involving game perceived themselves to be more able post-game than low perceived competence subjects who were in the ego-involving condition.

Hall (1990) examined the effect of a task- versus ego-involving situational goal structure and perceived competence on the attributions, perceptions of ability, and performance of male college students. The subjects were asked to perform a stabilometer task and their perceived competence was manipulated. Low perceived ability subjects performing under an ego-involving goal structure reported that they did not try as hard and expected to perform worse during the early trials as low perceived ability subjects in the task-involving condition or high perceived ability subjects in either condition. High perceived ability subjects in the ego-involving condition expected to do less well during the later trials. Low perceived ability subjects who performed in the ego-involving situation displayed lower performance than low perceived ability subjects who were assigned to the task-involving condition.

Chi (1993) conducted a laboratory experiment on the effect of dispositional goal perspectives, perceived competence, and objective outcome on performance and task choice. Male college students who were high in task orientation and low in ego orientation or high in ego orientation and low in task orientation (as assessed with the TEOSQ) were requested to perform an estimated VO2 max test on a cycle ergometer. Perceived cycling and fitness competence was then manipulated by giving the subjects bogus feedback.

The men were then requested to engage in two consecutive competitive races against an opponent of equal cycling ability. Half of the subjects were assigned to a win condition (i.e., they received bogus feedback that they won both races) while the other half were assigned to the lose condition (i.e., they received bogus feedback that they lost both races). Actual performance (in kilometers) during the two 6-minute races was recorded directly by a computer. In terms of the measure of task choice, the subjects were asked to indicate how challenging they would like their opponent to be (compared to his own and his present opponent's perceived cycling ability) if they were to compete against a same-sex and same-age peer in the next competition. This measure was taken before Race 1 and Race 2 and after Race 2.

Chi (1993) found a significant three-way interaction for goal orientation, outcome, and phase of assessment. As shown in Figure 3, high task-/low

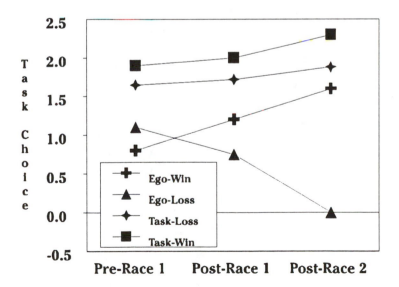

Figure 3. The interactive effects of goal orientations, outcome, and time of assessment on task choice.

ego-oriented subjects tended to select a more challenging opponent than
high ego-/low task-oriented subjects across the trials. Subjects who were
high ego-/low task-oriented and lost the races tended to select less challenging opponents that the subjects who were high ego-/low task-oriented and
won the races and the high task-/low ego-oriented subjects regardless of race
outcome. After losing the second race, the subjects who were high ego-/low
task-oriented selected a significantly less challenging opponent than what
was the case after Race 1.

Due to observed group differences in the subjects' cycling performance
in Race 1 (before outcome was manipulated), Chi (1993) conducted an analysis of covariance to partial out the initial variability in cycling performance.
The independent variables of interest were once again goal orientation, manipulated competence, outcome, and time of assessment. A three-way
interaction emerged (see Figure 4). High ego-/low task-oriented subjects
who received low manipulated competence feedback and lost the races performed significantly worse than the high task-/low ego-oriented subjects

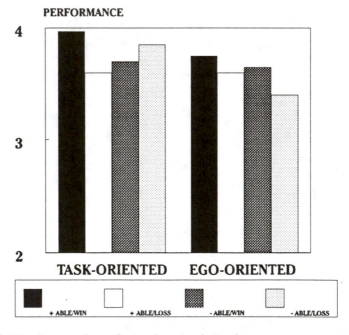

**Figure 4. The interactive effects of goal orientations, outcome, and per-
ceived ability on Race Two performance (controlling for
Race One performance).**

with low perceived manipulated competence and lost the races, and the high task-/low ego-oriented subjects who were in the high manipulated competence group and won the two races.

Treasure (1993) examined the effects of the manipulated motivational climate on children's self-reported achievement behavior, cognitions, and affect during physical education class. The subjects were 114 sixth and seventh grade children who were heterogeneous in terms of race and previous sport experience. After assessing their goal orientation, perceptions of ability, and attitudes toward the activity, the children were assigned to either a task-involving or ego-involving class condition. In the class, the children were taught soccer skills such as running with the ball, changing direction, dribbling, and passing and control.

Drawing from the work of Epstein (1989) and Ames and Maehr (1989), Treasure (1993) targeted strategies which were consistent with promoting either a task or ego achievement goal in the sport environment. Specifically, the intervention focused on five dimensions of the motivational climate, that is, the task structure, the reward system, the bases of grouping students, the evaluation procedure, and the nature of the time demands placed on the children.

In the ego-involving environment, the children engaged in the same unidimensional tasks. Communication and reward were provided in a controlling manner and the students had no input into class-related decision making. Rewards and recognition were public and based on the demonstration of superior performance. With respect to grouping, the children were assigned to competitive groups which stressed social comparison. The criterion underlying this selection was differences in the children's abiity levels. Children were evaluated in reference to how they performed on the soccer tests compared to the rest of the group. Finally, limited time was allotted for the learning of new skills and the teacher/coach spent the most time with the most competent children.

In contrast, there was diversity in the tasks and assignments in the task-involving soccer classes. The children were actively involved in the learning process and took part in decision making. Rewards were given privately to each child and were based on personal improvement and exerted effort. The children practiced their soccer skills individually or in small, cooperative groups. Evaluation was also individualized and focused on progress toward meeting personal goals. Self-tests, in which the children rated their own improvement and effort, were also administered. The task demands (in terms of time and complexity) coincided with the ability of the child and the teacher/coach spent equivalent time with all the children regardless of their soccer competence.

The intervention took place over 10 physical education class periods. At the conclusion of the investigation, the children's goal orientation and perceived ability were once again assessed. Further, the youngsters' self-reported achievement behaviors and cognitive and affective responses to the class were examined. In particular, Treasure (1993) measured their preference for challenging versus easy tasks, satisfaction with and interest in the soccer class, attitudes toward the class and teacher/coach, and beliefs about the determinants of success in soccer.

Treasure (1993) found that the high ability children who were assigned to the ego-involving condition significantly increased their perceptions of ability. The reverse was observed for low perceived ability in the ego-involving climate. The children who perceived their ability to be high and were in the task-involving climate also increased their perceived competence pre- to post-intervention. Albeit not significant, low ability children in the task group reported increased perceptions of ability over the course of the intervention.

Goal perspective theory predicts that maladaptive behaviors, cognitions, and emotional responses will be exhibited when individuals with low perceived ability are placed in an ego-involving situation. Treasure's (1993) results support this theoretical prediction. Low perceived ability children who were taught soccer skills in the ego-involving climate reported a less positive attitude toward the intervention and preferred to engage in less challenging tasks than all other subjects. These children also experienced less satisfaction and interest and indicated greater boredom than high ability youngsters in the ego-involving condition or those in the task-involving group regardless of their perceived ability.

A goal perspective analysis of motivation also implies that "trouble looms" for people placed in ego-involving environments even if their perceptions of ability are high. Aligned with this prediction, high perceived ability children who were assigned to the ego-involving group indicated that they prefer easy tasks when compared to the children in the task-involving climate.

In summary, the laboratory and field experiments conducted to date have provided preliminary support for the predicted effect of differences in goal perspectives on performance and other achievement behaviors such as task choice. This research has also suggested that goal perspectives impact the motivational processes of individuals involved in sport activities. In other words, variations in task and ego involvement (as resulting from differences in dispositional goal orientations or the manipulated motivational climate) have a significant influence on how people think and feel while engaged in sport-related tasks.

Future Directions

The goal perspective research has shown that individual differences in goal perspectives and the situational goal structure (whether perceived or actual) independently and in combination predict motivational indices. More work needs to be done which focuses on the interaction between dispositional and environment goals on achievement patterns. What is the consequence of placing a person who is high in task or ego orientation in an environment which is predominantly task- or ego-involving? The "matching model" of motivation would predict that a task-oriented athlete would be most content in a task-involving climate while an ego-oriented sport participant would exhibit optimal motivation in an ego-involving situation. In contrast, based on goal perspective theory, we would hypothesize that all individuals should demonstrate motivated behaviors in a mastery-focused atmosphere. Task-oriented people would be expected to exhibit adaptive patterns regardless of the prevailing climate. Further, we should see major motivational problems among ego-oriented persons who find themselves in an ego-involving context...especially if their perceived ability is low.

One of my doctoral students, Maria Newton, is addressing such questions in her dissertation research (Newton, 1994). Hopefully, through her study and subsequent work, we should have more insight into the interplay between dispositional and situational goal perspectives.

Our individual pronenesses for task and ego involvement are not borne in a vacuum. Rather, it is suggested that dispositional goal orientations are a product of previous socialization experiences (Nicholls, 1989). That is, the goal perspective which is adopted by young people should be a function of the goal perspective emphasized by significant others such as parents, coaches, teachers, and peers. In cross-sectional studies, we have found that the goal orientations of young athletes are not correlated with the self-reported goal orientations of their mothers and fathers in sport. Rather, young athletes' dispositional goal perspectives are strongly associated with the youngsters' perceptions of the goal orientation held by their parents (Duda & Hom, 1993; McNamara & Duda, in press; White & Duda, 1993).

Longitudinal work is needed which examines the influence of significant others on children's and adolescents' goal orientations over time. The assessments of perceived motivational climate created by coaches (Seifriz et al., 1992), teachers (Papapioannou, in press), and parents (White et al., 1992) which are available in the literature should be helpful in this area of investigation. Moreover, future studies are warranted which identify what young people use as informational cues when perceiving the goal perspective being emphasized by the important people in their lives.

An appealing feature of goal perspective theory is that it considers developmental changes in the concepts central to the framework and motivation per se. To be in a state of ego involvement, a person has to have a mature conception of ability (Nicholls, 1989; Nicholls & Miller, 1984). That is, she/he must be able to differentiate ability and effort and understand that ability is a capacity. When people possess a differentiated conception of ability, they realize that effort will only get them so far if competence is lacking. Nicholls and his colleagues have shown that younger children (up through the age of 10 years or so) are not able to employ a mature understanding of ability when they judge their competence and interpret achievement outcomes.

If in a state of task involvement, people are using an undifferentiated conception of ability. Ability and effort are not seen to covary in this instance. Rather, more effort is equated to more ability which results in subjective success. Younger children have been found to possess this less mature perspective on ability (Nicholls & Miller, 1984).

To date, these developmental changes in the understanding of ability have been examined only in the academic domain. Another one of my students, Mary Walling, is presently examining this issue in her doctoral research on children's conceptions of effort and ability in both sport and academic situations (Walling, 1994). If we hope to foster motivation to engage in sport and exercise among young people, much more work is needed on how children of different ages interpret sport activities (Duda, 1987).

All of the cited studies based on goal perspective theory in the sport domain (and almost all the sport research drawing from the other theories of motivation) have been nomothetic in design. If a theoretical framework on motivation truly captures the meaning of achievement experiences as well as people's actions within achievement contexts, it should have predictive utility at the individual level *and* in terms of aggregate data. Case studies testing the tenets of goal perspective theory should be considered in future research. More qualitative work on this topic is also warranted. For example, we have initiated a study in wich we will interview individuals who vary in their goal orientations and examine their achievement-related cognitions and behaviors.

Finally, in his recent work, Nicholls (1992) suggests that we need to consider the general as well as the specific in our work on motivation. The goal perspective research has shown that there are parallels and distinctions between findings stemming from studies conducted in the classroom versus sport, sport versus physical education, elite versus youth sport, etc. The differences between contexts, sports, and participants are important to our fuller understanding of motivated behavior. Subsequent research should examine goals, beliefs, values, and other motivation-related variables which are particular to specific sport activities and groups of competitors.

References

Ames, C. (1984). Competitive, cooperative and individualistic goal structures: A motivational analysis. In R. Ames & C. Ames (Eds.), *Research on motivation in education: Student motivation* (pp. 177-207). NY: Academic Press.

Ames, C. (1992). Classrooms: Goals, structures, and student motivation. *Journal of Educational Psychology, 84,* 261-271.

Ames, C., & Archer, J. (1988). Achievement goals in the classroom: Students' learning strategies and motivation processes. *Journal of Educational Psychology, 80,* 260-267.

Ames, C., & Maehr, M.L. (1989). *Home and school cooperation in social and motivational development.* Unpublished raw data. Project funded by the U.S. Office of Education, Office of Special Education and Rehabilitative Services, Contract No. DE-H023T80023.

Chi, L. (1993). *The prediction of achievement-related cognitions and behaviors in the physical domain: A test of the theories of goal perspectives and self-efficacy.* Unpublished doctoral dissertation, Purdue University.

Chi, L., & Duda, J.L. (1993). *Multi-group confirmatory factor analysis of the Task and Ego Orientation in Sport Questionnaire.* Manuscript under review.

Duda, J.L. (1987). Toward a developmental theory of achievement motivation in children's sport. *Journal of Sport Psychology, 9,* 130-145.

Duda, J.L. (1989). The relationship between task and ego orientation and the perceived purpose of sport among male and female high school athletes. *Journal of Sport and Exercise Psychology, 11*, 318-335.

Duda, J.L. (1992). Sport and exercise motivation: A goal perspective analysis. In G. Roberts (Ed.), *Motivation in sport and exercise* (pp. 57-91). Champaign, IL: Human Kinetics.

Duda, J.L. (1993). Goals: A social cognitive approach to the study of motivation in sport. In R.N. Singer, M. Murphey, & L.K. Tennant (Eds.), *Handbook on research in sport psychology* (pp. 421-436). NY: Macmillan.

Duda, J.L., & Chi, L. (1989, September). *The effect of task and ego involving conditions on perceived competence and causal attributions in basketball.* Paper presented to the Association for the Advancement of Applied Sport Psychology, University of Washington, Seattle, WA.

Duda, J.L., Chi, L., Newton, M.L., Walling, M.D., & Catley, D. (in press). Task and ego orientation and intrinsic motivation in sport. *International Journal of Sport Psychology.*

Duda, J.L., Fox, K.R., Biddle, S.J.H., & Armstrong, N. (1992).Children's achievement goals and beliefs about success in sport. *British Journal of Educational Psychology, 62*, 313-323.

Duda, J.L., & Hom, H.L. (1993). The interrelationships between children's and parents' goal orientations in sport. *Pediatric Exercise Science, 5*, 234-241.

Duda, J.L., & Nicholls, J.G. (1992). Dimensions of achievement motivation in schoolwork and sport. *Journal of Educational Psychology, 84*, 290-299.

Duda, J.L., Olson, L.K., Templin, T.J. (1991). The relationship of task and ego orientation to sportsmanship attitudes and the perceived legitimacy of injurious acts. *Research Quarterly for Exercise and Sport, 62*, 79-87.

Duda, J.L., & White, S.A. (1992). The relationship of goal perspectives to beliefs about success among elite skiers. *The Sport Psychologist, 6*, 334-343.

Dweck, C.S. (1986). Motivational processes affecting learning. *American Psychologist, 41,* 1040-1048.

Epstein, J. (1989). Family structures and student motivation: A developmental perspective. In C. Ames & R. Ames (Eds.), *Research on motivation in education* (Vol. 3) (pp. 259-295). New York: Academic Press.

Hall, H.K. (1990). *A social-cognitive approach to goal-setting: The mediating effects of achievement goals and perceived ability.* Unpublished doctoral dissertation, University of Illinois at Urbana-Champaign.

Hom, H., Duda, J.L., & Miller, A. (1993). Correlates of goal orientations among young athletes. *Pediatric Exercise Science, 5*, 168-176.

Huston, L., & Duda, J.L. (1993). *The relationship of goal orientations and competitive involvement to the perceived legitimacy of aggressive acts in football.* Manuscript under review.

Lochbaum, M., & Roberts, G.C. (1993). Goal orientations and perceptions of the sport experience. *Journal of Sport and Exercise Psychology, 15,* 160-171.

McNamara, W., & Duda, J.L. (in press). Goal orientations and perceptions of the purposes of sport among young male athletes and their parents. *Pediatric Exercise Science.*

Newton, M.L. (1994). *The effect of goal orientations and perceived motivational climate on the motivational responses of female athletes.* Unpublished doctoral dissertation, Purdue University.

Newton, M.L., & Duda, J.L. (1993a). Elite adolescent athletes' achievement goals and beliefs concerning success in tennis. *Journal of Sport and Exercise Psychology. 15,* 431 - 448

Newton, M.L., & Duda, J.L. (1993b). The relationship of goal orientations to mid-activity cognitions and post-performance attributions among bowling class students. *Journal of Sport Behavior, 16,* 4 - 12.

Nicholls, J.G. (1989). *The competitive ethos and democratic education.* Cambridge, MA: Harvard University Press.

Nicholls, J.G. (1992). The general and the specific in the development and expression of achievement motivation. In G. Roberts (Ed.), *Motivation in sport and exercise* (pp. 31-56). Champaign, IL: Human Kinetics.

Nicholls, J.G., & Miller, A. (1984). Development and its discontents: The differentiation of the concept of ability. In J. Nicholls (Ed.), *Advances in motivation and achievement: The development of achievement motivation.* Greenwich, CT: JAI Press.

Papaioannou, A. (in press). Motivation and goal perspectives in physical activity for children. In S.J.H. Biddle (Ed.), *Exercise and sport psychology: A European perspective.* Champaign, IL: Human Kinetics.

Papaioannou, A., & Duda, J.L. (1992). *Goal perspectives and motives for participation in physical education among adolescent Greek students.* Manuscript under review.

Rethorst, S., & Duda, J.L. (1993, June). *Goal orientations, cognitions, and emotions in gymnastics.* Paper presented at the Eighth World Congress of Sport Psychology, Lisbon, Portugal.

Roberts, G.C. (1992). Motivation in sport and exercise: Conceptual constraints and convergence. In G. Roberts (Ed.), *Motivation in sport and exercise* (pp. 3-30). Champaign, IL: Human Kinetics.

Roberts, G.C., Hall, H., Jackson, S.A., Kimiecik, J., & Tonymon, P. (1991). *Personal theories of ability and the sport experience: Goal perspectives and achievement strategies.* Unpublished manuscript, University of Illinois at Champaign - Urbana.

Seifriz, J., Duda, J.L., & Chi, L. (1992). The relationship of perceived motivational climate to intrinsic motivation and beliefs about success in basketball. *Journal of Sport and Exercise Psychology, 14,* 375-391.

Solomon, M., & Boone, J. (1993, May). *The impact of student goal orientation in physical education classes.* Paper presented at the meeting of the American Education Research Association, San Francisco, CA.

Stephens, D., & Bredemeier, B.J. (1992, November). *Toward an understanding of moral behavior in sport: An examination of lying, hurting, and cheating behavior in girls' soccer.* Paper presented at the Association for the Advancement of Applied Sport Psychology, Colorado Springs, CO.

Treasure, D. C. (1993). *A social-cognitive approach to understanding children's achievement behavior, cognitions, and affect in competitive sport.* Unpublished doctoral dissertation, University of Illinois at Urbana-Champaign.

Treasure, D.C., Roberts, G.C., & Hall, H.K. (1992). The relationship between children's achievement goal orientations and their beliefs about competitive sport. *Journal of Sport Sciences, 10,* 629.

Walling, M.D. (1994). *Developmental changes in the concepts of effort and ability in the physical domain.* Unpublished doctoral dissertation, Purdue University.

Walling, M.D., & Duda, J.L. (in press). The relationship of goal orientations to beliefs about and the perceived purposes of physical education. *Journal of Teaching in Physical Education.*

Walling, M.D., Duda, J.L., & Crawford, T. (in press). Goal orientations, outcome, and responses to youth sport competition among high/low perceived ability athletes. *International Journal of Sport Psychology.*

Walling, M., Duda, J.L., & Chi, L. (1993). The perceived motivational climate in sport questionnaire: Construct and predictive validity. *Journal of Sport and Exercise Psychology, 15,* 172-183.

White, S.A., & Duda, J.L. (1993, June). *The relationship between goal orientation and parent-initiated motivational climate among children learning a physical skill.* Paper presented at the Eighth World Congress of Sport Psychology, Lisbon, Portugal.

White, S.A., Duda, J.L., & Hart, S. (1992). An exploratory examination of the Parent-Initiated Motivational Climate Questionnaire. *Perceptual and Motor Skills, 75*, 875-880.

White, S.A., Duda, J.L., & Keller, M.R. (1993). *The relationship between goal orientation and the perceived purpose of sport among youth sport participants.* Manuscript under review.

Chapter 9

THE DEVELOPMENT OF GENDER AS A SOCIO-CULTURAL PERSPECTIVE: IMPLICATIONS FOR SPORT PSYCHOLOGY

Kari Fasting

Introduction: Gender Versus Sex

In the first part of this paper the task is to attempt to clarify the concept of gender; the second part discusses how gender has been treated in psychological research. The last part concerns sport psychology. Examples showing how gender has been treated in sport psychology are given attention. The paper closes with the implications for future research and practice in sport psychology.

According to Ann Hall (1990) some authors in United States started to use the term *gender* instead of *sex* about 25 years ago. According to her it was

> used to designate the psychological, cultural, and social dimensions of maleness and femaleness, whereas sex was used to designate the dichotomous distinctions between females and males based on physiological characteristics that are genetically determined. The

distinction therefore, between sex and gender was meant to clarify the biological versus the cultural. (p. 224)

This division and the interaction between sex and gender or between biology and culture is however not so clear. We really do not know where biology ends and culture starts. The meaning of a biological sex difference may also vary according to the culture through which it is mediated. For example the tendency towards greater physical strength in males tends to be exaggerated in Western industrialized countries in which boys are much more encouraged and motivated to participate in physical activity than are girls. A natural tendency towards greater muscular strength is therefore increased by the cultural factor: physical activity. In countries in which women customarily carry the physical burden, their muscles may be better developed than those of men (Eichler, 1980).

Today , gender seems to be widely used as a social construct. The latest research however focuses on the process by which this social construction of gender occurs or develops (Hall, 1990). New terms like gendering, gender belief system, and gender orders have occurred. A development from understanding gender as a variable, focusing on gender differences, to the understanding of gender as a perspective, or as a result, of a relational process seems to have taken place. This development has naturally taken on different forms in the different social sciences. According to Deaux (1984) psychologists have moved away from the sex differences and individual differences approaches to an emphasis on gender as a social category.

First of all it is important to realize that "the gender order is a dynamic process that is constantly in a state of change"(Messner & Sabo, 1990, p. 12). It can also be defined as

a set of power relations, whereby men, as a social group, have more power over women than women have over them; they are socially constructed, not biologically given; and they are not fixed, but rather are subject to historical change and can be transformed. (Hall, 1990, p. 226)

Famous male scientists (Bordieu, 1990; Goffman, 1977) have come to the conclusion that we live in a gendered society or that society is gendered. Goffman (1977) for example writes that the suppression of women is more serious and basic than the suppression of classes.

One can analyze women's as well as men's behavior from a gender perspective. Most research with such a perspective has however been done on women only. This is also true in sport research (Fasting, 1992).

As a result we have knowledge about women that we do not have about men. To get such knowledge about men is absolutely necessary for our understanding of the gender order or system. Diane Gill (1992) states that "if we hope to understand gender as a social category and process, we must consider the role of gender for both men and women. Certainly , gender belief systems operate for men in sport" (p. 156). She further states that gender plays different roles for female and male behavior.

By understanding gender as a perspective, situations and behavior may be studied even without the presence of males and females (Leira, 1992). Jennifer Hargreaves (1990) for example points out that "sport has important ethical and moral dimensions which are intrinsically related to gender but the connections are either ignored or glossed over: problems of drugs, violence, and commercialization all have important gender dimensions" (p. 288).

Gender and Psychology

The development of gender just described has been strongly influenced by the development of women's studies and the different feminist theories. Women's studies as a subject for research was developed as a result of a strong critique of the social sciences that emerged around 1970.

The essence of the critique was formulated as follows: "While general theories seemed appropriate for most boys and men in society, they seemed useless for explaining and predicting female behavior" (Ås, 1975, p. 143).

In psychology, data on female behavior were usually described as deviant, different, or difficult to explain, just because they did not fit the male-made theories. As a result, females were often excluded from the studies. One may therefore safely conclude that psychology was developed as generalizations and abstractions from men's experience and practices. Carolyn Wood Sherif (1979) used the standard procedures developed for studying achievement orientation as an example. They were, according to her, biased and inappropriate for studying achievement orientations of women. She focused on the fact that the indiscriminate use of tests developed primarily for males is not only biased, but also inappropriate as society changes. Their use assumes that the standards based on male performance in the past will be retained when the institutions in which performance is to occur will have changed by admitting women. She compared this situation with studies in cross-cultural research where the researchers attempt to use the methods and procedures developed in one culture to study a very different culture. It is believed that this comment is relevant for sport today because we have more knowledge about the psychology of women, concurrently as women's involvement and positions in sport and sport organizations have changed dramatically during the last 10 to 15 years.

Carolyn Wood Sherif (1979) also criticized the use of "sex" as an independent variable in psychology and described the situation as follows:

The variable sex is like a railroad boxcar : Everyone knows what it is called and what it is used for,but no one knows what is inside. Older psychologists had no doubt that it contained "biology". Modern psychologists follow suit, or add culture, or subtract biology as well. Result? Utter confusion in almost all discussions of the variable sex or sex differences. (p. 45)

Some years later Jacklin (1989) points out that gender changes as society changes, and that even the original conclusions on psychological sex differences for example in aggressive behavior and intellectual abilities cannot be supported anymore.

As a result of the critique that took place 20 years ago, and the new knowledge about women that came as a result of this, feminist psychology was developed.

Feminism is not a monolithic concept. Feminism can be and is divided into different forms. Feminist analyses have however something in common. They center around the relations between the sexes, and gender is therefore considered a key dimension of overall identity and a determinant of behavior.

The heritage from psychoanalysis, social learning theory, and cognitive theory is very important in understanding psychology's conceptions of gender today. This can be studied in the area of personality development and the development of sex-identity. The further development of these theories, the interaction between them, and the feminists' critique of them create the basis for our understanding of modern psychology's conceptions of gender.

Freud (1973, 1916) emphasized biology and early childhood, the social learning theorists focused on the environment and the consequences on behavior, and the cognitive theorists (Kohlberg, 1967) put emphasis on the individual's understanding of her or his environment.

The debate and discourse concerning which role gender (the meaning of gender) plays in different psychological theories have, according to Andenæs, Johansen, and Ødegard (1992) had one element in common: that the power relations between the sexes are overlooked. The question concerning the influence of gender (or the meaning of gender) became synonymous with the question of the existence of sex or gender difference, but the feminist analysis of androcenticsm in the field of psychology itself and the male-dominated society were never seriously taken into account.

It should be mentioned however that psychology, as opposed to the other social sciences, has never been criticized for having overlooked women and for not taking women into their analyses (Haavind, 1988). The criticism has concerned the field of psychology's view on women, particularly as mothers, who legitimitized a social arrangement where women were suppressed by men. This critique has partly been taken into account, and as a result the psychology has become sex-neutral. But the other important claims which concerned more focus on women's lives and the disproportion of power, as just mentioned, have not been adopted. (Andenæs et al., 1992).

In the 1990s, paradoxically, it is psychology's answer to the critique of 1970 that is criticized. By not including analysis of power-relations between women and men, psychological analysis may easily end up by repeating cultural interpretations. A main point in the critique of the discipline's sex or gender neutrality is that, as a result of trying to get rid of the traditional and normative views of women and men, the outcome is that the cultural norms for masculinity have become the norms for human beings (Andenæs et al., 1992).

In an interesting article by Wendy Hollway (1991) the psychologization of feminism is focused upon. She is critical of the development that has taken place and says that the only difference between feminist psychology's use of femininity and masculinity and the old patriarchal psychology of sex differences is that feminist psychology has re-evaluated femininity as superior. Her main point is that the theoretical focus on feminist psychology must be gender difference and not women only. It is important however to notice that by "gender difference" she does not mean the old psychology of sex differences which used the male as norm and problematized or pathologizised women through the measurement of sex differences. She represents the "new" gender perspective mentioned in the introduction. She focuses on the fact that studying gender difference involves doing research on men as well as women. A feminist psychology of men, understood in terms of gender differences, could theorize change and resistance to change in terms of the contemporary contradictions produced by gender difference in relations.

Postmodernism criticises the conception or understanding of gender in mainstream psychology as well as in feminist psychology. This analysis concentrates on difference and discourse, and there is a focus on language, subjectivity, and beliefs. The project for many feminist poststructuralists is to explore the variety of forms of femininity and masculinity. The emphasis on deconstructing femininity for example would imply the rejection of the usefulness of the categories of men and women in a social analysis.

In an article by Hare-Mustin and Marecek (1988) postmodern movements are applied to the psychology of gender. These approaches assert that meanings are historically situated and constructed and reconstructed through the medium of language.

Central in constructivism is that we actively construct the meanings that frame and organize our perceptions and experience. It therefore challenges the scientific tradition of positivism. As just mentioned, the "real " nature of male and female cannot be determined. Constructivism focuses our attention on representations of gender rather than gender itself. Hare-Mustin and Marecek (1988) ask: How much difference makes a difference? They state that psychological inquiry into gender has been along two main lines. The first inquiry reexamines gender with the goal of deemphasizing differences by sorting out "genuine" male-female differences from stereotypes (Hyde's meta-analysis of cognitive difference, 1981, Maccoby & Jacklin's review of sex differences, 1975). Most differences are therefore seen as culturally and historically fluid. If this phenomenon leads to that differences being minimized or completely dismissed from examination it is called *beta bias*. The other line , which can be labeled *alpha bias*, takes place when gender differences are exaggerated or maximized. Feminist psychodynamic theories (Chodorow, 1978; Eichenbaum & Orbach, 1983), which take as their goal establishing and reaffirming difference, and emphasize deep-seated and enduring differences between women and men in identity and relational capacities. Other examples are that gender differences in psychic structure may give rise to cognitive differences, for example in moral reasoning and in acquiring and organizing knowledge (Gilligan, 1982; Keller, 1985). This point of view is central in cultural feminism, a feminism that encourages women's culture and celebrates the special qualitites of women.

Andenæs et al. (1992) summarize today's situation as follows. The women's research has tried to redefine the gender differences through uncovering and reevaluation of women's experiences. At the same time some have tried to break down myths about gender differences particularly by analyses that focus on power relations between women and men. The future aim must be to challenge perceptions of similarities and differences between women and men that seem to make women's experiences invisible and mask power relations.

Gender and Sport Psychology

An interesting question is how the gender perspective can be applied to sport psychology. Let us first look upon how, and if, sport psychology has integrated the last 10-20 years' discussion concerning gender and psychology. What kinds of consequences has this debate in mainstream psychology, women's studies, and feminist psychology had on sport psychology?

In 1987 Fasting examined two of the best known journals of sport psychology: *The International Journal of Sport Psychology* and *The Journal of Sport Psychology*. The aim of the analysis was to determine if sport psychology had been influenced by knowledge and theories concerning women's research and feminist science.

Altogether 355 articles published in the time period 1980-1986 were analysed with reference to these criteria.

The main conclusions drawn from the analysis were:

Research in sport psychology so far has not internalized or been influenced by the amount of knowledge and theories from the women's perspective that has been published in recent years. Sport psychology is a heavily male dominated area, both with regard to the sex of the researcher and the subjects, as well as the design and methodology. (p. 260)

In 1991 Duda was editing a special issue of *The Journal of Applied Sport Psychology* focusing on "Gender, Sport and Exercise." In her editorial comments she wrote as follows:

Recent reviews of contemporary sport psychology work have indicated that the field has contributed little to our understanding of gender differences in behavioral patterns and psychological processes in the physical domain—and that a systematic inquiry into the psychological and behavioral antecedents and consequences of gender roles in the physical domain is sorely missing. (p. 2)

The critique that was raised against mainstream psychology around 1970s still seems to be relevant for sport psychology. Richardson (1989) illustrates this in a paper presented at the World Congress in Sport Psychology in Singapore in 1989. She states that faulty assumptions and generalizations about girls and women who engage in motor activities have been established and applied by sport psychologists, based on the use of a male-model format for assessment of psychological behaviors and physical performances, and a failure to include multidimensional approaches to sport achievement which provide for both qualitative and quantitative assessment. The latest work on gender and sport achievement by Eccles and Harold (1991) demonstrate however that gender influences children's sport achievement perceptions and behaviors at a very young age, and that these gender differences seem to be a product of gender role socialization.

Another example from sport psychology and sport sociology is the research concerning role-conflict and the female athlete. This research points out two concerns: 1) how male as well as female researchers' attitudes towards sport as a male preserve are established; 2) it illustrates that the knowledge produced by feminist research has not been integrated into the minds of many sport scientists. Similar concerns are seen in the use of sex-role orientation tests (such as Bem, 1984). Maria T. Allison (1991) demonstrated in a review article very clearly how the psychologically based role-conflict concept between the constraints of being an athlete and a woman, has reinforced that of a role conflict among female athletes.

In spite of the fact that this role conflict, or the ways one tried to measure it, does not seem to exist. Allison (1991) argues therefore that one has tended to perpetuate a construct which has no empirical foundations. This was demonstrated by Sage and Loudermilk as early as in 1979. The sex-role orientation tests, which were developed as a result of the critique of the personality tests measuring masculinity and femininity as bipolar concepts, have been criticizied for the same reasons. This has also been done from inside the world of sport science. (Hall, 1978, 1988). In spite of this fact, people still use the tests uncritically, and get their articles published in sport psychology journals. Many sport scientists seem not to be aware of the critique of the concept of androgyny itself and the stereotyping effect it may have concerning our conceptions of the content of masculinity and femininity. These examples raise questions concerning what kind of research sport psychologists should do. What kind of questions should be asked and what kind of knowledge should be developed or constructed through sport psychology as a sciences.

The same question is asked in an interesting chapter written by Alison

Dewar and Thelma Sternberg Horn (1992), as a response to R. Martens' epistemological critique from 1979 of sport psychology. Their paper is also one of the few examples, or perhaps the only one, where the authors base their discussion concerning research in sport psychology on postmodernist and feminist critiques of science.

Dewar and Horn (1992) see the need to contextualize the knowledge that is produced. In accordance with women-centered research they state that :

....sporting behaviors cannot be meaningfully isolated and studied independently of the contexts in which they are played. Sport has different meanings for different athletes, and their behaviors are developed within the contexts of these meanings. Sporting practices are not neutral and value free.... For example, there is evidence to show that sport is used to celebrate particular forms of masculinity (those that stress strength, speed and power) as natural rather than socially developed. (p. 18)

They state that we need to ask why researchers continue to focus on sex differences, and that with such a focus, one risks to reproduce sexism.

As mentioned earlier, little research in sport psychology until now seems to have been influenced by feminist critique and the latest developments in gender psychology. Gill summarized in 1992 the sport psychology research on gender by stating that it is remarkably limited in topic as well as publications.

One of the exceptions is a study by Brenda Bredemeier et al. (1991) titled the "Epistemological Perspectives Among Women Who Participate in Physical Activity." The study concerned women in five different activities (intercollegiate field hockey, individual non competitive activities, lesbian softball, bodybuilding, and expedition mountain climbing). Their ways of knowing were discussed in light of special themes focusing on the participants' thoughts of relations betweeen self and other: namely processes of cooperation and competition and issues of power and authority.

The authors used a women-centered, qualitative methodology in the study. The results showed great difference between the women. But all women in the study seemed to value cooperation regardless of how much or little they enjoyed competiton. The authors therefore state that "competition and cooperation seemed to be interdependent rather than dichotomous concepts" (p. 104).

As mentioned earlier women's as well as men's behavior can be studied with a gender perspective. As a result of a gender perspective on research on men, during the latest ten years, "men's studies" as a separate discipline has occurred. As a logical consequence we also have studies and research on masculinity and sport. This research seems first of all to have taken place in North America by sociologists. The most productive names are Don Sabo (Sabo, 1985, 1986; Sabo & Rufola, 1980) and Michael Messner (1987, 1990a, 1990b, 1992).

Men's studies use the feminist paradigm that holds the potential of liberating men as well as women. Messner and Sabo (1990) explain it as follows:

Men's studies scholars start from the premise that existing gender arrangements entail various costs for men (such as low life expectancy, emotional inexpressivity, and relational problems), yet males also enjoy significant privileges as a result of these arrangements. (p. 13)

Men's situation in today's Western society has also been described as follows by a man: "Our power in society as men not only oppresses women but also imprisons us in a deadening masculinity which cripples our relationships with each other, with women, with ourselves" (Segal 1990 quoted in Hargreaves 1990, p. 300).

From such a perspective it is clear that the sex-role stereotyping impovrerishes both men and women.

An article by Messner (1990b) about masculinity and sport demonstrates that he has integrated some of those perspectives mentioned in the first part of this paper. He tries in this article to explore the social meanings of sports violence. He states that to shed light on this problem it is important to explore the following:

How and why some men become violent: what meanings do men construct around their own violence against other men?

What is the broader cultural meaning of men's violence against other men? What role does some men's violence against other men play in the current state of play of the gender order?

Mike Messner published in 1992 a book titled *Power at Play: Sports and the Problem of Masculinity*. In this book he presents results of qualitative interviews with former top-level male athletes. He believes that the contribution of his study is that he shows that "sport does not simply and unambiguously reproduce men's existing power and privilege." (p.151). His interviews demonstrated several strains within the sport/masculinity relationship. Obviously, men's experience in athletic careers were not entirely positive, nor were they the same for all men. He states that masculinity is not a monolithic category, and focuses on three factors that undermine sports ability to construct a single dominant conception of masculinty. These are: 1) The "costs" of athletic masculinity to men (such as relational and health costs);

2) Men's different experiences with athletic careers, according to social class, race,and sexual orientation; and

3) Current challenges to the equation of sport and heterosexual masculinity.

In his analysis Messner mentions feminist psychoanalytic theory (particularly the work of Chodorow), which he believes can be an important component of a social constructionist theory of gender. He is referring to the fact that social structure and personality exist in a dynamic relationship with each other:

> Psychoanalytic theory suggests that young males are predisposed to define their masculinity through their achievements, rather than through initmate relationships with others .... My examination of the lives of male athletes proceeds from an anlysis of the dynamic interaction between the "internal" (conscious values and beliefs as well as the less conscious separation- attachment dynamic) and the "external (social institutions).... In short, masculine identity is neither fully formed by the social context nor caused by some personal dynamic put into place during infancy:Instead, it comes to be in the interaction between internal and the social. (p. 22)

Conclusions and Future Perspectives

So far we may conclude that the debate that has taken place in mainstream psychology, as a result of the feminist critique and the new knowledge concerning the psychology of gender, seems to have had relatively little impact on mainstream sport psychology.

This however does not mean research that has taken this knowledge and these perspectives into account does not exist, as has been shown in this paper.

According to Gill (1992) sound sport psychology research on gender beliefs and processes within the social context of sport and exercise could advance our overall understanding of gender and sport. To say that sport psychology is active in producing new knowledge about the psychology of gender would however not be correct. But it is a sub-discipline that also could contribute to this development, because sport and masculinity are so interwoven. The danger is however that the opposite may take place, that sport psychology will continue to use research methods and psychological tests that reinforce the stereotypes that exist in society about masculinity and femininity.

The paper will be closed by suggesting some areas for research. I would however like to focus on the fact that one should try to apply the knowledge one already has concerning the psychology of gender, to sport psychological practices. Since girls and boys are socialized differently and emerge into adult life with different attitudes, values and behaviors, it is clear that this must have some consequences for people who are working with them. At the same time it is important that those differences between women and men that have been proven to be myths are not taken into account in the work of practitioners. What is going on in practice in the field of coaching and sport psychology in this perspective is to a certain degree unknown. This could therefore in itself become an area for research.

Carolyn Wood Sherif (1979) wrote some years ago that the most underdeveloped problem area in psychological research was: "How people feel and experience themselves, and why, when, and how these self-experiences affect their actions" (p. 51).

This statement seems to hold for sport psychology of today. We have relatively little knowledge about female and male experiences , feelings, wants, attitudes and needs towards sport and in sport.

With reference to the epistemological question : What does one need to know in sport psychology or what kind of knowledge should be produced, one group of studies which should be carried out in sport psychology should concern inequality, oppression and power relations. This raises a lot of questions in different sport settings and concerns many different sporting roles. Questions in relation to racism and sexism are particular relevant for sport. As a social system sport is very white male-dominated, and female athletes for example are surrounded by male coaches, male leaders, and so forth. The Norwegian psychologist Hanne Haavind (1984) says that the concept of power is causal, in the sense that one person dominates another, but without this necessarily being intended. It is important to study how men dominate, how power is personalized, and thereby how the patriarchial system is maintained and legitimized. These should be crucial questions for sport. Both females and male feminists would agree that women are suppressed, but the suppression may take different forms, and not all of these are necessarily experienced as oppressive. How is it with the female athlete, or the female coach?

As mentioned in the introduction, most theories are developed and based on men's lives and experiences. This is particularly true for sport which until recently has been " the men's domain." Women's experiences, practices and consciousness in sport should therefore also be the starting point for theory development.

To develop theories in sport psychology based on research with a gender perspective will automatically raise questions concerning methodology and epistemology. Though many social scientists would claim that "positivisim" is dead, this is not true, at least not for sport psychology. It would be contradictory or very difficult however to do research with a gender perspective based on positivistic designs and methods. Questions concerning methods used in sport psychological research have gone on for a long time, and much research has moved out from the laboratory to the field. The use of tests only however cannot be a good measurement in validly analyzing female and male experiences or feelings in sport. The use of field studies and more qualitative techniques seems so far to be most useful, eventually in combination with different methods of data gathering.

As an important subdiscipline of psychology, sport psychology should also contribute to the development of mainstream psychology. I believe that sport psychology has some prerequisites in relation to other areas of psychology in developing new knowledge concerning the psychology of gender. Gender differences in sport should be redefined through uncovering and reevaluation of women's experience, at the same time as one should try to break down myths about gender differences in sport.

References

Allison, M . T . (1991). Role conflict and the female athlete; Preoccupations with little grounding. *Journal of Applied Sport Psychology, 3*, 49-60.

Andenæs, A ., Johansen, B. F., & Ødegard, T. (1992). Kjønnet som forsvant? Om betydningen av kjønn i psykologien. In A . Taksdal & K . Widerberg (Eds.), *Forståelser av kjønn* (pp. 51-87). Oslo: Ad Notam Gyldendal As.

Ås, B . (1975). On female culture-an attempt to formulate a theory of women's solidarity and action. *Acta Soc., 18*,142-161.

Bem, S . L. (1984). The measurement of psychological androgyny. *Journal of Consulting and Clinical Psychology, 42*, 79-87.

Bordieu, P. (1990). "Masculine/Feminine". In *Actus De la Researche N. Sciences Sociales, 84*.

Bredemeier, J . L ., Desertrain, G.S., Fisher, L.A., Getty, D., Slocum, N.E., Stephens, D.E. & Warren, J.E. (1991). Epistemological perspectives among women who participate in physical activity. *Journal of Applied Sport Psychology*, 187-207.

Chodorow, N. (1978). *The reproduction of mothering*. Berkeley, CA: University of California Press.

Deaux, K.(1984). From individual differences to social categories: Analysis of a decade's research on gender. *American Psychologist, 39*, 105 - 116.

Dewar, A., & Horn, T. S. (1992). A critical analysis of knowlege construction in sport psychology. In T . S . Horn (Ed.), *Advances in sport psychology* (pp. 13-22). Champaign, IL: Human Kinetics.

Duda, J . L. (1991). Perspectives on gender roles in physical activity. *Journal of Applied Sport Psychology, 3,* 1-6

Eccles, J. S., & Harold, R. D. (1991). Gender differences in sport involvement: Applying the Eccles' expectancy-value model. *Journal of Applied Sport Psychology, 3,* 7-35.

Eichenbaum, L., & Orbach, S. (1983). *Understanding women: A feminist psychoanalytic approach*. New York: Basic Books.

Eichler, M., (1980). *The double standard: A feminist critique of feminist social science*. London: Croom Helm.

Fasting, K. (1989). An analysis of research in sport psychology from the women's perspective. In M. Raivio (Ed.), *Proceedings of the Jyväskylä Congress - on Movement and Sport in Women's Life. Reports of physical culture and health 67* (pp. 17-21). Jyväskylä: Press of University of Jyväskylä.

Fasting, K.(1992, September). *Gender as an important perspectives in the study of sport sociology*. Invited paper presented at the '92 International Sport Science Congress, Korean Alliance for Health, Physical Education, Recreation and Dance, Seoul, Korea.

Freud, S. (1973). *Kvindeligheten. In Psykoanlysen - nye forelszeninger*. Copenhagen: Reitzel. (original work published in 1916).

Gill, D. L. (1992). Gender and sport behavior. In T. S. Horn (Ed.), *Advances in sport psychology* (pp. 143-160). Champaign, IL: Human Kinetic Publishers.

Gilligan, C. (1982). *In a different voice: Psychological theory and women's development*. Cambridge, MA: Harvard University Press.

Goffman, E. (1977). The arrangement between the sexes. In M.J. Deegan & M. Hills (Eds.), *Women and symbolic interaction*, Winchester: Allen & Unvin.

Haavind, H. (1984). Love and power in marriage. In H. Holter (Ed.), *Patriarchy in a welfare society* (pp.136-168). Oslo: Universitetsforlaget.

Haavind, H. (1988). Er det kjønnsnøytrale menneskesyn et vitenskapelig ideal? *Nordisk psykologi, 40,* 309-324.

Hall, A . M. (1978). Sport and gender: A feminist perspective on the sociology of sport. *CAPHER Sociology of sport monograph series*. Vanjer City, Ottawa. Ontario.

Hall, A . M. (1988). The discourse of gender and sport: From femininity to feminism. *Sociology of Sport Journal, 4*, (5), 330-340.

Hall, A . M. (1990). How should we theorize gender in the context of sport? In M. A. Messner, & D.F. Sabo (Eds.), *Sport, men and the gender order: Critical feminist perspectives* (pp. 223-241). Champaign, IL: Human Kinetics Books.

Hare-Mustin, R . T., & Marecek, J. (1988). The meaning of difference: Gender theory, postmodernism, and psychology. *American Psychologist, 43,* (6), 455-464.

Hargreaves, J . A. (1990). Gender on the sports agenda. *International Review for the Sociology of Sport, 25,* (4), 287-309.

Hollway, W. (1991). The psychologization of feminism or the feminization of psychology? *Feminism & Psychology, 1*, (1), 29 -37.

Hyde, J. S. (1981). How large are cognitive gender differences? *American Psychologist, 36,* 892-901

Jacklin, C. N. (1989). Female and male: Issues of gender. *American Psychologist, 44*, 127 - 133.

Keller, E.F. (1985). *Reflections on gender and science.* New Haven. CT: Yale University Press.

Kohlberg, L., & Ziegler, E. (1967). The impact of cognitive maturnity on the development of sex-role attitudes in the years four to eight. *Genetic psychology monographs, 75*, 89-165.

Leira, A. (1992). Hankjønn, hunkjønn, intetkjønn - ? Forståelse av kjønn i norsk kvinnesosiologi. In A. Taksdal & K. Widerberg (Eds.), *Forståelser av kjønn i samfunnsvitenskapenes fag og kvinneforskning* (pp. 171-201). Oslo: Ad Notam, Gyldendal AS.

Maccoby, E. E., & Jacklin, C. N. (1975). *The psychology of sex differences.* Stanford, CA: University Press.

Martens, R. (1987). Science, knowledge, and sport psychology. *The Sport Psychologist,1*, 29-55.

Messner, M. (1987). The meaning of success: The athletic experience and the development of male identity. In H. Brod (Ed.), *The making of masculinities: The new men's studies* (pp. 193-210). Boston: Allen & Unwin.

Messner, M . A. (1990a). Men studying masculinity: Some epistemological issues in sport sociology. *Sociology of Sport Journal, 7,* 136-153.

Messner, M. A. (1990b). When bodies are weapons: Masculinity and violence in sport. *International Review for Sociology of Sport, 25,* (3), 203-221.

Messner, M.(1992). *Power at play: Sports and the problem of masculinity.* Boston: Beacon Press.

Messner, M. A., & Sabo, D. F. (1990). Introduction: Toward a critical feminist reappraisal of sport, men and the gender order. In M. A. Messner & F. Sabo (Eds.), *Sport, men and the gender order: Critical feminist perspectives* (pp.1-17). Champaign, IL: Human Kinetics Books.

Richardson, P . A. (1989, August). *Sport psychology and women: A case for biased application of psychological theories and constructs.* Paper presented at the 7th World Congress in Sport Psychology, Singapore.

Sabo, D. (1985). Sport, patriarchy, and male identitiy: New questions about men and sport. *Arena Reviews, 2,* (9), 1-30.

Sabo, D. (1986). Pigskin, patriarchy and pain. *Changing Men: Issues in gender, sex and politics, 16,* 24-25.

Sabo, D. F., & Rufola, R. (1980). *Sports and male identity.* Englewood Cliffs, NJ: Prentice-Hall.

Sage, G., & Loudermilk, S. (1979). The female athlete and role conflict. *Research Quarterly, 50,* 88-99.

Sherif, C . W. (1979). Bias in psychology. In J. A. Sherman and E. T. Beck (Eds.), *The prism of sex: Essays in the sociology of knowledge* (pp. 37-56). Madison: University of Wisconsin Press; also printed in S. Harding (Ed.) (1987). *Feminism and methodology* (pp. 37-56). Milton Keynes: Open University Press.

Chapter 10

HEALTH AND WELLNESS: A SPORT PSYCHOLOGY PERSPECTIVE

Dieter Hackfort

About 1,800 years ago Juvenal, an ancient Roman satirist, had been invited to be a spectator in an arena and to enjoy himself by watching the fights of the gladiators. When he looked at the young muscular men and watched them brutally fighting each other he said to his host: *"Orandum est ut sit mens sana in corpore sano,"* which means: it would be nice if in such healthy bodies could also be a healthy mind.

Juvenal said this in a doubtful tone. He could not imagine that—after this experience in the arena—the young gladiators did not only have sound bodies but also a sound mind, that it could be possible to equally develop physical and intellectual power. He put the idea of the combination of physical and intellectual or moral power down in his papers (Satiren X, 356) as a wish to the gods. For an appropriate interpretation it is necessary to know that Juvenal was a famous and at that time notorious speaker and satirist in ancient Rome, who picked out and criticized human weaknesses with great eloquence.

This story should introduce situation analysis as a necessary procedure in order to understand the meaning of human actions and to develop appropriate explanations for goal-directed behavior. This situation analysis can demonstrate that Juvenal and not Homer as North, McCullagh, and Tran

(1991) have written (by the way, why should Homer the Greek produce this in Latin language?) had doubts and that the often given quotation "mens sana in corpore sano" (a sound mind in a sound body) is misleading.

Situation analyses refer to the person, the task at hand, and to the environment in which the person is acting. The fruitfulness of this concept will be demonstrated by focusing now on health and wellness from a sport psychology perspective.

Figure 1 provides a frame for understanding psychological health and wellness. Some authors regard psychological health and mental health as synonyms, some refer to mental health when focusing on cognitive processes, and some refer exclusively to anxiety and depression. Here mental health refers to cognitive processes whereas emotional health refers to mood, well-being/wellness and its opposite, mal-being and illness as subjective experiences. Fitness is regarded as an instrumental aspect of health—in a physiological as well as psychological understanding. The opposite of fitness is labeled "handicap," giving the term a special interpretation in this context.

Dimensions of Health

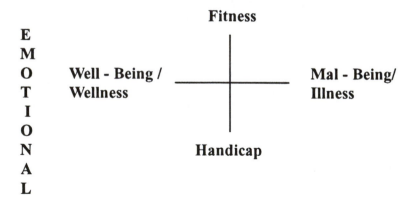

Figure 1. Instrumental and emotional aspects of health.

What can be contributed new about physical exercise and psychological health and wellness in addition to the enormous body of investigations and numerous contributions to this topic? Even if one adds a further experimental study or review, narrative review or meta-analyis, it does not seem that it would be very promising in improving our knowledge in this field. Perhaps it is now necessary to review the various reviews, secondary analyses, position statements, and consensus statements, and to provide a meta-review. It is not my favourite wish to do so but it seems unavoidable.

At present we cannot account for effects of physical exercise on psychological health (mental health and wellness) by "underlying mechanisms" and causal explanations. Various and different hypotheses are stressed but the results of the numerous studies conducted so far are inconclusive. It is not an extraordinary exception that for something of a certain effectivity an appropriate explanation is missing. Sime (1990) argues that "a great number of pharmacological treatments are used regularly in the absence of a known mechanism and with a risk of harm in prolonged use far greater than that present in most of exercise training" (p. 631). Theoretical progress seems to be possible at least not solely by further—and, if possible, better—experimental studies but for sure also with an—and if it is merely a crucial—understanding of the mind-body relationship in a broader philosophical frame. So, be invited to a short trip into philosophy.

Concepts of Mind-body Relationship

The fundamental philosophical positions are usually subdivided in monistic positions, of which Spinoza is the most prominent advocate, and dualistic positions, of which Descartes is the most prominent advocate. In a psychobiological approach these fundamental positions can be differentiated into six conceptualizations (see Bunge, 1980).

Idealism postulates a primacy of ideas over the physical world and—in an extreme interpretation—that only the mind exists. Our knowledge of the world is based on perceptions which are mental events. Physical objects that we assume to be the basis of our perceptions, do not exist but in our mind.

Materialism maintains that only the body exists. In this perspective there exists a real world of atoms and molecules whereas the mind is an illusion. A consequence of this position is that all psychological processes should be explained through physiological processes.

Animism declares that the mind controls the body but the mind is not affected by the body. Mental activity causes bodily phenomena but no physical

Table 1. Concepts of Mind-Body Relation

Title	Characterization by Symbols	Idea
Idealism		Only the Mind Exists
Materialism		Only the Brain Exists
Animism		Mind Controls Brain
Epiphenomenalism		Brain Controls Mind
Interactionism		Mind and Brain Interact
Emergent Dual Aspect		Mind is Part of Brain

Adapted from Bunge (1980,9).

event can cause a mental event. A consequence of this concept is that the soul survives the body.

Epiphenomenalism represents the opposite of animism: Bodily events cause mental events. Mental activity is regarded as being "secreted" from the brain like smoke produced by a fire.

Interactionism represents the predominant concept of a dualistic perspective. The fundamental idea is the existence of both body and soul, brain and mind, and physical and mental processes, which influence each other. The central question in this context is how the immaterial mind can influence the material body and physiological processes and how it is possible that these processes influence mental events.

Various concepts refer to an emergent dual-aspect explaining that the mind is a property of the brain but not a separate entity caused by it. The mind might be understood as a self-perception of the brain growing out of the special organization of the brain on a complex level as it is characteristic of human beings.

Returning to our problem to explain the psychological effects of physical exercise it might be appropriate to add a further understanding to the debate—even if this discussion demonstrated the limits of our knowledge and what we don't know rather than what we know for sure. A consequence of understanding human beings as biopsychosocial subjects is a description of phenomena of human life from three different perspectives: the biological, the psychological, and the sociological perspective.

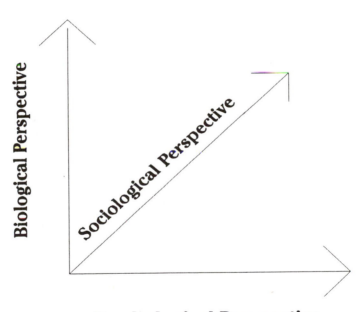

Figure 2. Three-dimensional perspective on health and wellness.

Each perspective has a special point of view, a specific background, history, and level of development. Consequently there are different levels of analysis, categorical systems, etc. Due to different discipline-specific terminologies, communication is difficult. But in principle "physiological", "psychological", and "sociological" denote certain systems of scientific approaches and description of the same subject.

Reviews

There are more than 30 reviews since 1960 referring to investigations on the relationship between physical exercise, fitness training, sports and psychologic effects (mental health, mood, well-being, anxiety, depression, self-concept, etc.). These include:

Abele and Brehm (1990), Abele, Brehm and Gall (1991), Brown (1990), Crews and Landers (1987), Cureton (1963), DeVries (1981), Dishman (1986), Folkins and Sime (1981), Hammett (1967), Hughes (1984), Petruzello, Landers, Hatfield, Kubitz and Salazar (1991), Knoll and Bös (1991), Layman (1960), Martinsen (1987), Mellion (1985), Mobily (1982), Morgan (1969), Morgan (1982), Morgan (1984), Morgan (1985), Morgan and O'Connor (1988), North, McCullagh and Tran (1991), Schlicht (1991), Schwenkmezger (1985), Scott (1960), Sime (1984), Sime (1990), Simons, McGowan, Epstein, Kuper and Robertson (1985), Sonstroem (1984), Stephens (1988), Tomporowski and Ellis (1986), Taylor, Sallis and Needle (1985), Van Andel and Austin (1984), Weinstein and Meyers (1983).

These are reviews already respected most by colleagues contributing subsequent reviews or the most updated reviews available. It is peculiar that in the 1970s there was no remarkable contribution review in this field of research. In the 1960s there were 5 published reviews. In the 1980s the topic became one of the predominant areas of research in sport psychology and most of the available reviews (21 are mentioned here) have been written in that time. Already 9 reviews have been published in this decade.

Until 1987 all reviews can be classified as narrative reviews. The first meta-analysis appears 1987 and to date there are 6.

For meta-analyses one can only refer to studies which are well-documented and which provide sufficient methodological and statistical information (see Glass, 1976; Wolf, 1986). The standard of a meta-analysis has to meet the standard of the analyzed empirical studies. Critique of meta-analyses refers to theoretical aspects and the primacy of theory in scientific research (e.g.

Hager, 1984; Lösel, 1987). The most frequent argument against meta-analysis is that of "comparing apples and pears". However, meta-analyses try to integrate quantitative results using a statistical strategy in order to come up with data-based evaluations. Thus it can be regarded as an alternative but not as a substitute for so-called narrative reviews. While for narrative reviews the criteria for selecting available studies often are not explicitly defined, meta-analyses are fixed primarily on statistical criteria for search in the research literature. While narrative reviewers sometimes overestimate the theoretical relevance of empirical (weak) studies and make subjective decisions on rejecting or accepting a hypothesis by the reported data, meta-analysis involves a certain danger of formulating somewhat strange hypotheses because it is possible to check it by statistical means. This signalizes an overestimation of empirical relevance of theoretical misleading assumptions.

An example for this is a meta-analysis by Schlicht (1991), who had the hypothesis that the kind of journal in which the study was published is a moderating condition of the global relationship between physical exercise and mental health. The meta-analysis revealed statistical effects and thereby evidence for this hypothesis and he concluded that the speciality of the journal is, among other factors, moderating the relationship. (It might be of interest if the data signalize the use of different criteria for judging manuscripts in journals in sport psychology, health psychology, and further journals.)

Review of Reviews

The results of these reviews—narrative reviews and meta-analyses—are not as homogenous as is expressed in the consensual statement published by Morgan and Goldston (1987) and altogether cause less optimism than is expressed in the position statement by the ISSP (1991). There are some enthusiastic narrative reviews (e.g., Abele & Brehm, 1990; Morgan & O'Connor, 1988) and meta-analyses or secondary analyses (e.g., Petruzello et al., 1991; Stephens, 1988). There are some skeptical reviews (e.g., Brown, 1990; van Andel & Austin, 1984). There are several critical narrative reviews (e.g., Hughes, 1984; Tomporowski & Ellis, 1986) as well as critical meta-analyses (e.g., Schlicht, 1991). This forces us to go more into detail and to discuss these in a more sophisticated manner.

The following scheme might be of some help for orientation in the physical exercise and psychological health relationship.

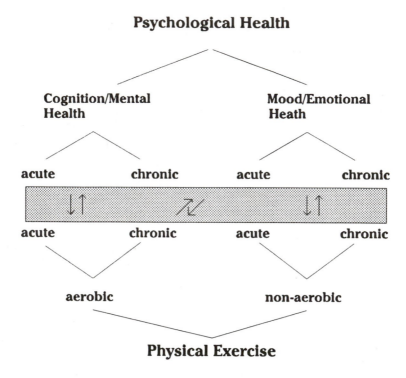

Figure 3. Frame of analysis of the relationship between physical exercise and psychological health.

Some reviews refer to "mental health" when looking for psychological effects and are based on a broad understanding of "mental health" (even animal studies have been included; see Brown, 1990). Components of mental health referred to are aspects of cognitive functioning (e.g., perception, memory), mood (well-being, anxiety, and depression), and personality factors or traits (self-concept, body image). Folkins and Sime (1981) and Hughes (1984), who based his conclusion exclusively on controlled experiments of the effects of habitual aerobic exercise (12 studies), screened more than 1,000 investigations and concluded that speaking about health protective effects of physical fitness training lacks empirical evidence and appropriate theoretical explanations. Only improvements in self-concept can be regarded as verified. This is confirmed by Sonstroem (1984), who reviewed 16 studies (most of them neither experimental nor quasi-experimental studies). He stated that the reviewed studies demonstrate that especially persons low in self-esteem make gains through physical exercise and that the reported effects partly can be explained by experimenter and subject biases.

Perhaps the most stressed relationship is between physical exercise and mood, wellness, anxiety, and depression. Morgan (1969; Morgan & O'Connor, 1988) in the United States and Abele and Brehm (1990; Abele et al., 1991) in Germany focus on this aspect. Their conclusions are enthusiastic but these reviews are to be qualified as highly selective in referring only to those studies which can support their hypotheses of a positive relationship (see also Schlicht, 1991).

Schlicht (1991) carried out a number of meta-analyses including 39 well-documented experimental and quasi-experimental studies. To sum up it can be said on the basis of the meta-analytical results that the probability to feel better is 14% higher in 100 persons involved in aerobic physical activities than in non-active persons. The results are based on a correlational analyses and thus it can be interpreted also in this way: Persons who feel well and healthy will engage in physical fitness programs with 14% higher probability than persons who feel less healthy. Furthermore, regarding statistical criteria, the data basis has to be evaluated as heterogenous and the results as inconsistent. As a consequence the general positive relationship postulated by Morgan and Goldston (1987) could not be verified.

A closer inspection brings up hints for necessary differentiations:
- In female subjects the relation ($RG=.14$) tend to be closer than in male subjects ($RG=.08$).
- In male subjects there is a relationship between aerobic exercise (e.g., jogging) and well-being, whereas in female subjects programs like jazz-dance, aerobics, and calisthenics result in psychologic benefits.
- In young subjects (age: 21-30; $RG=.18$) the relationship is closer than in older subjects (age: 31-50; $RG=.08$) and in the group of younger people there is a tendency for male ($RG=.25$) having more gain than female ($RG=.13$). Older subjects engaged in aerobic exercise seem to have the highest gain in mental health.

In spite of the data-based partial rejection of the consensus statement by such meta-analyses, the results in general seem to be very plausible and not far from common sense. Merely the relationship between aerobic training and mental health could be verified for older adults by experimental studies and statistical criteria. In male subjects there is a tendency to profit from aerobic exercise in well-being, and in females there is a tendency to profit from calisthenics and dance in well-being. It seems to be likely to hypothesize that personal motives could adequately explain these results.

Plausibilities and Contradictions

Instead of focusing merely on and analyzing exclusively causal relations between physical exercise and mental health variables by experimental strategies it should also be considered that human beings intentionally engage in specific activities and that they are goal-directed when starting a physical exercise program. Psychological categories as motive and volition are necessary to explain why and how a special activity is done. For example it is well known that for younger people "health" is not a significant motive (e.g. Fuchs, 1990), but it is for the elderly. Older adults engaged in sports are motivated to actively improve their health status by this activity. Those who maintain this engagement will do it because they are convinced that they do something effective to realize their intentions. This evaluation is recorded as a representation of mental health. Self-evaluations as measured by self-reports are psychological representations of health. Self-ratings of well-being are highly integrated judgements—subjective data of wellness and in this respect different from objective data but not less important, especially for a psychological perspective on health.

It seems to be a standard that a reviewer not only has to focus on methodological aspects, pointing out that there are primarily descriptive, correlational, and cross-sectional studies and that longitudinal studies are missing but also to deplore the methodological deficits and serious methodological problems, such as:

- inadequate sample size and description of initial (physical and psychical) fitness of the subjects.
- failure to assign subjects randomly to experimental and control groups.
- control of biases of experimenter and subject. "Experimenter demand and subject expectancy biases are especially likely to occur in this field of research because many experiments and subjects have an a priori belief that exercise produces psychological benefits" (Hughes, 1984, p. 67). Self-report measures seem to be especially sensitive for such influences.
- poor choices of instruments to measure psychological constructs. Instead of objective measures and sport-specific instruments (for a discussion see Hackfort & Schwenkmezger, 1989), global self-rating scales or questionnaires have been used and standardized psychological tests are often

not convenient because they are designed for clinical populations.

- lack of designs with a control group, placebo conditions, double or total blind designs.

- insufficient documentation and descriptions of methods, type or/and intensity of the exercise program, and reports on exercise-induced changes in fitness.

Sport psychological research in this area seems to be dominated by types of studies which are classified as generally uninterpretable by Cook and Campbell (1979):

- One-group posttest-only design (lack of pretest or control group: no comparison possible).

- Posttest-only design with nonequivalent groups (lack of pretest: differences could be simply due to selection).

- One-group pretest-posttest design (internal validity: statistical regression, maturation, etc.).

Van Andel and Austin (1984) concluded that "after a critical analysis of the studies ... nearly half were one-group preexperimental studies, which tend to have built-in selection bias and will statistically reflect a regression effect on the posttest" (p. 216). Possible designs and solutions for experimental studies in field settings are provided by Cook and Campbell (1979), for example, quasi-experimental designs for nonequivalent control groups and time-series studies.

One common conclusion of nearly all reviews, narratives as well as meta-analyses, is to point out the need for more and better experimental studies. Is this obviously the only or only obviously appropriate strategy to overcome the problems and to enrich our knowledge in this field of research?

Further differentiations should lead to more definite results and a better understanding of the "underlying mechanisms". Intensity and duration of physical exercise programs and the health status of the persons involved should be considered. But this does not seem to reduce significant inconsistencies as well.

Morgan (1985) argues on the background of results growing out of his investigations on self-estimation, anxiety (state), and depression, that

- psychologic effects should be expected not before a period of 10 weeks of exercise and

- a certain kind and intensity (vigorous, 70-80% of maximal aerobic power) would be necessary.

It is worth mentioning that he often cited a study by Greist et al. (1979)

referring to "running as treatment for depression" and that he also based his conclusions in this context on the study, which is of low methodological standard (see Schwenkmezger, 1985) due to for example, the lack of a control group, a very small sample size of the experimental group, a lack of registrations of physical fitness, and the missing of statistical characteristic values.

Quite opposite to these results Steptoe and Cox (1988) found that: "high-intensity exercise led to increase in tension/ anxiety..., whereas positive mood changes ... were seen following low-intensity exercise only" (p. 329).

In addition their results demonstrated no differences between fit and unfit groups in mood changes. Those effects of mood changes already appeared after single bouts of exercise (four 8-min exercise trials on a bicycle ergometer).

Van Andel and Austin (1984) refer exclusively to studies on physical fitness defined in terms of cardiovascular efficiency, aerobic fitness programs of adequate intensity (elevation of the heart rate to approximately 70% of capacity) and duration (minimum 15-20 minutes). They focus on experimental and quasi-experimental studies and conclud that:

- such exercise programs conduce improved sleep, self-confidence, body image, and less anxiety in female junior college students (not in male subjects).
- such programs may serve as a coping strategy for reducing a special kind of anxiety, such as somatic anxiety (see Bahrke & Morgan, 1978; Schwartz, Davidson, & Goleman,1978).
- "mildly depressed individuals appear to respond more favorably to fitness training than those who are deeply depressed" (p. 216) and
- geriatric clients demonstrate significant changes in mental health variables,although they did not achieve aerobic conditioning. "Group participation and social acceptance appear to be important contributors to the personality changes in the individuals" (p. 217).

Stephens (1988) found in his secondary analysis of four surveys (2 in Canada and 2 in the United States) over a period of 10 year that:

- the level of physical exercise is positively correlated with mental health (defined as positive mood, well-being, and relatively infrequent symptoms of anxiety and depression) and positive changes in mood (wellness).
- women and the elderly (age 40 years and over) have more gain from exercise than men and younger people.
- sedentary persons who become moderately active have more gain than

those who are already moderately active and increase their exercise level.

Finally he stated that "physical activity relates about as strongly to mental health as does education" (p. 43), and "it not only applies to the superfit and to neurotics but also extends to the general population" (p. 43).

Stephens (1988) offered three plausible explanations for those correlational findings:

(1) Physical activity causes mental health.

(2) Good mental health is a reason to exercise.

(3) Physical activity and mental health are influenced by a third variable. It seems that sex and age are associated with such variables (see the better gain in women and the elderly).

Conclusion

In addition to the differentiations already mentioned in the task component—the kind of physical exercise, its intensity, duration, and frequency—we have to differentiate further aspects in analyzing the situation.

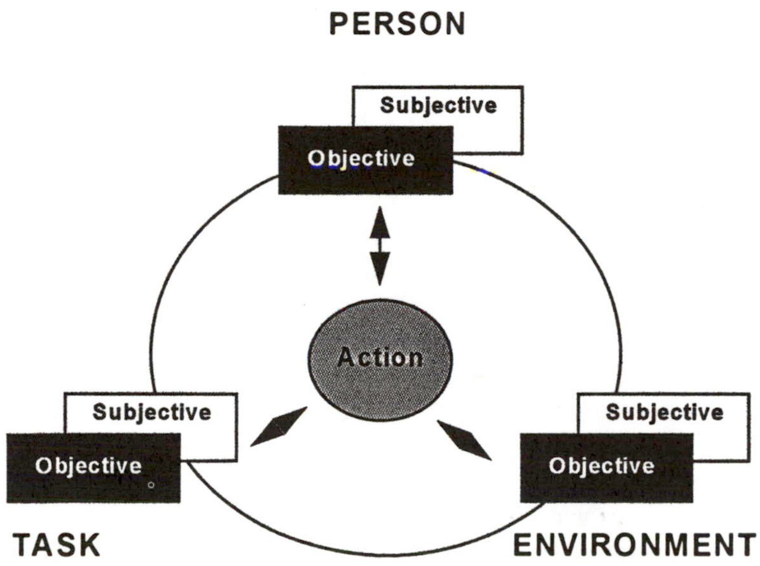

PERSON

Figure 4. Determinants of an action situation.

Personal components (such as sex; age; traits, e.g., hardiness, optimism, and locus of control) are emphasized by researchers in health psychology to be possible predictors of health-oriented behavior. Furthermore, environmental components have to be regarded. It might be possible that more introverted persons gain especially from social settings (social support) and more extroverted persons might be affected by the special outfit and "ambiance" associated with body shaping and fitness studios.

Figure 4 illustrates that not only the objective person-task-environment constellation has to be taken into account from a psychology perspective but also the subjective representation (perception, evaluation), which also is a determinant for intentional behavior.

To date we are used to differentiate exercise programs according to physiological criteria: aerobic, anaerobic or non-aerobic. Psychological criteria are neglected, for example, affordances in concentration, psychological endurance, the emotional potential associated with special activities and so on.

Most of our knowledge in this domain is based on correlational evidence. Even in the experiments there has been no evidence that physical exercise programs cause psychologic effects. The observed changes have merely been associated with the participation in such programs. Despite this we are busy to find "mechanisms" and causal relations for explanations and it is emphasized by every reviewer that we need more appropriate experimental studies. How can we manage to consider the differentiations in appropriate experimental designs? In experiments we have to reduce complexity and in this case the reality of sports. In doing so we reduce the conditions and number of interacting variables and the potential of effect sizes. The better the standards of experiments are met the more artificial is the situation. The more the situation is structured by the experimenter the more are the actions of the subject partialized and decoupled from any sense.

While the principle of unidirectional causality might be an appropriate orientation in natural sciences (e.g., physiology) and is used to explain physiological effects of physical exercise, alternative possibilities should be considered that might also be or even be more appropriate for explanations in social sciences and offer adequate principles to explain psychological benefits of sports activities, for example, conditional and final explanations (see Hackfort, 1990). The study by Farrel et al. (1986) provides a hint for this. Before conducting an ergometer test an opioid antagonist was given to the experimental group and a placebo to the control group, but both groups reported a significant reduction in tension. This experiment was carried out to test the endorphin hypothesis. From a medical view the experiment lacks verification of the causal relation. From the psychological view it should be considered that the subjects do have certain expectations and perhaps have been active on the bicycle ergometer because they had the intention to reduce tension. It might be possible that both explanations (causal explanation: reduction in tension by drug, and final explanation: reduction in tension due to intentional actions on a bicycle ergometer) are appropriate in their special context.

From the perspective of action theory it is fundamental to analyze the situation (a) in its objective determinants and (b) in its subjective determinants, that is, to consider the interpretation of the acting subject (definition of the situation; see Nitsch & Hackfort, 1981). If we do not consider the definition of the situation by the subject it is difficult to explain why anxiety was heightened in some persons exercising on a bicycle ergometer in the study by Steptoe and Cox (1988). With respect to a definition of the situation as a test situation in which performance is of some importance—as it is appropriate—the anxiety- inducing effect can be well understood and the data are far away from being astonishing.

References

Abele, A., & Brehm, W. (1990). Sportliche Aktivität als gesundheitsbezogenes Handeln: Auswirkungen, Voraussetzungen und Förderungsmöglichkeiten [Sports activity as health oriented behavior: Effects, preconditions, and interventions]. In R. Schwarzer (Ed.), *Gesundheitspsychologie* (pp. 131-150). Göttingen: Hogrefe.

Abele, A., Brehm, W., & Gall, T. (1991). Sportliche Aktivität und Wohlbefinden [Sports activity and well-being]. In A. Abele & P. Becker (Ed.), *Wohlbefinden. Theorie - Empirie - Diagnostik* (pp. 279-296). Weinheim: Beltz.

Andel, van G.E., & Austin, D.R. (1984). Physical fitness and mental health: A review of the literature. *Adapted Physical Activity Quarterly, 1*, 207-220.

Bahrke, M.S., & Morgan, W.P. (1978). Anxiety reduction following exercise and meditation. *Cognitive Therapy and Research, 2*, 323-333.

Brown, D.R. (1990). Exercise, fitness, and mental health. In C. Bouchard, R.J. Shephard, T. Stephens, J.R. Sutton, & B.D. McPherson (Eds.), *Exercise, fitness, and health* (pp. 607-626). Champaign, IL: Human Kinetics.

Bunge, M. (1980). *The mind-body problem: A psychobiological approach.* New York: Pergamon Press.

Cook, T.D., & Campbell, D.T. (1979). *Quasi-experimentation: Design and analysis issues for field settings.* Chicago: Rand McNally.

Crews, D.J., & Landers, D.M. (1987). A meta-analytic review of aerobic fitness and reactivity to psychosocial stressors. *Medical Science and Sports Exercise, 19* (Suppl.), 114-120.

Cureton, T.K. (1963). Improvement of psychological states by means of exercise-fitness programs. *Association of Physical and Mental Rehabilitation, 17*, 14-25.

DeVries, H.A. (1981). Tranquilizer effects of exercise: A critical review. *Physician and Sports Medicine, 9*, 46-55.

Dishman, R.K. (1986). Mental health. In V. Seefeldt (Ed.), *Physical activity and well-being* (pp. 304-341). Reston, VA: American Alliance for Health, Physical Education, Recreation and Dance.

Farrel, P.A., Gustafson, A.B., Garthwaite, T.L., Kulkhoft, R.K., Cowley, A.W., & Morgan, W.P. (1986). Influence of endogenous opioids on the response of selected hormones to exercise in humans. *Journal of Applied Physiology, 61*, 1051-1057.

Folkins, C.H., & Sime, W.E. (1981). Physical fitness training and mental health. *American Psychologist, 36*, 373-389.

Fuchs, R. (1990). *Sportliche Aktivität von Jugendlichen* [Sports activity by young people]. Köln: bps.

Glass, G.V. (1976). Primary, secondary and meta-analysis of research. *Educational Researcher, 10*, 3-8.

Greist, H.H., Klein, M.H., Eischens, R.R., Faris, T., Gurmann, A.S., & Morgan, W.P. (1979). Running as treatment for depression. *Comprehensive Psychiatry, 20*, 41-54.

Hackfort, D. (1990). Empirical social science oriented research in sport science. *International Journal of Physical Education, 27* (1), 25-32.

Hackfort, D., & Schwenkmezger, P. (1989). Measuring anxiety in sports: Perspectives and problems. In D. Hackfort & C.D. Spielberger (Eds.), *Anxiety in sports* (pp. 55-74). Washington, DC: Hemisphere.

Hager, W. (1984). Metaanalyse: Zahlen als Psychologieersatz? [Meta-analisys: Numbers instead of psychology] *Psychologie in Erziehung und Unterricht, 31*, 64-70.

Haken, H. (1983). *Synergetics: An Introduction.* (3rd edition). Berlin: Springer.

Hammett, V.B.O. (1967). Psychological changes with physical fitness training. *Canadian Medical Association Journal, 96,* 764-767.

Hughes, J.R. (1984). Psychological effects of habitual aerobic exercise: A critical review. *Preventive Medicine, 13,* 66-73.

International Society of Sport Psychology (1991). Physical activity and psychological benefits: An ISSP position statement. *Newsletter, 2,* 1-3.

Knoll, M., & Bös, K. (1991). *Eine Analyse empirischer Untersuchungen aus dem Bereich 'Sport und Gesundheit'* [An analysis of empirical studies on 'Sports and Health']. Vortrag auf dem dvs-Workshop 'Literaturrecherche in sportwissenschaftlichen Datenbanken' am 21.11.91 in Köln. Hektographie.

Layman, E.M. (1960). Contributions of exercise and sports to mental health and social adjustment. In W.R. Johnson (Ed.), *Science and medicine of exercise and sports* (pp. 560-599). New York: Harper.

Lösel, F. (1987). Methodik und Problematik von Meta-Analysen. - Mit Beispielen aus der Psychotherapieforschung [Methodology and the problem of meta-analysis — Examples from research in psychotherapy]. *Gruppendynamik, 18,* 323-343.

Martinsen, E.W. (1987). The role of aerobic exercise in the treatment of depression. *Stress Medicine , 3,* 93-100.

Mellion, M.B. (1985). Exercise therapy for anxiety and depression. *Postgraduate Medicine, 77,* 59-66.

Mobily, K. (1982). Using physical activity and recreation to cope with stress and anxiety: A review. *American Corrective Therapy Journal, 36,* 77-81.

Morgan, W.P. (1969). Physical fitness and emotional health: A review. *American Corrective Therapy Journal, 23,* 124-127.

Morgan, W.P. (1982). Psychological effects of exercise. *Behavioral Medicine Update, 4,* 25-30.

Morgan, W.P. (1984). Physical activity and mental health. In H.M. Eckert & H.J. Montoye (Eds.), *Exercise and health* (pp. 132-145). Champaign, IL: Human Kinetics.

Morgan, W.P. (1985). Affective beneficence of vigorous physical activity. *Medical Science and Sports Exercise, 17,* 94-100.

Morgan, W.P., & Goldston, E. (1987). Summary. In W.P. Morgan & E. Goldston (Eds.), *Exercise and mental health* (pp. 155-159). Washington, DC: Hemisphere.

Morgan, W.P., & O'Connor, P.J. (1988). Exercise and mental health. In R.K. Dishman (Ed.), *Exercise adherence: Its impact on public health* (pp. 91-121). Champaign, IL: Human Kinetics.

Nitsch, J.R., & Hackfort, D. (1981). Streß in Schule und Hochschule - eine handlungspsychologische Funktionsanalyse [Stress in school and college — a functional analysis out of action psychology perspective]. In J.R. Nitsch (Hg.), *Stress. Theorien, Untersuchungen, Maßnahmen* (S. 263-311). Bern: Huber.

North, T.C., McCullagh, P., & Tran, Z.V. (1991). Effect of exercise on depression. *Exercise and Sport Sciences Reviews, 18,* 379-415.

Petruzello, S.J., Landers, D.M., Hatfield, B.D., Kubitz, K.A., & Salazar, W. (1991). A meta-analysis on the anxiety-reducing effects of acute and chronic exercise. *Sports Medicine, 11,* 143-182.

Schlicht, W. (1991). Sport und seelische Gesundheit [Sports and psychological health]. Meta-Analysen zum Zusammenhang zweier summarischer Konstrukte. Hektografie.

Schwartz, G.E., Davidson, R.J., & Goleman, D.J. (1978). Patterning of cognitive and somatic processes in the self-regulation of anxiety: Effects of meditation versus exercise. *Psychosomatic Medicine, 40,* 321-328.

Schwenkmezger, P. (1985). Welche Bedeutung kommt dem Ausdauertraining in der Depressionstherapie zu? [What about the meaning of aerobic exercise in the therapy of depression] *Sportwissenschaft, 15* (2), 117-135.

Scott, M.G. (1960). The contributions of physical activity to psychological development. *Research Quarterly, 31,* 307-320.

Sime, W.E. (1984). Psychological benefits of exercise training in the healthy individual. In J.D. Matarazzo, S.M. Weiss, J.A. Herd, N.E. Miller, & S.M. Weiss (Eds.), *Behavioral health: A handbook of health enhancement and disease prevention* (pp. 488-508). New York: Wiley & Sons.

Sime, W.E. (1990). Discussion: Exercise, fitness, and mental health. In C. Bouchard, R.J. Shephard, T. Stephens, J.R. Sutton, & B.D. McPherson (Eds.), *Exercise, fitness, and health* (pp. 627-633). Champaign, IL: Human Kinetics.

Simons, A., McGowan, C.R., Epstein, L.H., Kuper, D.J., & Robertson, R.J. (1985). Exercise as a treatment for depression: An update. *Clinical Psychology Review, 5,* 553-568.

Sonstroem, R.J. (1984). Exercise and self-esteem. In R.L. Terjung (Ed.), *Exercise and sport sciences reviews* (pp. 123-155). Lexington: Collamore Press.

Stephens, T. (1988). Physical activity and mental health in the United States and Canada: Evidence from four populations surveys. *Preventive Medicine, 17,* 35-47.

Steptoe, A., & Cox, S. (1988). The acute effects of aerobic exercise on mood: A controlled study. *Health Psychology, 7,* 329-340.

Tomporowski, P.D., & Ellis, N.R. (1986). Effects of exercise on cognitive processes: A review. *Psychological Bulletin, 99* (3), 338-346.

Weinstein, W.S., & Meyers, A.W. (1983). Running as treatment for depression: Is it worth it? *Journal of Sport Psychology, 5,* 288-301.

Wolf, F.M. (1986). *Meta-analysis: Quantitative methods for research synthesis.* London: Sage.

Chapter 11

PSYCHOLOGICAL OUTCOMES OF SCHOOL SPORT: A NON-PSYCHOLOGIST'S VIEW

Francisco Sobral

«Hébertism» Revisited

In 1925, Georges Hébert, a French vessel lieutenant and author of the Natural Method of physical education, published *Le sport contre l'éducation physique [Sport Against Physical Education]*, a book that is probably his masterpiece and a very influential work for decades. There, Hébert made some critical statements concerning the evil influence of sport on the "sound" physical education of children and youths. A major emphasis was put on the objectionable moral and social consequences of sport.

Hébert had no relevant background in psychology, but as it often occurs, he trusted enough his common sense and intuition as to assess the psychological outcomes of sport. His views were largely naïve and opinionative but highly valuable in a historical perspective.

"While the natural athlete reveals a quiet mood," he argued, "the artificial athlete appears to be thrilled, restless, irritable" (1925, p. 46). "In its present form, sport is rather a school of nervousness than source of stillness and balance" (p. 47). Hébert also blamed the fact that sport competition is grounded on emulation, "a very frail pedagogical procedure" (p. 52), and attempted afterwards a national character approach by saying that "sport is anglo-saxon in its essence. Excellent as to stimulate a temperament colder than ours, it can only raise vanity, envy, selfishness and distrust from our natural disposition" (p. 90).

These words seem very remote indeed. Nowadays, sport invades everyday life and physical education curricula are no more immunized against it. On the contrary, sport stands for the main, if not the only, content of school physical education. Moreover, children and youths currently join sport programs many researchers and educators recognize to be too severe either in physiological or psychological terms. They participate in competitive top sport and experience an increasing pressure in a setting ruled by the adults' values and expectations. Champions at the Olympic Games are increasingly younger, meaning intense training in childhood and early adolescence. Criticism has grown around the world, but the trend towards an earlier specialization in sport shows no deceleration.

Journals and conferences often handle the issue of children in sport in a binary, yes or no perspective. The general idea drawn out of the literature is that the sporting child is the natural fact. Conferences aim to disclose which are the reliable indicators of his/her potential of performance, and how to optimize them. Researchers and coaches are both concerned about readiness for sport. This concept encompasses the match between the child's current level of maturation and the demands presented by a specific sport branch (Malina, 1984). Parents, educators and media are prone to praise the sporting child; oppositely, they blame his/her non-sporting age peer as someone who presents a worrying, deviant behavior.

School reflects more or less this social attitude towards sport. Nevertheless, many teachers are still skeptic about the virtues of sport as a mean of education, and fear it may bring into school the same immoderation we often recognize in the sport at large.

The Limitations of the Biological Paradigm

Before we move to consider the benefits of school sport in terms of psychological outcomes, as listed among the teachers' expectations or in the rhetoric of pedagogy, we ought to examine why sport is so deeply rooted in the contemporary culture. One has to admit that modern sport meets some essential needs of mankind and fits into the human pattern of growth.

As Bogin (1986) pointed out, the pattern of human growth displays three main characteristics: a prolonged period of infant dependency, an extended childhood, and a rapid and large acceleration in growth velocity at adolescence. These traits provide a prolonged period for brain development; time for acquisition of technical skills; and time for socialization, play, and the development of social roles and cultural behavior. For many years, the biological paradigm in physical education underlined the potential of sport as a factor intervening upon growth and maturation. Actually, the pioneering investigations of Kohlrausch (1924, 1929) and Bach (1925) spread out the idea that regular and moderate to intense exercise could induce an increase of skeletal growth (longitudinal and transverse), beside the well-known effects on muscular development. Further research suggested, however, that the taller and stronger athletes in all age groups were rather a consequence of selection than the result of training. The lack of control for maturity kept hidden differences accounted for by maturation pace and genetic endowment.

The selective pressure may act upon biological traits at a very early stage of sport experience even in the school setting, as we have observed in the Azores Growth Survey (Sobral, 1993). School girls aged 10 to 12 years, selected to represent their islands on a basis of a multi-sport competence, have been found to be significantly taller than their counterparts in the population at large. Furthermore, their mean stature was also above the value reported for their average age male peers in the same population. Although schoolgirl athletes did not differ significantly from the population for sexual dimorphism in other body dimensions, those who presented such a characteristic were found to perform significantly better in some athletic events.

Similar data reported in other investigations suggest that our findings may be probably more than an accidental fact. Since physical educators and coaches usually employ the same activities and criteria to assess children's success in sport, it appears very likely that in school sport selection for physique may also prevail, particularly when training experience is still too short to account for noticeable motor and physiological adaptations.

Most people appointed the low intensity of exertion, and the small number of hours per week granted to physical education in regular schooling as the main causes of such a failure to enhance the biological potential of juveniles. Yet, the idea that extra time of physical education and sport could induce significant gains in motor fitness and work capacity of schoolboys and girls turned out to be a chimera, following the evidence brought out by Kemper et al. (1974), which has been confirmed in further investigations. Then, exercise and sport in schooldays have surely to be justified beyond the boundaries of the biological paradigm, since a satisfactory degree of physical fitness is all one has to expect about a healthy child living a healthy life, as Malina stated in a personal remark.

Nevertheless, physical education and school sport ought to encourage a health concern in individuals from an early age, providing the opportunities to learn practical and joyful activities to be adopted later in the life, "by the time the body commits its first treacheries," to quote the Belgian-born novelist Marguerite Yourcenar, in her novel *Memoirs of Hadrian*.

School Sport and Movement Culture

The failure of the biological paradigm, as witnessed by both educators and researchers, gives a chance to a different conceptual scheme of school sport as a pathway to a movement culture (cf. German *Bewegungkultur*). As Crum (1992) states, movement culture "refers to the way in which a social group deals with the issue of corporeality and embodiment, and the need and desire for movement apart from moving behavior in the frame of labour and direct life maintenance." Although movement culture is thought of to be time and place dependent, mass media contribute nowadays to spread out stereotypes that arouse new needs and trigger phenomena of identification among children and youths, making movement culture much more universal than before. In Portugal, for example, baseball was practically unknown until the day our children were introduced to it by a television series. Softball is currently present in the official curriculum and the very first attempts to promote baseball in some communities are now being done. Despite serious constraints in terms of facilities and equipment, one can foresee a more cosmopolitan sport education in a near future, which is amenable to a wider motor repertoire and culture of movement. This appears to be a valuable cognitive and cultural outcome of school sport, provided physical educators are quite aware of the importance of it and pay enough attention to the mobility of their pupils' interests.

School Sport and Federation Sport: Servitude and Identity

In order to fulfill its purpose of cultural enrichment, while accounting for the acquisition of a healthy life-style, school sport has to struggle for its own identity. This may imply the refusal of some elements, habits and representations inherent to the federation sport which stands as the main reference for children and youths. It is not easy to deal with the potential of contagion carried by the «great sport», and teachers experience too often the dilemma between *pedagogialism* and cultural realism. They try to implement strategies of protection rooted in the values and principles of pedagogy, shaping school sport according to the needs and capacities of their pupils, and they risk to gain from them anything but lack of interest and withdrawal.

It is a hard issue, indeed, because sport and education are based on opposite and conflicting philosophies. Since the dawning of the 19th century, the philosophy of education that informs our schools is undoubtedly democratic and egalitarian. Whenever it claimed the need to consider the subject's own individuality (regarding, for example, his/her pace of learning and proposing, therefore, a pupil-fitted teaching strategy), it acted still on behalf of the egalitarian maxim: every normal man is born equal not only in rights but also in duties and potential of basic competencies. Hence, schooling is bound to promote a common knowledge suitable for the diverse social needs and roles, employing the means most likely to accomplish this goal.

I admit this view may be outmoded, but its inertial influence is much more present in teachers than we are inclined to concede.

Sport, on the contrary, seeks for the difference. It drives naturally to elitism and meritocracy. "First is first, second is nowhere", as Sebastian Coe, the former Olympic and world 800 and 1500 meters record holder, is said to have been taught from his father and coach according to the Portuguese sports newspaper 'Record'. The attempt to conciliate these two philosophies calls forth the physical educator's tragic experience. I say *tragic* in the old Greek sense, meaning something we incur beyond our own will and power, and are not able to escape despite the full consciousness of it.

I see this tragic experience as the conflict between J.-J. Rousseau and Darwin; between *equality* (as the right of each child to participate independently of his/her talent) and *selection* resulting from differential success; between the pedagogical reasoning, founded on a science of ethical standards, and the logic of sport that is much more concerned with biology and, therefore, founded on the facts of Nature. For instance, *dropout*, an ubiquitous flaw in youth sport, has much to do with sport in its natural, *wild* stage, while sport participation under protection is evidence of the *domestication* of sport according to some criteria deeply rooted into the philosophy of education. This is a highly metaphorical speech borrowed from Darwin's theory of natural selection, I agree, but I also believe it meets the main contradiction between education and sport.

Play versus Formal Sport

It is in this ideologically conflicting setting that school authorities summon the children to participate in training programs and competitions "within the spirit of education". In Portugal, school sport is a voluntary activity, complementary to the P.E. compulsory curriculum. Each student is free to choose between sport and any other activity (e.g., archaeology, computer science, drama, depending on the availability of a leading teacher). School sport is intended to be a space where participation prevails upon excellence, and joy upon stress and anxiety. Cooperation is also esteemed as a value higher than competition. Nevertheless, the activities still follow too closely the formalism we observe in the federate sport and some undesirable behaviors may occur when and where school sport is the only relevant social event in the community.

We carried out research on children aged 10 to 14 years who were regularly involved in school sport programs (Sobral, 1992). Searching for the variety and level of participation in other cultural activities, we found that only 1.2% of the boys were affiliated to a folklore group, 3.6% reported to be members of a musical society, 6.1 % were Boy Scouts, while 10.9% spent some leisure-time in activities organized by the local church. However, 35.3% were affiliated to the local sport club, rather as supporters than athletes. Girls still reported a lower level of participation, their corresponding percentages ranging from 1.2 to 6.2 in the 10 categories considered in the questionnaire.

These figures depict the importance of school sport in a large, densely populated region of northern Portugal, and explain to some extent why, despite the educational command, school sport may be also exposed to the evil influences originating from the stereotypes of federation and professional sport. Owing to the lack of alternative, rewarding cultural occupations, communities tend to overrate their children's experience in sport, either in or out of school.

There is a tendency to foster the idea that sport is merely a variety of play, thus putting into action a similar drive both in children and adults. Those who advocate this conception reckon that sport is a much more complex activity; they do not find, however, any essential difference between play and sport. We ignore whether children also assign different meanings to play and sport, nor do we know when they start to discriminate between these two patterns of activity. Hence, any decision concerning this problem stays too conjectural, based on a formal analysis conducted by an external observer, instead of a child's subjective account of the progress towards the stage in which play and sport assume distinct significances.

Sport and Quest for Excitement

If one seeks for psychological outcomes of school sport, it seems suitable to apprehend before how sport can meet some of the psychological needs acknowledged in children and youngsters. Every textbook dealing with the fundamentals of physical education and sport pedagogy includes a long list of properties intrinsic to sport and allegedly relevant regarding the psychological development of the human being, and its general development as well. That is a rather fragmentary interpretation, unable to lead to a more general theory concerning the early sport experience. Such a theory must be eclectic, since no single scientific pursuit is able to seize the nature and implications of this multidimensional phenomenon, and founded on intertwined arguments originated from sociology, ethology and psychological anthropology.

Goodger and Goodger (1989) focused the capacity of sport to generate excitement, agreeing with Loy (1981), who refers to sport as "intrinsically appealing," owing to its problematic outcome that "lends tension and excitement to a sporting contest" (pp. 262 -294). The quest for excitement in our contemporary societies is due, according to Elias and Dunning (1986), to the numerous restraints of the 'civilizing process,' demanding affect-control and sublimatory response.

Excitement, however, should be attained through events and activities socially acceptable, even if this implies to turn to symbolic practices, deprived of dangerous consequences for oneself or the other group members. Elias and Dunning assume that play and sport fulfill the same tendency of humans to engage in primitive activities transformed, by a socialized inhibitory process, into controlled, well-tempered source of excitement, tension and feat. This assumption is deeply rooted into Browne's ethological theory of play, which emphasizes the role of instincts genetically inherited from our remote ancestry, explaining thus three ever-present elements in games and sports: territory, hierarchy and weapons.

In the ethological perspective, then, play and sport work as *substitute activities* that, beside the above-mentioned sublimatory role, may also signal the possession of some attributes and competencies before the grown-up persons, as we can see among primitive groups by occasion of the initiation ceremonies honoring the adolescent transition.

It is encouraging, when attempting a holistic approach of play and sport in children and youths, to find congruent arguments pertaining to so different scientific pursuits as sociology and ethology. Nevertheless, one has to solve a preliminary problem respecting the dynamic causes that conduct children to sport other than instinct and phylogenetic impregnation. In fact, a basic assumption in ethology states that any innate behavior typical of a species survives the long process of evolution only when it represents some adaptive advantage. Such a solution, I believe, emerges from a biocultural model of sport participation.

Sport, Culture and Human Development

Sport is a quasi-universal trait of culture, while archaeological evidence exists that play has been quite early present among the activities of mankind. Thus, it seems very likely they both serve a basic developmental function either in a phylogenetic or ontogenetic perspective. The quest for tension and excitement, for example, probably derives from the need of some degree of unspecific arousal that makes the subject ready for action. The primitive men had their lives permanently endangered by animal and human predators, and survival was too much a matter of vigilance. Play would have been then advantageous to promote a kind of preparatory state making defense or escape easier, allowing also the refinement of tools and tactics to be used in the struggle for existence.

At this point, my speculations lack empiric evidence about configurations of play in populations undergoing different stages of social organization. One should ask, for example, at what extent nomadism and sedentism mould the group's repertoire of games and peculiar sporting contests; or how much time and importance they accord to playful activities. About 10,000 years ago, the settlement of populations, with the advent of agriculture and domestication, had a dramatic impact on human life-style, introducing a more elaborate culture and influencing our evolutionary past, where many of our behavior patterns are rooted (Malina, 1987). The question is still pertinent regarding the contemporary populations, but few investigations have been devoted to following the ways children and youths adopt new habits of play and physical activity because of social and cultural change. The same applies to the lack of comparative studies focusing the forms and density of play in urban and rural settings; in gypsy communities, nomadic and sedentary; in different ethnic groups sharing a common space of living, etc., as it has been extensively done with respect to the somatic and discrete motor traits. In the field of human movement and sport sciences, research on play and sport in a developmental perspective stays too descriptive and confined to single-disciplinary, single-method approaches.

Intensity and Context

In the lines above, I have dealt with a few highlights of a comprehensive theory of play and sport as calling patterns of activity printed in the biocultural evolution of mankind. I shall now tackle the main lines children and youth sport present both in the school and federate settings.

Telama (1988) developed a similar analysis among Finnish schoolboys and girls, and concluded that one of the main differences in school and competitive sport refers to time consumption in effective exertion. He found children reached an average amount of 17 to 18 hours of activity in the physical education class in a semester, approximately the same amount their age-peers involved in ice-hockey training used in a week. The picture may vary somewhat across the countries, according to the particular organization of physical education and school sport. In Portugal, where school sport is optional, sessions may have a configuration much more similar to the competive sport training, but this depends basically on the effectiveness of teaching and the goals attached to it. Often, it depends also on the specific sport branch. Actually, in this age period, performance and volume of training are not significantly different in school and club athletes, excepting for a few sports like gymnastics, swimming, or soccer. It is not rare that school athletes win open tournaments, for example in badminton or wrestling, but, undoubtedly, the time alloted for school sport is far from adequate to fulfill the goals of competitive sport.

Nevertheless, in the metropolitan area of Porto, almost 30% of boys and girls engaged in school sport spent more than 5 hours per week in sport activities, in and out of school. The sample comprised 146 boys and 125 girls whose ages ranged from 10 to 15 years (Sobral, 1992). It seems very likely that, for these youngsters, extra-school sport lacked consistency in terms of training and competition, considering that participation in both settings is hardly compatible or interesting for the excelling athlete.

The same applies to the intensity of training, whose levels are normally very low in comparison with those set in the sport club. This fact is an obvious consequence of different contexts and goals, with school sport much more inclined to promote learning and fun instead of titles and excellence. Accordingly, the levels of psychological pressure on children are different too in both settings, as well as the corresponding parental attitudes and involvement. Figure 1 summarizes other differential characteristics between school and federation sport.

Thus, anxiety, one of the negative features most often reported in competitive children and youth sport, arouses little, if any, concern in school. The nature of incentives assures that the main reason to stay in or quit the school group is simply the degree of satisfaction experienced in the activity. Also, the fact that school sport is not conflicting with the family's life-style nor the child's school work prevents much of the stress usually felt by the young outstanding athlete in some sport branches.

SPORT SETTING

School Federation

	School	Federation
Planning of training	Short term	Medium and long term
Competitive density	Low	Moderate to high
Anxiety-producing potential	Low	Moderate to high
Incentives	Inner	External
Interference in everyday life	Irrelevant	High or very high

Figure 1. Typical differences in children's sport according to the context of practice.

Some Facts and Figures

Whether a consequence of a natural impulse or culturally imprinted by strongly effective media, sport is a distinctive issue of adolescence in modern urban societies. As the pubertal age comes near, children, and boys particularly, become more receptive to the athletic experience and sport fetishes. On the track of auxology, I try to understand the call of sport in two ways:

- As a consequence of the great acceleration of the growth process, bringing about new capabilities for strenuous exertion and the acquisition of motor skills, as well as a state of psycho-physiological overexcitement, certainly with peaks and downs, induced by the so called 'neuro-endocrine storm'.

- And as an opportunity to fulfill some of the adolescent's basic developmental needs, in terms of the self-and social adjustments.

Prior to both hypotheses, one has to consider the adolescent growth beyond its strict biological features. Actually, the child is not a passive spectator of his or her own body changes, nor do the latter have their consequences confined to cells and corresponding functions. From the very first sign of puberty, to grow up is also to be aware of the changes suddenly installed by the growth process, and not every child is equally prepared to deal with its unsteady body image. The same may be said about the codes, values and behaviors the adult's world attaches to the new body status.

Despite the current knowledge concerning the psychological aspects of adolescent growth, parochialism is still too strong as to prevent from a more holistic research on children in sport, and I happen to quarrel a lot with colleagues and post-graduate students who resist to include psycho-social variables in their research designs, intimidated by the ever likely charge of invading the fields of neighbouring sciences. As far as this attitude prevails, it appears quite hard to distinguish between the psychological outcomes and the psychological prerequisites of sport, for example.

As Conger (1973) stated, "developmental change and the need to adjust to it cause adolescents to focus concern on physical aspects of the self," and "the adolescent who perceives himself as deviating physically from cultural stereotypes is likely to have an impaired self-concept" (p. 109). If sport allows, in some way, to overcome this kind of maladjustments, one should expect a fairly high percentage of children and youths in school sport scoring positively in body-image and body-satisfaction questionnaires. Such a percentage, however, keeps unknown the part of a negative selection, say, the auto-exclusion from sport by those children whose body-image raises deep feelings of refusal or dissatisfaction.

In the National Research Project on School Sport, FACDEX (Sobral, 1991), an adapted version of the KAS Questionnaire (Mrazek, 1987) was employed to assess fears and apprehensions related to health and illness, pains and doctor visiting, body appearance and body efficiency. The results of the preliminary applications in 190 school sport participants aged 10 to 15 (90 boys and 100 girls), published by Bento and Graça (1992), show that fears related to physical appearance rank very low in both sexes (Figure 2). No significant differences were found between sexes for any of the latent dimensions, but when the subjects were assigned to two age groups (10-12

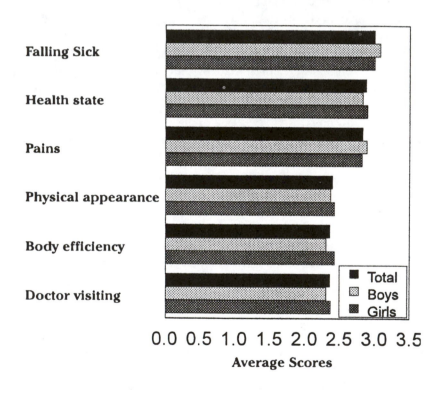

Figure 2. Fears and apprehensions relative to health and body in boys and girls active in school sport, assessed by the adapted KAS Questionnaire (Bento & Graça, 1992).

and 13-15 years), the physical appearance became a matter of higher concern, and the difference turned out to be significant at $p < .05$ (Fig. 3).

We looked for associations among the six categories of fears and apprehensions isolated by Bento and Graça and seven somatic traits in a small subsample of 20 boys and 51 girls. The selected somatic traits were body weight, standing height, body-build index (weight/height^2), endomorphy, mesomorphy, ectomorphy (according to the Heath-Carter anthropometric somatotype method), and sum of skinfolds measured at five sites (triceps, subscapular, spinal, abdominal and medial calf). Despite the small number of subjects and the preliminary nature of the analysis, some results are worth drawing our attention for further research.

While in boys no significant correlation coefficient was found, girls yielded some meaningful associations. For example, the fear of falling sick appeared significantly correlated with body-build index , mesomorphy and ectomorphy . Although r's are very small, they suggest clearly that the less bulky and muscular girl may be more afraid of falling sick than her stronger counterparts. The fact that mesomorphy and ectomorphy also correlate significantly with the concern about general health state provides additional likelihood to that hypothesis. Girls with higher scores in ectomorphy and smaller weight for height were also less confident about their body efficiency (r's significant at $p < .05$).

The correlation coefficients calculated for boys and girls together confirmed the above-mentioned hypotheses about fear of falling sick and (a)

	Ages		
Fears & apprehensions	**10-12**	**13-15**	*F-test*
Falling sick	2.91	3.18	1.60
General health state	2.83	2.83	-
Pains	2.81	2.70	0.44
Physical appearance	2.15	2.43	5.10 ($p < .05$)
Body efficiency	2.16	2.28	0.90
Doctor visiting	2.25	2.06	1.24

Figure 3. Changes according to age in boys and girls active in school sport (Bento & Graça, 1992).

body-build index, and (b) ectomorphy; and general health concern and ectomorphy, at the .05 probability level.

Beside the small number of subjects, we do not know whether these results are specific of children active in school sport or shared with their nonactive age peers. Nevertheless, sport at school is still granted the potential to facilitate self-adjustment and the attainment of the pubescent's own identity on the basis of an active body experience, as well as emotional balance towards the intriguing messages from his/her changing shape and function.

Another issue concerning the psychological outcomes of school sport focuses the social adjustment enhanced by the diverse situations of dual and group interaction, and of objective assessment of one's abilities as well. Competitive sport, either in school or within a federation program, provides an irreplaceable opportunity to tally the child's perceived competence and expectations with its actual and potential level of performance. At the first stage of their sport experience, most children cannot set realistic performance goals, and such an inability may lead to disappointment and dropout in the medium term.

Among the development tasks appointed to adolescence, most psychologist and sociologist authors include peer identification, social sensitivity and external interests and activities, which physical educators contend as being met by an educationally built sport. It is very hard, indeed, to ascertain whether these arguments are tall stories or deep wishes, before we can gather enough objective evidence from purposeful cross-sectional and longitudinal investigations, matching youngsters active and non-active in sport. Regarding Portuguese schoolchildren, social experience, together with relaxing and fun, was the most commonly appointed as the basic motive for involvement in sport. In a specific branch of the National Research Project on School Sport, Serpa (1992) administered the Participation Motivation Questionnaire of Gill, Gross, and Huddleston (1983), and found that affiliation, recreation and group-goal achievement were much more relevant for Portuguese youngsters compared with their North American counterparts, who are seemingly more prone to emphasize skill development and competition (Serpa, 1992).

Another matter of concern in our investigations on adolescent growth and sport from a biocultural perspective deals with ethnicity and sexual maturation. In Portugal, as in many other European countries, most suburban schools are crowded with youngsters of African and Asian descent, who experience serious problems of adaptation to the European cultural standards. They grow up according to specific biological patterns, despite the conceivable interference of their actual environment, and attach different meanings and values to the sequential stages of pubertal development. They also live in poor economic and hygienic conditions, and housing and family stability are far from satisfactory. Hence, absenteeism and disruptive behavior follow their inability to adjust to regular schooling. Sport is thought of as a means to overcome this situation, but one has to ask, how far and specifically the black or Asian adolescent responds to the call of sport in the school setting?

Within our post-graduate research program, Silva (1992) studied the motives for participation in school sport among white and black girls in relation with menarche (*status quo* assessed). She found that black girls living in a suburban area of Lisbon experienced menarche onset significantly later, although the difference between blacks and Whites was smaller than the figures reported in the literature (Eveleth and Tanner, 1976). White girls did not show significant changes in sport participation and motivation before and after menarche, but the phenomenon accounted for a decrease of Black girls' involvement in school sport. While active in sport programs, subjects in both groups grant similar importance to being with friends and enjoyment.

In Portugal, data relative to the factors that drive school children and youths to sport, as well as their psychological and biosocial characteristics at the beginning of their sport experience, are growing in a fairly promising rate. Long-lasting outcomes, however, are still obscure and speculative, owing to the lack of follow-up studies. Investigation proceeds aiming to approach sport as an essential feature of the contemporary school-life, and an ever present cultural force that raises the need of a cooperative, multi-disciplinary pursuit.

References

Bach, F. (1925). Brustumfang und Leibesübungen, *Anthropol. Anz., 23* (4),199.

Bento, J.O., & Graça, A. (1992). Educação da Saúde e Conceito de Corpo, In F. Sobral & A.Marques (Eds.), *FACDEX, vol.2: Relatório Parcelar, Área do Grande Porto* (pp. 77-87). Lisboa: Ministério da Educação, DGEBS.

Bogin, B. (1986). *Patterns of human growth.* Cambridge: Cambridge University Press.

Conger, J.J. (1973). *Adolescence and youth.* New York: Harper & Row.

Crum, B. (1992, Dec.). *The identity crisis of physical education: To teach or not to be, that is the question.* (Paper presented at the IV Conference SPEF, Oeiras, Portugal.

Elias, N., & Dunning, E. (1986). *Quest for excitement.* Oxford: Blackwell.

Eveleth, P.B., & Tanner, J.M. (1976). *World wide variation in human growth, International Biological Programme: 8.* Cambridge: Cambridge University Press.

Gill, D., Gross, J., & Huddleston, S. (1983). Participation motivation in youth sports. *International Journal of Sport Psychology, 14,* (1).

Goodger, J.M., & Goodger, B.C. (1989). Excitement and representation: Toward a sociological explanation of the significance of sport in modern society, *Quest, 41,* 257.

Hébert, G. (1925). Le sport contre l'éducation physique [*Sport against physical education*], Paris: Librairie Vuibert.

Kemper, H.C.G., Ras, J.G.A., Snel, J., Splinter, P.G., Tavecchio, L.W.C., & Verschuur, R. (1974). *The influence of extra physical education.* Haarlem: De Vriesenborch.

Kohlrausch, W. (1924). Über der Einfluss Funktioneller Beansprung auf das Langenwach-stum von Knochen, *Münchner Med. Wschr., 71,* 513.

Kohlrausch, W. (1929). Zusammenhangen von Korperform und Leistung Ergebnisse der anthropometrischen Messungen an den Athleten der Amsterdammer Olympiade, *Arbeitsphysiologie, 2,* 187.

Loy, J.W. (1981). An emerging theory of sport spectatorship: Implications for the Olympic Games. In J. Segrave & D. Chu (Eds.), *Olympism* (pp. 262 - 294). Champaign, IL.: Human Kinetics.

Malina, R.M. (1984). Readiness for Competitive Sport. In Maureen R. Weiss & D. Gould (Eds.). *Sport for children and youths* (pp. 45 - 50). , Champaign, Il.: Human Kinetics.

Malina, R.M. (1987). Physical activity in early and modern populations: An evolutionary view. In R.M. Malina & H.M. Eckert (Eds.), *Physical activity in early and modern populations* (pp. 1 -12). Champaign, IL.: Human Kinetics.

Mrazek, J. (1987). Das Gesundheitskonzept von Jugendlichen. *Brennenpunkte der Sport-wissenschaft* BSW (Sankt Augustin), *1,* 105.

Serpa, S. (1992). Motivação para a Prática Desportiva. In F. Sobral & A. Marques (Eds.), *FACDEX, vol. 2: Relatório Parcelar, Área do Grande Porto* (pp. 89-97). Lisboa: Ministério da Educação, DGEBS.

Silva, M.I.V. (1992, Dec.). *Influência do Sexo e do Estatuto Menarcal na Motivação para a Prática Desportiva*. Paper presented at the IV SPEF Conference, Oeiras, Portugal.

Sobral, F. (1991). *FACDEX: Desenvolvimento somato-motor e factores de excelência desportiva na população escolar portuguesa*. Lisboa: Ministério da Educação, DGEBS.

Sobral, F. (1992). O Estilo de Vida e a Actividade Física Habitual. In F. Sobral & A. Marques (Eds.), *FACDEX, vol. 2: Relatório Parcelar, Área do Grande Porto* (pp. 65-76). Lisboa: Ministério da Educação, DGEBS.

Sobral, F. (1993). Sexual dimorphism and motor performance of female children, with a remark on elitism and negative selection. In J.W. Duquet & J.A.P. Day (Eds.), *Kinanthropometry IV* (pp. 205 - 211). London: E. & F.N. Spon.

Telama, R. (1988). Sports in and out of school. In R.M. Malina (Ed.), *Young athletes: Biological, psychological and educational perspectives* (pp. 205 -221). Champaign, IL.: Human Kinetics.

Chapter 12

PRACTICE CONCERNS UNIQUE TO PROFESSIONAL SPORT

Bruce C. Ogilvie

Introduction

Presently there appear to be few opportunities for graduate students majoring in sport psychology to experience the special issues relating to service within professional sport organizations. Developing the skills necessary to remain effective in the roles team psychologist may be called upon to play requires a variety of training experiences rarely offered in graduate programs. There will be a range of crises of a particular social-psychological nature that are unique within these highly complex organizations. Particular reference would be the value of having graduate training in the area of organizational psychology. The consultation crises selected for presentation are intended to illuminate practice issues that typically fall outside formal training presently offered in graduate sport psychology programs. It is true some consultation issues the practitioner may confront are similar to those occurring within intercollegiate or elite athlete programs. An emphasis will be placed upon services that one might be called upon to address that have the potential for placing the team consultant's role in jeopardy. The abbreviated case histories may serve to begin our examination of the specific training of future sport psychologists.

Glyn Roberts and Wayne Halliwell edited a Special Theme Issue in *The Sport Psychologist* titled "Working With Professional Teams." (*The Sport Psychologist*, 1990). This volume presented articles by psychologists with extensive experience working with professional teams. Kenneth Ravizza, Ronald E. Smith and Jim Johnson, Harry Dorfman, baseball; Cal Botterill, Wayne Halliway, hockey; Jame E. Loehr, tennis; Sandy Gordon, cricket; Robert Rotella, golf; Fredrick Neff, football; and Daniel Gould and Laura Finch, bowling. These authors presented excellent reviews of their practice philosophy and the personal values that formed the basis for their service. Each author offers a representative sample of the issues and problems the consultant may confront within these sports.

Each author reinforced the nature of responsibilities that become a fact of life when providing services as team consultant. Particular reference was made to both ethical and moral considerations when the goal is that of acting in best interest of coaches, management and players. In early publications the capacity to maintain the desired role as an effective consultant was described as akin to "walking the razor's edge," (Ogilvie, 1977, 1979), the implication being that functioning as a service person will depend greatly upon the consultant's training and ability to identify potential threats from a variety of unanticipated sources. Throughout the hierarchy of the team there will be individuals each with a private agenda. These agenda will reflect the various administrative roles played by each member within the organization. Professional survival may often depend upon one's skill in identifying each agenda and then modifying consulting behavior accordingly. From the multiple of factors that may be operating during team services we could focus our attention upon the financial implications inherent in terms of the role the consultant might play. Whether we accept it or not the consultant is intimately involved with individuals in whom the organizations have great financial investments. Protection of their capital investment will be a primary concern.

The following examples of critical incidents have been chosen as representative examples of unique issues and crises confronted within the professional sports world. The particular issues and crises were selected because each exemplifies the highly volatile issues that may arise in team sports. The presentation of errors, mistakes and poor judgment while under contract to these professional teams hopefully offers content of educational value. In the absence of mentors and literature to provide guidance these consultation experiences represented trial and error approaches. Years exploring and experimenting in ways of providing service within numerous professional organizations did provide a most challenging learning laboratory. It is not possible to extend appreciation to the head coaches, general managers, owners and numerous others within the professional organization who acted as mentors.

Educational Setting

The recommendations and guidelines that will be discussed represent learning experiences as a consultant in professional sports of baseball, football, basketball, hockey, golf, skiing, tennis, ice skating, and race car driving. The two examples are selected from professional basketball. The first question might be with regard to the service commonalities to be found within individual as compared with team sports. Experience confirms that working with individual sports persons may result in a reduction in the number of extraneous factors that can operate to extenuate counseling concerns. When the golf or tennis professional seeks service often, responsibility is restricted to the client and their agent. There have been occasions where sponsors and parents have by the nature of their relationship to the client compounded the problem. More frequently it has been the focused one on one relationship with the individual athlete. Ideally this client-athlete relationship would be based totally upon the collaborative efforts of psychologist and athlete. When services extend to the entire team or organization, functioning within the APA ethical code becomes a continuous challenge. The cases selected reinforce this reality

Critical Incident

Introduction

The first critical incident represents consultation experience within a professional basketball organization. The presentation of the issues inherent in this service situation may serve as a means of calling attention to a number of complex threats to the consultant in terms of professional survival.

Particular reference will be made to the maintenance of privileged communication. Professional survival will depend greatly upon the development of skills in protection of privileged communication. Honoring such communication may become an issue should the coach request your presence at practice to evaluate a particular problem he is having with one of his players. You may be required to travel on the road with the team because the coach is confused with regard to a particular player's behavior. There may be a request to sit with the coaching and scouting staffs while they converse about the possible selections available in the national player draft. Even greater pressure may be experienced should the general manager or owner seek counsel with regard to decisions that affect the team. The following is an example of a request to reprocess the possible effects of administrative decisions that have already been made.

CASE I - Professional Basketball

This consultation experience represented an example of being asked to review the effects upon the team and community when a decision had already been made to trade a veteran player. In this situation management requested counsel with regard to the means of tempering possible negative community reactions. In an ideal counseling situation the team consultant would have a reliable foundation for anticipating what might be the negative ripple effect of such a decision. In this case there was absolute certitude that the veteran was an idol to the fans. He had been a team leader and confidant to other team members. He had been the media favourite even though the team had been struggling for years. Also, a strong personal positive bond existed with this particular athlete. How then does the consultant guard against the influence of personal feelings and maintain a capacity to be objective when examining the best course of action?

It is difficult to convey the professional danger inherent in such a consultation setting particularly the threat to the consultant's future effectiveness that such service requirements might engender. It will be such critical incidents that force the consultant to reevaluate his/her competence in terms of providing best solutions. Certainly it would be ideal to beg off temporarily and take time to sit with a colleague and explore the most viable solutions. The reality of this situation was that a press release had been prepared and management's only interest was to soften the effects of their decision. Their expectation was, based upon your training you will contribute to a solution that will reduce the possible traumatic effects within the organization. Their secondary concern, to find an approach that would placate the feelings of the veteran they are about to trade. There may be concern for team's and coaches' feelings but each are given lower priority.

It is apparent that becoming a party to this decision-making process places the consultant in a position that could challenge his future relationship with the entire team. In this example the decision concerned a year journeyman who had been the mature heart of the team. The team had struggled but failed to make the playoffs for a number of years. Any effort on the consultant's part to cushion the negative aftereffects of such a trade must capitalize upon a number of sophisticated counseling skills. To be seen as a party to this decision-making process will have direct ramifications throughout the entire organization. To be placed in such a position will force the consultant to engage in some form of self-appraisal. Certainly high on the self-evaluation list will be effectiveness in past experiences when confronted with such a request. At this critical juncture the counselor is obligated to examine the extent to which he/she possesses the required skill and training to function effectively in such a role. A most significant, and probably the most important factor, will be having sufficient experience to anticipate the long-terms effects of being a party to the final decision. Like so many unique situational crises within professional sport few graduate programs offer formal preparation with regard to team intervention issues.

Chosen Course of Action

Management was asked for permission to be the person to convey their decision to this veteran player. It was stated that this would only be done if full disclosure of the contractual relationship with the new team would be made available. They were asked to share all knowledge as to what his role might be with the new team and how he was to fit into their program. This request was based upon considerable insight into the personality of this unusually mature athlete. It was felt that minimizing the negative effects of the decision would best be served by appealing to his strengths and using these strengths to buffer the effects upon his fellow teammates. During this private meeting it became evident that he had been keenly aware of possible trades. He stated that having had to remain in the dark with regard to his future caused him the most distress. He obviously did not want to be traded but he was quick to begin to examine what this might mean in terms of his long-range goals. The secondary stresses at this time were almost too numerous to mention. Moving his children from a school they loved, his wife's adjustment to an entirely new environment, selling his home, finding new quarters, helping his children to adapt and find new friends, etc. A particular stress was the reality that he had to be on a plane the next day and be at practice ready to contribute. The anticipated strengths of this veteran were much in evidence when he chose to break the news to his fellow teammates and then provide whatever buffer effect with regard to their feelings of loss. The maturity he exhibited reduced the negative fan response and disarmed the media.

<u>On Being Traded</u>

In professional sport one learns very quickly that being traded to another team is something almost every veteran dreads. There are the few exceptions of players who beg to be traded, particularly those who are not getting their share of playing time. For those traded against their will it has sometimes been possible to temper the blow to their ego by examining the possible positive factors that may accrue from being traded. There may be chance for more playing time; the new team may have a greater chance of making the playoffs; playing in a major city may offer a greater chance for exposure and therefore greater economic gain. These and other such possible positive accidents associated with the trade can ameliorate negative feelings. The consultant must be sensitive to both the social and psychological ramifications of being traded. The athlete has purchased a home; children are going to be forced to leave a school to which they have become attached. A wife must now seek to reestablish a social network or find a new part-time job. There are an infinite variety of cost factors that produce stress for the entire family. Independent of any of these factors the veteran will be expected to be performing at a level of his personal best the next day. Not only must he be ready to practice, but to be a contributing team member immediately.

There will be exceptions when the general manager chooses to convey the painful message of a trade. Experience within the professional sport clearly supports that it is the head coach who chooses this responsibility. Coaches have often expressed that they feel it is an act of betrayal not to take responsibility for this painful duty. Depending upon the relationship which exists between consultant and coach this may be an occasion where the coach may seek to work out his feelings before meeting with a player. There have been occasions where the head coach has been reduced to tears when confronting this unpleasant responsibility. The stressfulness of the occasion intensifies should the head coach not have played an active part in the decision-making process. As a service person confronting such issues the experience is much like wading one's way through a minefield. Every step in the ameliorating process requires forethought and a sensitive insight into personal dynamics of each of the actors involved. A single misstep can terminate your effectiveness within the entire organization.

CASE II - External Threats When the Issue is Team Underachievement

There will be few crises that increase the complexity of the consultant's role like those that are the consequences of a losing season. It is not possible to enumerate all the external stresses or their sources when the team, coach and management must continue to function in a totally non-reward situation. On such occasions individuals and even organizations may often retreat to pathological reactions. In past publications reference has been made to the "unholy defensive trinity" of denial, rationalization and projection (Ogilvie, 1990). When a team is on a losing cycle you may be forced to function in the middle of a form of chaotic disintegration. One of the many ways this may be expressed is that each division within the organization may seek to place responsibility by means of projection. There seems to inevitably be a quest within each level of the power structure to designate a scapegoat. The forms that such projection take clearly reinforce the reality that one is practising in a business first and a team sport second. The primary goal of professional sport is to generate income.

The example of underachievement is selected consultation experience within professional basketball. Most organizations offer a flowchart generally including the following: Owner or Board of Directors, General Manager, Asst. General Manager, Coaching Staff, Director of Player Personnel, publicity-promotions, radio-TV personnel, team physician, and trainer.

The threats which contribute to excessive defensive reactions within the organization are those reflected by negative media and fan attitudes and responses. As the number of fans begins to decrease and the media begin to convey despair with regard to the team's future, avoidance of the performance reality is no longer possible. This will be the occasion in the season where buried feelings such as resentment, anger, hostility and negative stereotypes begin to surface. Independent of the causes of the decrement in team play the first solution on the part of management may be that of sacrificing the head coach. This can occur even when an objective evaluation of the team may find injuries to key veteran players, inability of high draft choices to compete at the professional level, and absence of talented players at key positions such as point guard, etc. may be contributing factors. Here the analogy of walking in a minefield becomes even more pertinent. When confronted with the potentially highly volatile management behaviors there will be occasions where the consultant's primary loyalties will be tested.

Before proceeding it should be stated that each consultant must define where his/her primary loyalties reside. There has never been a question for this consultant; the Head Coach has been the member of the organization in whom primary loyalty has been invested. The most meaningful and constructive professional relationships have been those where an emotional bond of respect and trust has developed between consultant and head coach. A number of these have endured over 20 years, one lasting 34 years. It is recommended that the consultant define his/her role as primarily that of serving the needs of the head coach. The experience of this consultant is that this fundamental commitment will in no way limit one's capacity to honour one's professional responsibilities to team or management.

Critical Issues Involved in Breakdown of Team Morale

A breakdown in team morale presents a number of consultation challenges particularly with regard to loyalty and competence. Management or the coaching staff may seek your counsel by posing questions that will generate insight into causes of collapsing morale. In the role of team psychologist there will be few responsibilities that possess the threat to professional integrity such as that of attempting to intervene in such team issues. The foregoing comment reflects direct experience as a consultant for such issues occurring both within elite university teams as well as professional teams.

A consultation failure will serve as an instructional model with regard to the complex issues that may be associated with breakdown of team morale. The terminal effects of attempts to be of service to this particular team crisis were as follows: The general manager became alienated, the head coach eventually was fired and the team psychologist's contract was terminated. Returning to earlier remarks with regard to future graduate training it is strongly recommended that actual case study seminars of such failures offer an excellent opportunity to enhance counseling skills. Such training experiences though extremely informative are not a substitute for practical field experience under supervision.

Based upon hindsight the failure with this team could be characterized by a number of professional oversights. The most damaging was that of not doing sufficient homework with regard to causality before setting up the team meetings. The second less than professional act was to agree to begin the solution-seeking process traveling with the team on the road. A third serious failure was in not gathering the available hard data with respect to the reported negative behavior of individual team members. If it were possible to prioritize the professional mistakes the list would be headed by an initial acceptance of management's conclusion that the media had accurately analyzed the team's problem. How anyone at that time with twelve years' experience within professional sport could have given credence to such an information source is now unthinkable. It was extremely shortsighted not to have first taken time for one-on-one conferences with each of players— particularly the players that the media had reported as "the heart of the problem." Lack of foresight was also demonstrated by not determining exactly what each player actually had communicated to the press.

No attempt will be made to rationalize the nature of services or the unacceptable level of professional conduct during this consultation experience. A lack of sound judgement was that of acceding to the general manager's demand for a quick solution. Reacting to this pressure resulted in a failure to discover that the (problem) players were being judged based upon false premises. In retrospect it is clear that there were violations of fundamental principles that underlay working effectively with groups. An important violation was that of assuming the problem as defined by management was based upon facts. This assumption functioned to undermine the provision of an exploratory environment where the group defines, or identifies, the problem. A most critical oversight was that of not getting in tune with the level of hostility and resentment within the team. The ego deflation that the poor season had generated had stripped a number of players of their pride. This emotional pain was contributing to exceedingly high levels of negative stereotyping of their teammates. Whether such forms of projection were justified or not attempts to deflect blame had become a generalized psychological defense.

It was under such circumstances that management refused to permit the players to have a choice with regard to attendance at the group sessions. This form of management manipulation only added fuel to the anger and resentment within the team. Their interpretation was that management was merely looking for scapegoats. They saw such sessions as only serving the purpose of placing blame.

The critical reader might say, "How could you have presumed to be able to accept responsibility for resolving such a complex team problem?" At this point presumption was based upon over ten year's practical experience working with business and clinical groups plus posdoctoral group training. Also past experience utilizing the group process method in the treatment of team issues had proven to be an effective strategy in the past. Though somewhat naive the premise at that time would have been "we can solve anything if we will only sit down and talk together." This premise still obtains but with the qualification that the psychological and social groundwork must precede problem confrontation. The first step in laying the groundwork should have been that of creating an environment where open, non-judgmental discourse can occur. In this case the magnitude of the team problem and pressure for an immediate solution interacted to cloud professional judgment. Though this is not intended as an excuse for less than professional conduct the volatile nature of the crisis could not be anticipated until actually experienced during the first team meeting. The emotional component most evident at this time was rage.

In actual practice in field situations you will find that it is often difficult to design or control the environment in which you are forced to function. This is particularly pertinent to the case under discussion. The General Manager in order to guarantee total attendance insisted that team meetings be held in the locker room immediately before practice. Once again the players were denied a choice. A locker room may be ideal for planning game strategies or the offense and defense for the night, but not as an environment which encourages open communication. The locker room is a citadel for concentration on how to win the game not exploring feelings of resentment and betrayal. Once again the urgency of the problem negated the use of sounder clinical judgement. This was a team that had been slated to make the playoffs and now found themselves eliminated by mid-season. They were playing to a shrinking population of fans while enduring the assault of three major newspapers. After the third session the players took it upon themselves to protest attendance at the group meetings. In this number of sessions it had not been possible to even get them to agree to the groundrules that would provide the structure for identifying the true nature of the problem. Even getting the communication process started by admonishing each to speak only to his feelings, what he was experiencing and to avoid placing blame or making reference to other players led to open attacks. As those who chose to identify the problem experienced a number of personal assaults eventually no one volunteered.

After approximately 12 hours it became apparent that there was little to be done to start the healing process. The sessions were interspaced with games that the team was losing badly. Fan and press abuse became like salt on their wounded egos. As team performance deteriorated the head coach became more verbally abusive. It is certain that as a veteran coach he was imagining management behind closed doors making a decision about his future. As his security became more threatened his hostility became more overt.

A counseling decision was made to offer the team a final apology for being a less than effective professional and then withdraw from the problem. The coach was soon released and the psychological service contract terminated. This ending was made more painful in the light of what had been a most rewarding four-year relationship.

What are Some Lessons From the Foregoing Failure?

It would necessitate an entire chapter to present in a detailed manner every specific factor that underlies the failure to meet adequate professional standards when confronting this team morale problem. Rather than flying in one afternoon and being thrown into the breach the following approach would have been preferable.

a. Management would be informed that no contact would be made with the team or individual members until a fuller evaluation of the nature of the crisis had been completed.

b. Access to every member in the organization that might contribute valuable insights would be assured.

c. The first formal session of exploration would be with the head coach (and his staff at his discretion).

d. During practice or some convenient moment the team captain would be approached with regard to his interest in discussing the problem.

e. Whatever data, interpretations, and inferences that had been gathered during the search for causality would be explored first with the team captain.

f. The team captain would be asked if he would support sharing these data with the entire team. Most importantly, he would be asked to call a team meeting where the team could explore relevant issues.

g. Upon agreement he would be asked to test the team's willingness to have the team psychologist present while the team searched for the most viable solutions.

Once consensus had occurred with regard to the nature of the problem and options in terms of solutions had been spelled out a meeting with the coach and team captain would be requested. At this meeting the team captain would be provided with an opportunity to share the team's consensus as to the nature of the problem. Depending upon the degree of clarity and the extent to which the coach felt he could remedy the causes of the team or individual members discontent a team meeting would be arranged. At this coach-team meeting the agenda would cover those issues and factors in prioritized order that could form the basis for reintegration of team morale. The role of team consultant would be reduced to that of clarifying issues, refocusing when communicates got off the track, inviting deeper exploration of options while keeping the communication problem centered. The goal, and hopefully, the end product of discourse would be general acceptance of a cognitive-behavioral strategy that leads to constructive solutions.

The Importance of Spelling Out Areas of Competence

Inevitably there will be occasions where the consultant may be asked to aid in the resolution of critical internal problems of an extremely complex nature. Should the consultant feel adequately trained to become a partner to the resolution process it is imperative that he/she define the role he/she will play. The least threatening areas of service will be providing coaches with helpful insights about their players or answering the call for individual player attention. Still one may confront challenges which produce considerable ambivalence. The service challenge may force a direct confrontation with one's competences, where one's loyalties must reside, and even if one has the adequate background, experience or training to consider becoming a party in the quest for a solution. The following example contains all the foregoing issues plus a number of other that are unique professional team concerns.

CASE III - When the Request for Service Intrudes Upon Established Loyalties

The final example represents an occasion of being asked by the team owner to meet privately to discuss issues with regard to the head coach's behavior. In practice you may find that such concerns may be limited to on-court conduct or may extend into the coach's personal life. If ownership considers your contract to include obligations for services within your competence beyond those specifically related to the team then such a request may be felt to be justified. In this example the owner had every right to request counsel because the contract explicitly stated that services would include mental hygiene issues within the organization. Performing the function of a referral agent where problems indicated such a need for services had been included in the service contract.

The number of factors that can contribute to professional ambivalence is extensive. As stated earlier for this consultant the strongest loyalty commitment is always to the coach. In this case a personal and professional relationship had extended over a 2 1/2 year period. The owner's only comment before seeking the meeting was with regard to the coach's loss of behavioral control during recent games. He also questioned the coach's control of his alcohol consumption.

With these brief statements as to the owner's concern what became the professional obligations of the team consultant? Before we explore appropriate conduct it should be stated that no one else in the organization was informed about the requested meeting.

In this example a bond of support and trust had developed whereby the coach had exposed extensive privileged information. He chose on occasion to use our relationship for therapeutic purposes. His style of using counsel was of the intermittent variety, reaching out only when his stress threshold had been breached. He retained total control of these encounters and terminated them when he felt he had derived whatever he had needed at the moment. What he wanted most was an extension of his perception as to the nature of the problem he was confronting. As a service person the feelings toward this man were of a very protective nature. There was so much about him to be liked. The greatest threat to his professional career was his intermittent lack of emotional control. His emotional responses to players who refused to perform consistently, bad calls by the officials, andclose losses were internalized as volatile negative energy. He was ranked in the coaching profession as an outstanding teacher and coach. His overall performance record over the years was above average. He was considered to be technically advanced. Most important the team was succeeding under his direction. With just those few brief insights into this coach's character what role should the consultant play when confronted with the owner's request?

It is difficult to convey the magnitude of responsibility should the team consultant find himself/herself in such a position. In this case loyalty to the coach took precedence over the owner's concerns. The decision was made to first apprise the coach of the request for the meeting. He was asked to recommend how his conduct should be analyzed and how he would defend it. A first determination was made as to what he would prefer to be shared about him during this meeting. He was presented with the opportunity to outline those things that he would prefer not being raised. He was then asked to describe how he saw himself on those occasions where he felt out of control. Finally he was presented with an opportunity to suggest how each member of the organization could provide him with emotional support.

In our forthcoming meeting with the senior executive considerable negative feelings did surface. The meeting did force this coach to begin to seriously reflect upon his recent emotional outbursts. He found certain of his responses totally out of character. Each loss of control had seemed to result in lessening of his self-esteem. The session terminated with exploring ways the organization could reduce the stress he was experiencing and help him with his control. It was recommended that the coach and executive meet alone and review all we had learned. The result of this meeting was the setting of well-defined limits with regard to his conduct before the public. These boundaries proved to be extremely effective throughout the rest of the season. This also provided the occasion for examining other stressful issues in his life. A recommendation was made for him to seek private counseling. With some reluctance he accepted this recommendation.

The foregoing is consistent with the philosophy that with sensitivity and human concern the team consultant can effectively provide services without ever violating ethical or contractual commitments. It is true we can learn by doing, but how much better prepared we would be if in our graduate training we could be exposed to extensive case histories and explore best approaches to problem resolution. Having graduate students role play a variety of scripts of actual consultation experiences would be a preferred form of training. Through the critiquing real consultation experience transfer of training could be maximized.

Graduate Training Recommendations

It is strongly recommended that provision be made for course offerings that reflect the consultation realities for those seeking to become practitioners in the art/science of sport psychology. Those sport consultants seeking to practice within professional sport would benefit greatly from courses content that is most represented within graduate course offered in industrial organizational psychology. Much of the knowledge and many of the counseling skills that increase effectiveness in industry settings will be directly applicable within the professional sport world.

This consultant receives frequent requests for recommendations as to the composition of formal service contracts. It is evident that few graduate students have had an opportunity to confront the responsibility of defining a formal contract. An opportunity must be provided where graduates have experience, under supervision, preparing a contract that protects their professional integrity. Such a document must provide a sound basis for legitimate expectation of the consumer. It must take a form that will eliminate any ambiguities with regard to any and all services to be rendered. In its final form it must be the reference source that protects both the consumer and the practitioner. There is no better foundation upon which to define professional obligation than that offered within the APA ethical and practice guidelines. Defining the obligations inherent in privileged communication, limiting practice to areas of proven competence, meeting the training standards with regard to specialized services offered should be part of any contract.

Once again the case study method would provide the most effective learning environment for the development of contract development skills. It will be through the review of the unexpected, the unplanned for, and the complex social, psychological and economic realities within professional sport that insight and skills will evolve.

References

Ogilvie, B.C. (1977). Walking the perilous path of the team psychologist. *The Physician& Sportsmedicine, 5* (4), p. 113.
Ogilvie, B.C. (1979). The sport psychologist and his professional credibility. In Klavora& Danniel (Eds.) *Coach, athlete, and sports psychologist* (p. 103). Toronto: University Toronto Press.
Ogilvie, B.C. (1990, August). *The practice of medicine can be injurious to your physical and mental health.* Presentation to AAOS, Anaheim, CA.
Roberts, G., & Halliwell, W.(Eds.). (1990). Working with professional athletes [Special issue]. *The Sport Psychologist, 4* (4).

Chapter 13

THE DEVELOPMENT OF A COGNITIVE-BEHAVIORAL BETWEEN-POINT INTERVENTION STRATEGY FOR TENNIS

James E. Loehr

Support for the use of sport specific cognitive-behavioral pre-performance routines to enhance competitive performance has been established (Boutcher & Crews, 1987; Cohn, Rotella & Lloyd, 1990; Crews & Boutcher, 1986a; Gould, Weiss, & Weinberg, 1981; Lobmeyer & Wasserman, 1986; Pelz, 1988;). In 1984, no tennis specific cognitive-behavioral model existed that could be used by players, coaches, or sport psychologists to enhance competitive performance. From my perspective as a practicing sport psychologist, specializing in work with tennis players, the development of a between-point performance training strategy could prove to be of considerable value in helping tennis players more effectively manage competitive stress and achieve Ideal Performance State control during competition. An Ideal Performance State is conceptualized as the optimal condition of mental and physical arousal for the execution of motor skills (Loehr, 1983).

Pre-performance routines combine both cognitive (covert) and behavioral (overt) strategies and typically involve a specific progression of mental and physical steps preceding the execution of the desired motor skill. In 1986, the effects of such a performance routine on the accuracy of the tennis serve was investigated (Moore, 1986). The study showed slight improvement in accuracy of the serve when a precise cognitive/behavioral routine was followed. The study, however, did not explore the impact of the pre-performance routine under competitive match conditions. The effectiveness of such cognitive/behavioral strategies in helping players perform optimally under pressure has not as yet been determined in tennis.

The Between-Point Factor

According to official men's professional tour (ATP) statistics, the average length of time the ball is in play (during point time) on hardcourts is 6.5 seconds, on clay is 8.2 seconds, and on grass is 2.7 seconds. The average between-point time on hardcourts is 28.5 seconds, on clay is 21.0 seconds, and on grass is 27.4 seconds. In a 4-hour match, the average play time is less than 16 minutes on grass, less than 26 minutes on hardcourts and less than 34 minutes on clay. Such statistics underscore the importance of the between-point time in tennis. Although this non-playing time consumes 80 to 90% of the total match time, the idea that players' patterns of thinking and acting between points might play a significant factor in during-point motor skill execution had been given little consideration by coaches or players. Prior to 1984, the between-point time in tennis was viewed essentially as unimportant down-time. The notion of training players to think and act in specific ways between points to enhance competitive success during points represented a new training direction for most coaches.

Separating Poor from Good Competitors

Considerable agreement exists among tennis coaches regarding the identification of players possessing good competitive skills. When coaches at the Nick Bolletteri Tennis Academy were asked to select the 5 best competitors out of 138 players in residence, coaches consistently selected the same players. When asked to list the poorest competitors, a similar consensus was evident.

Of particular significance was the finding that when asked to list the reasons why a particular player was a poor or good competitor, coaches consistently pointed to patterns of thinking and acting between points to explain the competitive differences.

Explanations of poor competitors included "always thinking negative during competition," "looks lazy," "poor on-court image," "too casual," "gets upset at everything," "shows no fight," "poor intensity," "never thinks," "mind wanders everywhere," "goes crazy when he doesn't play well," "too nervous and shy," "looks weak and unmotivated."

Explanations of good competitors included "always very positive during competition," "great competitive image," "clear thinker under pressure," "always fights hard," "never shows weakness," "never gives up," "great intensity," "stays focused."

In an effort to further clarify the criteria coaches were using to separate poor from good competitors, coaches were asked to review video tapes of matches of both good and poor competitors. The video-taped material was edited into two separate versions. Version I included during point time only and Version II included between-point time only. Coaches first reviewed Version I and were asked to identify patterns of behavior they used to separate poor from good competitors. Comments regarding biomechanics, movement skills, shot selection and tactics were common but coaches found it extremely difficult to identify positive and negative competitive habits by observing during point time only. Separating poor from good competitors based solely on during point time proved very difficult for the coaches sampled.

The coaches' response to Version II, however, was very different. Positive and negative patterns were quickly identified. Coaches were clearly relying heavily on between-point information to explain competitive differences between good and poor competitors. It was very easy for coaches to separate good from poor competitors based on between-point behavior.

Using Top Players as the Model

To further explore the meaning and importance of between-point patterns of behavior, video tapes of between-point time for top playing professionals were intensively studied.

Included in the analysis were tapes of Jimmy Connors, Ivan Lendl, Boris Becker, Stefan Edberg, John McEnroe, and Bjorn Borg. Female pro's included Steffi Graf, Martina Navratilova, Chris Evert, Gabriela Sabatini and Pam Shriver. The purpose of the video analysis was threefold: first, to detail patterns of between-point behavior characteristic of highly successful competitors; second, to look for commonalities among the top players in terms of the between-point time; and third, to compare common behavioral patterns of top competitors with those of poor competitors in the hope of identifying critical differences.

Video Analysis

Video analysis of the top players commenced as soon as the point was over and continued until the ball was struck by the server marking the beginning of the next point. The analysis consisted of the following:
1. Average time taken between points for each player.
2. Physical reaction of each player immediately following a point in terms of shoulders, head, eyes, racquet, etc.
3. Each player's walk, position of arms, hands, racquet at all times, movement patterns, eye patterns, verbal behavior and posture.
4. Pre-performance rituals initiated by each player just prior to the start of the point.

Although tedious and time consuming, this analysis provided many critical insights. Among them were the following:
1. Top players showed considerable discipline and precision in their behavioral patterns between points.
2. Top players rarely projected weakness in their body language between points.
3. Top players followed remarkably similar between-point behavioral routines.

Of all the top players studied only John McEnroe showed substantial variations.

Of particular interest, however, was the finding that against Bjorn Borg, John McEnroe's between-point behavior was very consistent with the patterns of the other players. John has stated repeatedly that his finest competitive performances occurred against Borg.

The same video analysis system used with top competitors was employed with players identified as poor competitors residing at the Nick Bollettieri Tennis Academy. The poor competitor sample consisted of 9 boys ranging in age from 14 to 18 and 8 girls ranging from 12 to 17. The following conclusions were made after review of the video material.

1. Compared to top competitors, poor competitors were less disciplined and less precise in their behavioral patterns between points.

2. Compared to top competitors, poor competitors had a greater tendency to engage in the overt expression of negative emotion, and were more likely to outwardly portray negative feelings and emotions such as fatigue, helplessness, disillusion and self-criticism.

3. Compared to top competitors, poor competitors used less time between points (greater tendency to rush), were less likely to follow a consistent pattern of behavior prior to the start of each point and were more likely to allow their eyes to wander between points.

More Data Collection

The clear differences between top and poor competitors in terms of their behavioral patterns between points were certainly encouraging. However, much more information was needed before a truly meaningful between-point training system coud be developed. Many critical questions remained unanswered. Exactly why do the behavioral differences exist and precisely what role do such differences play in competitive success? What is the impact of specific between-point behavioral patterns on Ideal Performance State control? Of great importance also was the question of whether cognitive differences exist between top and poor competitors in the same way behavioral differences were found to exist.

In an effort to gather more information pertaining to these questions, top juniors residing at the Nick Bollettieri Tennis Academy at the time were selected for further testing and analysis. Several of those included in the sample are currently highly successful touring pros. These included Jim Courier, Andre Agassi, David Wheaton and Monica Seles. Over a six-month period, approximately 50 practice matches were scheduled for the purpose of gathering between-point data. All matches were video taped and all players wore heart rate monitors that could be down loaded into a central computer and synchronized to video replay. Synchronization of heart rate data with video data provided insight into the way between-point time connected to physiological recovery. The impact of cognitive/behavioral between-point routines on physiological recovery could be studied as well as the impact of the overt expression of various positive and negative emotions on heart rate. Match charting data was also synchronized with heart rate data to explore the possible connection between heart rate recovery patterns between points and error production during points.

The data collected tended to support the following conclusions:

1. Heart rate data provided relevant feedback regarding psychological and physiological arousal levels as well as psychological and physical recovery.

2. Changing emotional states clearly impacted heart rate response pattern between points.

3. High heart rate patterns not punctuated by between-point recovery (reduction in heart rate) were associated with higher error production and poorer play.

4. High linear heart rate patterns were associated with intense negative emotional states such as anger and fear as well as extreme fatigue.

5. Low heart rate patterns not punctuated by during-point arousal (increases in heart rate) were associated with higher error production and poorer play. This pattern occurred when players either gave up (tanked) or were generally unmotivated.

6. The best performances typically occurred when players experienced moderate to high arousal punctuated by rhythmic between-point recovery cycles (reductions in heart rate of 6 to 25 beats).

7. Highly linear heart rate patterns were associated with increased error production and poorer play.

Cognitive Strategies of Top Players

Studying the cognitive patterns of top competitors between points proved far more difficult than studying behavioral patterns. Answering the question of whether thinking patterns of top competitors differ significantly from those of poor competitors between points is fraught with procedural obstacles. Understanding how and what successful competitors were thinking and visualizing between points, however, was critical to the development of a truly meaningful between-point intervention strategy.

The following methods were used to collect data:

1. Wireless microphones and video analysis

Practice matches were videotaped and players were asked to think out loud between points. Remote microphones enabled researchers to record all resulting verbal behavior on videotape.

2. Player recall with video replay

Players watched videotapes of previous matches of themselves and were asked to attempt to recall what and how they typically were thinking between points.

3. Player recall without video replay

Players were asked to describe their thinking patterns between points without the use of video replay. The following questions were asked: What are your typical habits of thinking between points? Are you aware of any particular sequence of things you think about, stroke corrections, tactics, concentration strategies and so forth? Do you visualize between points? If so, when and how? Are you aware of following any particular routine in your thinking between points?

Based on data collected from amateur and professional players residing at the Nick Bollettieri Tennis Academy over a 5-month period, the following tentative conclusions were drawn:

1. Compared to top competitors, poor competitors tend to be less disciplined and less precise in their cognitive patterns between points.

2. Compared to top competitors, poor competitors have a greater tendency to engage in negative, pessimistic thinking and self-criticism between points.

3. Compared to top competitors, poor competitors were less likely to follow a clear-cut sequence of thinking and visualizing between points.

Top competitors were more likely to be disciplined, positive thinking and patterned in their thinking between points than poor competitors. Top competitors were also more likely to engage in some form of visualization prior to the start of each new point.

From the interviews, it quickly became obvious that although top and poor players were engaging in a wide variety of cognitive activities between points, little conscious attention or personal reflection was typically given to between-point mental activity.

As a general rule, however, good competitors were able to describe their between-point mental activities and patterns in greater detail and were more aware of the importance of following a specific routine than poor competitors.

A Four-Stage Sequence

Both the behavioral and cognitive between-point data supported the development of a four stage training sequence.

Stage 1 - Positive Physical Response

Begins as soon as the point is over and lasts 3 to 5 seconds.

This stage was named Positive Physical Response because of the strong, positive behavioral patterns occurring during this time frame. Examples are pumping-up with a fist following a great shot, physically rehearsing mistakes, acknowledging an opponent's exceptional shot by clapping, and quickly turning away from a mistake and continuing to act confident and positive.

The Positive Physical Response Stage of top competitors apparently acts to facilitate the continuous flow of positive emotion from one point to the next and reduces the chance that anger, disappointment or any other disruptive emotional response might interfere with between-point recovery.

The heart rates of players typically remained constant or continued to slowly increase during this stage. Sudden increases in heart rates typically followed a pumping up sequence.

Recommended Behavioral Sequences for Stage 1:
1. Racquet out of dominant hand (for relaxation).
2. Racquet carried by the throat between thumb and forefinger, with head slightly elevated. Racquet not to be carried by the handle because of the negative image.
3. Quick, decisive turn away from mistake.
4. Shoulders back and broad.
5. Head up with chin parallel to the ground.
6. Arms hanging freely at sides, 3 to 5 inches away from body.
7. Eyes forward and down.
8. High energy, confident walk.
9. Physical rehearsal of mistakes (optional).
10. Pumping-up (optional).
11. Acknowledge great shot by opponent (optional).

Recommended Cognitive Sequence for Stage 1:
1. Think "no problem" or "let it go" in response to a mistake.
2. Think about the correction following a mistake or missed opportunity (optional).
3. Think "yes" or "come on" to build momentum and increase arousal following a good shot.

Stage 2 - Relaxation Response

Begins 3 to 5 seconds after the point ends and lasts 6 to 15 seconds depending on how physically and/or emotionally stressful the previous point was. This stage was named the Relaxation Response Stage because of the declining heart rates typically occurring during this period.

The purpose of Stage 2 behavioral and cognitive activities is to facilitate physiological and psychological recovery from the stresses of the previous point and to adjust arousal levels to an optimal range prior to the start of the next point.

Although Stage 2 activities generally serve to lower arousal, under conditions of insufficient arousal when players feel flat emotionally, unmotivated, etc., activation rather than relaxation strategies are to be used.

Although increases in arousal levels by players during Stage 2 were evidenced in the testing, it was rare. Under the typical pressure of match play, Stage 2 was associated with the lowering of arousal.

Recommended Behavioral Sequence for Stage 2:

1. Eyes to the strings (the strings, a neutral stimulus, become the trigger for relaxation).

2. Deep breath synchronized to the eyes going to the strings.

3. High energy walk until across the baseline, then slow, relaxed walking behind the baseline.

4. Never stop moving (keep legs moving to facilitate physiological recovery).

5. Contract and relax specific muscles--stretch, bend, shake hands and feet.

6. Eyes on the strings or on the ground at all times but head should remain up and shoulders back at all times maintaining the look of confidence and control.

7. More time is to be taken in Stage 2 under conditions of high physical or emotional stress.

8. When the need exists for increased arousal rather than relaxation, players are to continue Stage 1 activities such as pumping-up, running in place, jumping up and down, physically rehearsing strokes, etc.

Recommended Cognitive Sequence for Stage 2:

1. Think "relax," "calm," "easy," "loose," or "settle down," etc. Develop a trigger word that initiates and facilitates the lowering of arousal.

For many players, continuous repetition of a particular phrase such as "only-the-ball" has the same desired effect.

2. Focus should remain very present centered. Thoughts of past or future points during this time generally interfere with recovery.

3. No analysis, problem solving, or critical thinking is recommended when lowering arousal is needed.

4. To increase arousal, players are to focus on challenging and stimulating thoughts such as "come on, let's get going," or "come on, fight, move, aggressive" during Stage 2.

Stage 3 - Preparation Response

Begins after completing the appropriate arousal adjustment in Stage 2. Players are to move toward the baseline to serve or toward the return-of-serve position, stop and raise their eyes to the opposite side of the court. The raising of one's eyes signals the end of the Relaxation Stage and the beginning of the Preparation Stage. The Preparation period lasts only 3 to 5 seconds and serves to insure that the players know the score and is very clear about what the player know to do before the point starts.

After they have calmed down from Stage 2 and can think clearly, players are encouraged to step outside themselves for just a few seconds and do a reality check. They are to think rationally and logically like a good coach. This is the only time in the entire between-point sequence where players are to engage in logical, objective thinking. Match play data and interview reports clearly underscored the hazards of thinking too much between points as well as not thinking at all.

Heart rates typically cease to decline during this stage and often begin to show a gradual increase.

Recommended Behavioral Sequence for Stage 3:

1. Stop approximately 2 to 3 feet behind the baseline when serving. Move into the return of serve position when returning.

2. Lift eyes to the opposite side of the court. The focus of the eyes should not be the opponent but rather the intended target for the serve or return.

3. Verbalize the score out loud when serving (optional).

4. Project the strongest, most confident and aggressive image possible. The message sent by the appearance of the physical body should be "I am confident, I will win this point!"

Recommended Cognitive Sequence for Stage 3:
1. Register the score.
2. Consciously decide what you're going to do on the next point. Think like a coach. Example: "serve and volley, be aggressive, first serve in." With only 3 to 5 seconds, thinking must be clear, precise and decisive.

Stage 4 - Ritual Response

Begins as soon as the player moves to the baseline to serve or begins movement of his/her feet for the return of serve. The length of this final stage is 4 to 8 seconds. The purpose of the Ritual Response Stage is to bring the player to the highest state of mental and physical readiness just prior to the start of each point. The goal is to produce a state of intense concentration that will lead to a highly instinctive and automatic form of play.

The heart rate of players typically continued to slowly rise during this stage.

Recommended Behavioral Sequence for Stage 4:
1. Bouncing the ball one or more times prior to serving.
2. A full one-second pause just after the last bounce on the serve.
3. Stimulate hands and feet prior to returning serve by contracting and relaxing hands on the racquet handle and by moving from foot to foot.
4. Sway back and forth from foot to foot after stimulating hands and feet on return of serve to keep muscles relaxed and ready.
5. Execute a split step to maximize balance and create muscle readiness with slight stretch reflex as one's opponent strikes the ball on the serve.

Recommended Cognitive Sequence for Stage 4:
1. Mentally rehearse the serve or serve return and visualize the ball going to the intended target.
2. Bring focus to the present and allow one's attention to become totally absorbed with the ball.

It should be noted that if the server faults on the first serve attempt, players should return to the Stage 4 position but allow 5 to 7 seconds between first and second serves.

The minimum time required to complete all four stages is 16 seconds and the maximum allowable time is 25 seconds. Players taking less than 16 seconds invariably experience a variety of competitive problems related to rushing.

Training Progressions

The learning progressions followed in teaching the four stages are the same regardless of the level of player skill. The learning sequence is as follows:

Step 1

Review a specially prepared video tape of the between-point habits of top professional players. The original video tape included footage of over 25 players including Connors, Lendl, Becker, Edberg, Navratilova, Graf, Evert and Sabatini. The short version took approximately 20 minutes and the long version took 1 hour.

Step 2

Review video tape of the client in competition and compare between-point habits with top professionals. If client does not have competitive match data on video tape, a match should be arranged and video taped. Using the world's best professionals as models is very motivating and convincing. Allow approximately 30 minutes for the comparative review.

Step 3

Move on-court and rehearse all 4 stages without a ball. Players are taught in great detail how to carry their head and shoulders, how to walk, carry their racquet, breathing patterns, eye control, etc. Players are asked to become great actors or actresses. The average time for learning all 4 stages is 1 hour. At the end of the training session, players compete against an imaginary opponent (shadow box) and the sequence is videotaped (3 to 5 minutes). The training sessions concludes with a brief video review of the imaginary competition.

Step 4

Player shadow-boxes for approximately 25 minutes and the trainer provides feedback on precision and accuracy of the stages. Material is video taped and reviewed. Shadow- boxing is very demanding physically. Player is now learning how to think and act under relatively high levels of physical stress. No emotional stress has been introduced yet. Session lasts 1 hour. Players wear heart rate monitors to enhance their understanding of how the stages relate to recovery.

Step 5

Player competes by playing points but does not keep track of score. Trainer actively makes adjustments and corrections in the 4 stage progressions during play. Material is video taped and players wear heart rate monitors. Session lasts 1 hour. This is the first introduction of competitive stress. Player should now be thinking and acting in highly specific ways in the presence of physical and emotional stress.

Step 6

Expose player to increasing levels of competitive stress and closely monitor 4 stage sequences. Matches are video taped and heart rate monitors are periodically used.

Step 7 - Full Tournament Competition

Approximately 10 to 12 hours of training is required to complete all 7 steps. This can be done in 3- to 4-day time frame or spread over 2 to 3 weeks. A 2- to 3-week period generally produces the best long term results.

Although significant competitive improvement is often evident following the 10- to 12-hour training program, the most enduring positive effects occur after the sequence becomes habitual and automatic. This usually requires 30 to 60 days of focused practice.

Results and Discussion

Since 1986 literally hundreds of amateur and professional players have been exposed to the training method with encouraging results. Positive results have been documented with competitors as young as 8 and with nearly every level of competitive skill from beginner to world class. Several highly visible professional players have publicly attributed significant performance gains to the between-point training including Gabriela Sabatini, Jim Courier, Shuzo Matsuoka and Brenda Schultz. This intervention strategy has clearly been the most effective of any I have thus far employed for helping tennis players build competitive skills, improve concentration and focus, control nervousness and temper, and generally help players manage competitive pressure more effectively.

Because of the positive results achieved with several highly celebrated players, requests from a number of Tennis Federations worldwide to have their national coaches and players learn the training system have been received. During the past 5 years, such requests have been fulfilled in Japan, Germany, Spain, Great Britain, Greece, Holland, Italy as well as several South American countries.

National coaches and Area Training Center coaches from the United States Tennis Association (USTA) have regularly been exposed to the training systems as well as players attending USTA National Training camps.

Training programs have also been regularly conducted at the request of the United States Professional Tennis Association (USPTA) and the United States Professional Tennis Registry (USPTR), the two principal teacher training organizations within the United States.

The feedback from coaches and players regarding the between-point intervention strategy has thus far been very favorable. Modifications to the basic system are made each year based on feedback from coaches and players worldwide as well as my own personal experience with players.

The training system in essentially its current form was published in *World Tennis Magazine* in February of 1990 and in *The Mental Game*, 1990. A training video was produced in 1989 and has been translated into several languages. The written and video materials have proven useful in accelerating the learning process.

A slightly modified training system has been developed for doubles.

Summary

The between-point intervention strategy described in this paper essentially teaches players how to think and act under pressure.

At its most basic level it is a stress management system. The model was based on the intensive study of the cognitive-behavioral habits of many of the game's most successful competitors. The position taken by the author was that the best way to manage stress during competition would be to model those experiencing the highest level of competitive success. The between-point cognitive-behavioral habits of top professional competitors were used as the basis for developing the 4-Stage training system described in this paper.

The intent in launching the investigative effort was not to design a research project suitable for journal publication but rather to simply improve my effectiveness as a sport psychologist specializing in tennis. The intent was to deepen my understanding of between-point variables so that more effective and relevant training interventions could be introduced in my work with players.

Future research is needed to determine the overall effectiveness of this intervention strategy. It is the hope of the author that sport psychology researchers will become interested in systematically investigating the cognitive-behavioral model presented in this paper.

References

Boutcher, S.H., & Crews, D.J. (1987). The effect of a preshot attentional routine on a well-learned skill. *International Journal of Sport Psychology, 18,* 30-39.

Cohn, P.J., Rotella, R.J., & Lloyd, J.W. (1990). Effects of a cognitive-behavioral intervention on the preshot routine and performance in golf. *The Sport Psychologist, 4,* 33-47.

Crews, D.J., & Boutcher, S.H. (1986a). Effects of structural preshot behaviors on beginning golf performance. *Perceptual and Motor Skills, 62,* 291-294.

Gould, D., Weiss, M., & Weinberg, R.S., (1981). Psychological characteristics of successful and nonsuccessful Big Ten wrestlers. *Journal of Sport Psychology, 3,* 69-81.

Lobmeyer, D.L., & Wasserman, E.A. (1986). Preliminaries to free throw shooting: Superstitious behavior? *Journal of Sport Behavior, 9,* 70-78.

Loehr, J.E. (1983, January). The ideal performance state. *Science Periodical on Research and Technology in Sport* (pp. 1-8). Bu-1.

Loehr, J.E. (1990, Feb.). Stop choking. *World Tennis magazine* (pp. 24-30).

Loehr, J.E. (1991). *The mental game.* NY: Penguin.

Moore, W.E. (1986). *Covert-overt service routines: The effects of a service routine training program on elite tennis players.* Unpublished doctoral dissertation, The University of Virginia, Charlottesville.

Pelz, D. (1988, July). Make it routine. *Golf Magazine, 7,* 48-51.

Subject Index